EMPIRE

EMPIRE

**A Tale of
Obsession,
Betrayal,
and the
Battle
for an
American
Icon**

MITCHELL PACELLE

John Wiley & Sons, Inc.

New York • Chichester • Weinheim • Brisbane • Singapore • Toronto

Copyright © 2001 by Mitchell Pacelle. All rights reserved.
Published by John Wiley & Sons, Inc.
Published simultaneously in Canada.

This publication is designed to provide accurate and authoritative infor-mation in regard to the subject matter covered. It is sold with the under-standing that the publisher is not engaged in rendering professional services. If professional advice or other expert assistance is required, the services of a competent professional person should be sought.

Library of Congress Cataloging-in-Publication Data

Pacelle, Mitchell.
    Empire: a tale of obsession, betrayal, and the battle for an American icon / Mitchell Pacelle.
       p. cm.
    Includes bibliographical references and index.
    ISBN 0-471-40394-6 (cloth: alk. paper)
    1. Yokoi, Hideki, 1913-   2. Empire State Building (New York, N.Y.) 3. Real estate development—New York (State)—New York.   4. Real estate developers—New York (State)—New York.   5. Real estate devel-opers—Japan.   6. Businesspeople—Japan.   I. Title.

HD268.N5 P33   2001
333.33'873'097471—dc21   2001045312

The Empire State Building design is a registered trademark of the Empire State Building Company.

To Laura

CONTENTS

A white stretch limousine braked at a midtown Manhattan curb on the afternoon of August 11, 1997, and a frail old man shuffled out of an office building, trailed by an entourage of a half dozen. He was a small man, perhaps five feet two, his hair dyed jet-black, slicked back, and parted down the middle. As always, he was dressed impeccably, this afternoon in a two-button blue suit, a crisp white shirt, and his trademark bow tie, a clip-on. Although 84 years old, Hideki Yokoi was still a vain man.

The two and a half years Yokoi had just spent in a Japanese prison hospital had not been kind to him. A stroke had left him unsteady on his feet. But on this blessedly cool summer afternoon, the second day of his first ever visit to the United States, Yokoi carried himself as if he was still one of Japan's wealthiest men. With the aid of a silver-handled walking stick, he made his way to the limousine—he had insisted on the white stretch—and climbed inside. His driver nosed the unwieldy vehicle into the crush of cabs and pointed it down Fifth Avenue.

Beside the old man sat a beefy former New York City cop with a six-shot Colt tucked into a shoulder holster under his blazer and another pistol at his ankle. Accompanying him was an ex-Army man who also wore a handgun holstered under his jacket. Yokoi had insisted on the firearms. As always, two Japanese women shadowed Yokoi, tending to his every need. There was Yokoi's New York trial lawyer, Raymond Hannigan, a weekend surfer whom Yokoi had met only a day earlier. Guiding Yokoi's colorful posse was Yokoi's top strategist and unlikely mentor in the ways of the Western world: Peter Bal, a 37-year-old painter, sculptor, and sometime rock musician who divided his time between New York and Paris. The closest Bal had previously come to the business elite had been during the week he spent as a bicycle messenger on Wall Street. But Bal was half Japanese, and distantly related to Yokoi. In Yokoi's insular world, family and loyalty were everything.

As the limousine made its way down Fifth Avenue, Yokoi leaned toward the window and gazed up. The Empire State Building rose serenely into the late afternoon sky. Although long since vanquished in the contest for the world's tallest building, this monument to American hubris in the Roaring Twenties still had the almost magical capacity to fill people with wonder and joy, even jaded Manhattanites long since deadened to the scale and brawn of the city. There was something enduring about the way the Empire State Building towered over the midtown skyline, a rock-solid sentinel that, when the late afternoon sun hung low, seemed to shimmer with power and glory. Its profile—the soaring limestone tower with its streamlined crown that glowed in the twilight like a dream—was etched into the mind's eye of nearly everyone who had ever laid eyes on it. Was there another structure in the world with more iconic heft? The Brooklyn Bridge, perhaps. The Eiffel Tower. The Great Wall of China.

Yokoi was hardly the first powerful man to find it enthralling. Over the years, the Empire State Building had exerted an almost magnetic pull over a certain kind of person, the kind who once had nothing and now had everything. To Yokoi, who for years had been pursuing a quixotic quest to rise above his roots as a shadowy Tokyo businessman, it was quite simply the world's ultimate trophy. Buying it, he believed, had gained him a spot on the world stage. With all the indignities he had suffered in recent years, Yokoi was determined not to let anyone wrest this prize out of his bony grasp.

Yokoi's car stopped beside a hydrant in front of the sky-scraper, and Yokoi stepped onto a sidewalk thronged with New Yorkers hurrying home. If this had been Tokyo, busi-nessmen would have stopped in their tracks. There would have been whispered conversations and furtive glances. In postwar Japan, Yokoi had earned a degree of infamy that few businessmen would envy. Ruthless investment practices and runaway land values had made him a billionaire. But in the eyes of his compatriots, Yokoi was a shady character who asso-ciated with disreputable men. Worse still, his reputation had forever been tarnished by a single shameful event, a calamity that had impelled him to formulate the secret plan that had brought him to New York.

Here in New York, however, where surely not more than a few dozen people knew who he was, Yokoi could enjoy the blessed anonymity of a tourist. Bal scurried into a shop for a disposable camera. Yokoi struck a pose in front of the limou-sine, the skyscraper soaring up behind him. He posed with his aides, his lawyer, his bodyguards. Then he shuffled off to inspect his prize. The building was dirty, he complained, the construction scaffolding unseemly. He assessed the quality of the building's shops. Eventually, he joined the throng of tourists streaming through the lobby, part of a sea of more than 3 million visitors who cross the building's marble lobby each year. When he returned to his handlers, Yokoi held a small bag containing an Empire State Building mug and a snow globe.

The very next day, Yokoi slipped away from his entourage with a bodyguard and interpreter to visit his skyscraper once again, taking his place in the ever present line of tourists waiting to ride to the observatory. When Yokoi emerged onto the eighty-sixth-floor terrace, he was, like most tourists, mesmerized. He studied the panorama for a long time, smiling. It is impossible to know what Yokoi had come to think of his best-known possession and the trouble it had brought down upon him like a poisonous fog. If nothing else, in his controversial life, Yokoi had perfected the art of never expressing regret. By any objective measure, however, the Empire State Building had brought him little more than misery.

For years, Yokoi had managed to keep the peculiar constellation that he called his family—a messy universe in which even the number of children he had fathered and the women who had borne them was a topic of considerable debate—from spinning into disarray. Now it was all ending so badly. Buying the Empire State Building had torn his family asunder, had turned his sons and daughters against one another. It had prompted his beloved daughter, Kiiko, and her husband, to double-cross him, Yokoi believed. Yokoi, never a forgiving man, had reacted to the perceived betrayal with characteristic abandon. Now, as he gazed out over the metropolis, he was mired in the consequences of his own base instincts. If Yokoi had misgivings, though, they weren't apparent on the crowded observation deck. To his bodyguard, Yokoi seemed simply elated that the building was his.

Stories of eccentric men and women and their powerful obsessions are stunningly common in the world of Manhattan real estate. But the chaos Yokoi brought upon New York's best-known building may well go down as one of the strangest real estate tales the metropolis has ever produced. Yokoi had been eager to punish his daughter and her husband, to make them pay dearly for their lack of respect. He had succeeded in chilling fashion. Three years had passed since he had even spoken to Kiiko. She had been shut away in a jail cell in France. Yokoi, too, had been away, locked in a cold prison hospital outside Tokyo. Now he was ready to fight with every last ounce of his strength to stake his claim on the Empire State Building. As Yokoi turned away from the stone parapet 86 stories above Fifth Avenue to return to his limousine, he had no way of knowing that he would never set foot in his prized property again.

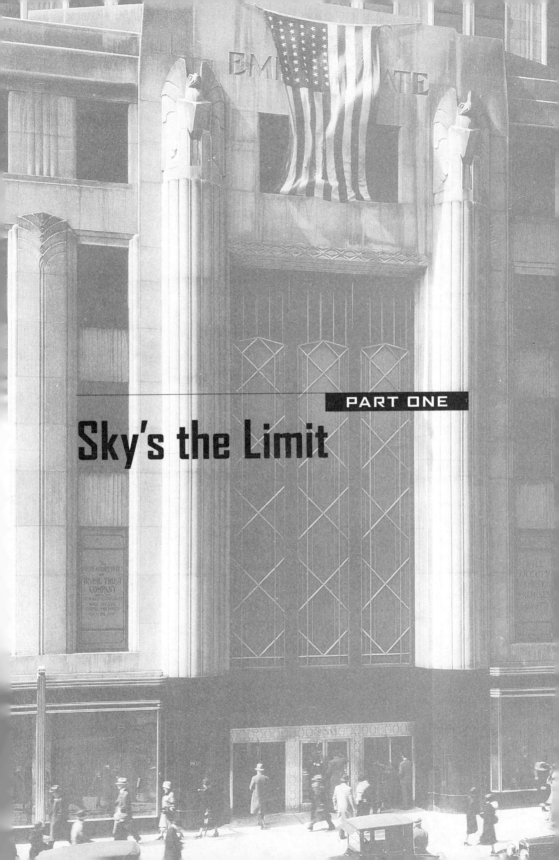

PART ONE

Sky's the Limit

The Deal and the Deception

How many millions might a man be willing to spend to raise his ego a quarter mile high? How much to lay claim to the heart and soul of New York City? What would a respectable businessman pay? Not a shadowy character looking for legitimacy or attention. On August 21, 1991, almost six years before Hideki Yokoi gazed in triumph off the top of the Empire State Building, Kurt A. Reich turned the questions over in his head. For the 15 years he had been buying and selling commercial property for Prudential Insurance Company of America, Reich had been trying to fathom what drives men to buy trophy real estate, to pay beyond reason for the opportunity to affix their names to spectacular buildings. On this morning, it was not a matter of idle curiosity. As the real estate gold rush of the 1980s was fading into bust, and financial pressure on the insurance company mounted, Prudential had decided to sell the Empire State Building, and Reich was waiting to meet the mysterious couple who had bid more than anyone else.

The ego buyers had indeed been out in force, because the world's most famous skyscraper, curiously enough, was likely to sell for a price that—in the lofty world of Manhattan real estate—was little more than a song. Thirty years earlier, Prudential had gutted the building's profit potential. It had leased the entire building—for 114 years, an eternity in real estate—to an investment company controlled by a pair of Manhattan real estate titans. Each year, the two moguls paid Prudential a paltry $1.9 million in rent for the 2.5-million-square-foot building, giving them both a motive to cling to their lease with the tenacity of Park Avenue millionaires in rent-controlled apartments. Whoever bought the Empire State Building now would face the prospect of wrangling with two of Manhattan's most difficult real estate magnates: Peter Malkin, an iron-willed Harvard-educated lawyer who was exacting to the point of annoyance, and Leona Helmsley, a notoriously volatile woman who was sowing terror through the billion-dollar real estate empire assembled by her ailing husband, Harry. What Prudential was selling, in truth, was little more than sizzle: the right to boast, "I own the Empire State Building."

Reich and a young investment banker from Salomon Brothers, Gregory White, had worked the numbers time and again. No sensible investor, they reasoned, would park money until the year 2076 for anything less than a 7.5 percent return. Unencumbered by the lease, the building might fetch $600 million to $800 million, they figured. But no matter which way they looked at it, the Empire State Building, saddled with that long-term lease, was worth only about $25 million to a rational buyer. How much more could Prudential squeeze from the ego factor? White boldly conjectured another $15 million to $25 million. But who was to say? Putting an asking price on the skyscraper, White advised, would merely stifle the imaginations of potential buyers. If someone wanted to overbid, he told Reich, it wasn't Prudential's business to worry about why.

One Salomon banker had even floated a proposal to organize a New York State lottery with the Empire State Building as grand prize. Who wouldn't put down $5 for a crack at owning the world's most famous skyscraper? The numbers could be astounding, he had argued. But Prudential had scotched the proposal as far too risky.

Just before bringing the 102-story landmark to market, Reich gathered his bankers to ponder the unknowable. Each of them anted up $10, mulled over what the skyscraper would fetch, and secretly jotted a number on a slip of paper. A few guessed in the high twenty millions. Others guessed the low thirties. Reich wrote down $39 million. Head banker White, who had been talking up the cgo-play strategy, figured he ought to put his money where his mouth was. White wrote $39.5 million, and stuffed his guess into the envelope.

Reich wasn't sure what to expect as he waited for the Japanese woman and French-American man who had bid $41 million. The names Nakahara and Renoir had meant nothing to him. He punched the numbers into his calculator. The lease payments from Malkin and Helmsley would give the couple a scant 4.6 percent annual return on the purchase price. Reich didn't consider it his job to stop people from making foolish deals.

Reich could find no one who knew anything about Renoir and Nakahara. They were an enigma. Ordinarily, when Prudential was unloading, say, strip malls or suburban office buildings, it cared about little more than whether a potential buyer could come up with untainted cash. But the Empire State Building was a different matter. Prudential feared a firestorm of negative publicity if it sold the landmark to the wrong buyer. Under the circumstances, the seemingly ludicrous economics of the Renoirs' bid bore careful scrutiny, Reich decided. He wanted to put a question directly to the bidder. Why?

When Renoir and his wife arrived at Reich's spacious

office on the twentieth floor of New York's Rockefeller Center, Reich rose to his feet and introduced himself. Renoir—a ramrod-erect 44-year-old with close-cropped hair, a boxer's face, and a penetrating gaze—handed Reich a card identifying himself as president of Lehman Brothers' asset management arm in Japan. Renoir told Reich he had come as a representative of his wife's family. Kiiko, a short, attractive woman whose dark hair curled around her face like a helmet, smiled demurely, then sank into a chair. "We understand you have an interest in the Empire State Building," Reich began. "Obviously, it's a remarkable asset. Why are you interested?"

Kiiko handed Reich a portfolio of pictures. Reich flipped through them, incredulous. He saw European castles, lots of them. "My father collects them," said Kiiko. Her billionaire father, who wished to remain anonymous, she said, had assembled a portfolio that included nine French châteaux, four British castles, a Spanish palace, and the second-largest private residence in America, a sprawling behemoth on Long Island. "The Empire State Building is just one of the buildings he wants," she said matter-of-factly. Renoir picked up the story. Kiiko's aging father, he told Reich, had made a fortune by manufacturing uniforms for the Japanese Imperial Army during World War II and by producing soft goods for American occupying forces after Japan's defeat. Later, he branched into real estate, snapping up treasures from Japan's royal family. Finally, he had been active in the stock market, taking runs at undervalued companies, not unlike the noted American raiders T. Boone Pickens and Carl Icahn. Reich, ever alert to potential controversy, interrupted. Renoir reassured him that his father-in-law hadn't been tainted by his takeover activities. The Empire State Building, Renoir concluded, would be another one of his collectibles.

To Reich, the bizarre story seemed a plausible enough statement of motive. After all, Prudential was looking for someone with a world-class ego. And from what little he could tell from the snapshots, this bidder appreciated grandeur. But Reich's gut was telling him something else. There was something unsettling about this couple. Renoir seemed brash, a little too slick, even shifty. Perhaps, thought Reich, he was just reacting to Renoir's French accent. Or to Kiiko's strange disengagement. As he bid the couple good-bye, Reich couldn't shake the feeling that something wasn't being said. Was it that Renoir had trouble looking him in the eye? We'll need to find out more about this family patriarch, Mr. Nakahara, Reich decided after the meeting.

Soon Peter Malkin received a telephone call from an investment banker at Salomon. At 57 years old, the gangly six-foot three-inch Malkin had long ago emerged from the shadow of his late father-in-law, one of Manhattan's most respected property kingpins. By dint of inheritance and shrewd investments, Malkin controlled some 20 million square feet of commercial property, from Manhattan office buildings and retail properties to suburban apartment buildings and shopping centers. In an industry known for the rough edges of its dominant figures, Malkin was, at least on the surface, a notable exception. Erudite, civic-minded, and impeccably mannered, Malkin seemed less the product of his native Brooklyn than of the exclusive Greenwich, Connecticut, neighborhood where he had settled. Malkin took old-fashioned shoeshines at his desk and, when discussing his colleagues, seldom failed to attach a "Mr." or "Mrs." to their names. But some people in Malkin's business and social circles also associated him with a steely determination about matters large and small, a willingness, for example, to personally reproach people who violate the restrictions on leaf-blowing machines in his neighborhood of million-dollar homes. In short, he was not a man to be easily bullied.

As holders of the Empire State Building's lease, Malkin and

Leona Helmsley were themselves the most logical buyers of the building. Their lease gave them almost absolute control of the building for 85 more years. Buying the bricks and mortar would consolidate their position, remove the potential headache of a troublesome new owner, make it easier for them to sell their valuable position outright. But in earlier meetings with Salomon's White, Malkin had been cagey. "I can be the best buyer," he had assured White. Nonetheless, he had bid only $32 million. White had warned him not to assume no one would bid higher. Malkin simply hadn't believed him.

Malkin was astonished to learn from a Salomon banker that a $41 million bid had come in from Asia. The banker assured him the bid was real.

"Well, I can't match that," Malkin replied. He hung up his phone, crestfallen. He had figured he could afford to bid more for the building than was economically reasonable, to protect the lease. But why, he wondered, would anyone else?

With Malkin apparently unwilling to engage in a bidding war, Prudential's Reich turned his attention back to the Renoirs. Prudential had a rule against selling buildings to anonymous buyers. Imagine the embarrassment that would come from selling the Empire State Building to, say, a blind trust backed by a Columbia cocaine cartel. Prudential would need to know exactly where any money for the Empire State Building was coming from, and Reich felt he hadn't gotten an adequate explanation from the Renoirs. He told White to pump his Salomon colleague in Tokyo for more information on Mr. Nakahara, the family patriarch. White's colleague, who had a commission riding on the deal, assured him the family company was solid.

Something else also nagged at Reich: the potential fallout from selling such a cherished landmark to a Japanese buyer of any sort. Recent years had seen a tsunami of Japanese purchases of American trophy properties, many at prices that left American real estate veterans bewildered. But the Japanese purchases of Rockefeller Center and the Pebble Beach golf course had sparked a xenophobic backlash, as commentators fretted that an all-powerful Japan was consuming America's corporate lunch and then moving on to its cultural treasures. White played down the concern. The building couldn't be loaded onto a boat and moved back to Japan, he told Reich. Reich met with his bosses at Prudential to discuss the prospects of negative press. If the high bid came from Japan, the group decided, so be it.

On August 23, 1991, Prudential signed a contract to sell the Empire State Building to an investment company set up by Renoir and Nakahara, pending approval of the buyer by Prudential's board of directors. Both Reich and White remained uneasy. Getting further information about Nakahara from Salomon's Tokyo office was like pulling teeth, White confided to Reich. White didn't want some enterprising reporter to uncover skeletons after the deal was closed. Both men pressed for more information from Japan. Finally, White began to get to the truth about Kiiko's father, the mystery billionaire. His name wasn't Nakahara, after all. It was Hideki Yokoi. When White's office punched the name into a computerized news search, it surfaced like a stink bomb. White was livid. He phoned Reich immediately. "Now we know why we're not getting a straight story," he told Reich. He rushed uptown to Reich's office.

"The guy you're selling to is probably financially credible," he informed Reich. "But you might want to think twice about doing business with him." White showed Reich newspaper accounts of an inferno that had gutted a massive Tokyo hotel in 1982, killing 33 guests. Yokoi owned the hotel. He'd been arrested, convicted of gross negligence, and was facing a jail term. Hideki Yokoi, the articles suggested, was one of Japan's most hated businessmen. And that's not all, White told Reich. Yokoi had long been said to consort with Japan's notorious criminal underworld, the *yakuza,* White said. He cautioned

Reich that he had no idea whether the rumors were valid. But Reich had heard enough. This was hardly the caliber of buyer he was seeking. He told White he would urge his superiors to kill the deal. Shortly after White returned to his office, Reich telephoned. The deal was off.

Reich phoned Renoir's lawyer with the news, offering no explanation. "If you and your client would like to discuss the reasons, we can meet in my office to do so," Reich told the lawyer. To Reich's astonishment, he never again heard from Jean-Paul Renoir or his wife. Reich couldn't help feeling that Prudential had avoided catastrophe by the narrowest of margins.

There were those at Prudential who wanted to fire Salomon over the fiasco. But faced with the time-consuming process of starting again, Prudential relented, so White set about salvaging the sales process. He telephoned Peter Malkin and told him the deal had collapsed. He asked Malkin if his bid was still on the table.

"Absolutely," said Malkin, his hopes rekindled. When he hung up, Malkin was convinced the deal would break in his direction after all.

Within days, however, Salomon unearthed another prospect, a Wall Street investor named Oliver Grace Jr. Remarkably, Grace bid $39 million, nearly matching Renoir's bid. And he had pedigree. Onetime New York mayor William R. Grace had been his great-great-uncle, and industrial magnate Peter Grace was his second cousin once removed. White ordered an exhaustive background check. At one time, White discovered, Grace had mounted a hostile tender offer for a closed-end mutual fund. It was a controversial move, but hardly extreme in the cutthroat 1980s takeover world. Reich wondered why a man with Grace's savvy and connections would offer so much for a property with the meager income stream of the Empire State Building. Was this another ego trip? Reich told White he wanted to meet Grace directly.

Given the Grace family's stature, Reich was expecting a man with Wall Street polish. The man who presented himself to Reich had the slightly unkempt look of an eccentric professor, a bit overweight, his hair askew. Reich seated him in a conference room. He asked Grace why he wanted the Empire State Building. Grace paused for a moment, then looked Reich in the eye and explained in a soft voice that he planned to put the building into a trust for his children and grandchildren. When the lease to Helmsley and Malkin expired in 2076, the building would soar in value, to the benefit of his offspring. It struck Reich as a perfectly plausible motive. Reich invited Grace to join him in his office. Reich shut the door. "At $40 million, I'll do the deal," Reich told Grace. Grace agreed. But he warned Reich that he didn't want his name to surface. "This is the Empire State Building," Reich replied. He couldn't make any guarantees, but he'd do his best. He assumed Grace was embarrassed to be overpaying.

On November 27, 1991, the deal closed. The Empire State Building was sold through a web of offshore trusts to E. G. Holding, a shell company set up by Grace. At a celebratory party, Salomon Brothers bankers passed out cufflinks engraved with the building's signature profile, and the bankers expressed relief about averting disaster. It would be some time before Reich concluded that underneath Oliver Grace's soft edges and quiet demeanor had lain a gifted liar.

Nearly two years, in fact, would pass before Grace's lie began to unravel.

One day, celebrity developer Donald Trump phoned Malkin at his office. By all appearances, the two real estate kingpins had practically nothing in common. With the exception of the Empire State Building, the bulk of the Manhattan portfolio Malkin and his partners controlled was distinguished primarily by drabness and age, and Malkin himself seemed stuck in the bygone era when real estate men preferred that their names be unspoken and their vast fortunes untold. Trump, on the other hand, had turned attention-getting into a sort of core business philosophy, and he never tired of telling people that the Trump name added immense value to his glass office and condominium towers, which to some critics resembled gold ingots.

"I wanted you to know, I'm buying the Empire State Building," Trump told Malkin.

"Really?" said Malkin, not missing a beat.

"Yeah, it's the most amazing story," continued Trump. "Marla goes to this exercise class. And one day, the young Japanese girl on the bicycle next to her tells Marla that her father had given her the Empire State Building as a birthday present."

"That is an amazing story," agreed Malkin. "First of all, do you know that we have a lease on the property until 2076?"

"Oh, I know that," responded Trump. "But I'm talking about the ownership of the building."

"Well, as far as I know, the building is owned by a corporation that is the nominee for Oliver Grace Jr.," said Malkin, who had ferreted out the secret on his own. "E. G. Holding Company. I don't know of any Japanese owner. I think you may have something wrong here."

Trump seemed taken aback. "I'll check with my lawyers," he said, and hung up. Before long, Trump called back. He had checked with his lawyers, he told Malkin. It was true. He was buying the Empire State Building.

Now Malkin didn't know what to believe. Trump plowed ahead. "It was the greatest deal in the world. I didn't put up a dime," he said. The skyscraper had great potential, he continued. The top could be converted into apartment condominiums. Trump Empire State Building Tower Apartments, said Trump, would be fantastic. They would sell for thousands of dollars a foot. A huge price. With his name and his promotion, Trump told Malkin, it would be amazing. Trump reminded Malkin that New York law wouldn't allow Malkin, as the building's lessee, to attempt such a condominium conversion himself. "You and I together could create something terrific," Trump told him.

"Well, Donald," Malkin said, "I don't think this would really make too much sense. We have over 3 million people a year who go up the elevators that are used for those tower floors, to go to the observatory. These would be tourists of all kinds and descriptions." Not the kind of people that owners of deluxe condominiums would want to share elevators with, Malkin suggested.

Trump told Malkin that if he couldn't do that, he would do something that would result in an increase in the rent. The somewhat menacing implication was not lost on Malkin.

"You can't do that, Donald," Malkin said. "The lease goes to 2076, and it's a fixed rent."

Trump hinted that he could force a change in the lease by demonstrating that the building had not been properly maintained.

"Donald, that won't work either," continued Malkin, "because we're in the middle of this huge, almost $60 million improvement program for the building, which is more than we paid for it, and it's been going on for almost three years already."

"We'll see," said Trump. He hung up.

What in the world was going on? Malkin wondered. Malkin had been under the impression that he had solved the puzzle of Prudential's anonymous buyer two years earlier when he ferreted out the name of Oliver Grace. If there was even a kernel of truth in what Trump had told him, he had been sorely mistaken. The mystery, it now seemed, had only deepened. Malkin puzzled over Trump's claims: Trump is buying the building from someone I didn't even know existed. Trump isn't putting up a dime. And if we don't cooperate and convert the building into condominiums, I'm going to have a problem with the lease. Malkin realized that he was in the dark on the most basic question of all: Who really owned the Empire State Building?

Reaching for the Sky

O n August 29, 1929, Alfred E. Smith, a backslapping Irish American with a bulbous nose and an unlit cigar perpetually clamped in his stained teeth, gathered reporters at his suite at Manhattan's Biltmore Hotel. Few of them knew what to expect from the 55-year-old former governor of New York. Nearly 10 months had passed since Smith's political career had ended in a thudding loss to Herbert Hoover in the presidential election. The defeat had left Smith restless and badly in need of a job. Smith, who had risen from a rough-and-tumble neighborhood of fishmongers below the Brooklyn Bridge, had watched his friends get very, very rich. Manhattan was riding the biggest bull market in the history of the nation. Everywhere in the city, people were building pyramids of wealth on borrowed money. Smith was eager for a share of it.

Smith told the reporters he had decided to head a new company that would erect the tallest building in the world. The Empire State Building, as Smith called it, would rise 80 stories, or nearly 1,000 feet, above Fifth Avenue on the site of the landmark Waldorf-Astoria Hotel. It would eclipse the Woolworth Building, the stately queen of the New York skyline, by some 200 feet. It would be one of the largest real estate undertakings in the history of the country. Smith said he would take charge of the construction, and when it was done, he would run the enormous building.

Pie-in-the-sky real estate schemes were nothing new in 1920s New York. And Smith, the reporters knew, had not a shred of real estate experience. Yet the instant Smith identified his backers, his plan gained gravity. Smith was fronting for two of America's richest men: Pierre S. du Pont, chairman of Delaware's E.I. du Pont de Nemours and Company, and financier John Raskob. Smith's partners had already plunked down $16 million for the land, he said, and expected to spend up to $44 million more to complete the skyscraper. Engineers had projected that it could be completed in an astonishingly short 18 months. In a city fueled by speculative frenzy, the news spread quickly. The governor was taking a flyer on real estate.

The three men were about to take a frightening leap of faith. Filling 80 floors with paying tenants would require a monumental act of salesmanship. In that respect, Raskob could have chosen no better front man than Al Smith, whom he hired at $50,000 a year, a princely sum in comparison to the $10,000 a year Smith had been drawing as governor. Smith lacked book learning, having left school at 14 to work in the fish market after the death of his father. His voice was still thick with the accent of the tenement neighborhood where he had come of age. But in working his way up the ranks of New York's notorious Tammany Hall political machine, Smith had mastered the art of winning people over. "Al could sell the Brooklyn Bridge to the Atlantic Ocean," a fellow Democrat once said.

Like Smith, Raskob was a devout Roman Catholic who had

risen far. He was the kind of self-made man Smith had always admired. Born in Lockport, New York, to a French father and Irish mother, Raskob at first seemed destined for an undistinguished life of clerical drudgery. But in the summer of 1900, not long after Raskob turned 21, Pierre S. du Pont offered him a job as secretary and stenographer.

What the Rockefellers were to oil, the Astors to real estate, and the Vanderbilts to railroads, the du Ponts of Delaware were to gunpowder. They had cornered the market. Pierre, who worked in the family powder plant, was a big man, perhaps six feet tall, 200 pounds, bald and owlish. He liked to read organ music, raise flowers, and entertain in the indoor gardens of Longwood, his sprawling home near Wilmington. Although childless, he possessed a wide paternal streak. One male secretary took to calling him "Daddy." Pierre, in turn, called him "son."

Recognizing Raskob's facility for finance, Pierre began relying on him more and more. It was Raskob's good fortune that soon after he arrived, the du Pont family drama would unfold in a way that would make him rich beyond his wildest dreams. After a death in the family led one du Pont faction to propose selling the family business, Pierre joined forces with his cousins Alfred and Coleman to take over the company. Coleman then sold his stock in the company to Pierre and several other directors, including John Raskob. The coup left Pierre and his right-hand man, Raskob, in control of a vast industrial empire.

By then, Raskob had developed into an astute investor. He had accumulated stock in the then troubled General Motors Corporation and had convinced Pierre to invest the future profits of the du Pont company into the same. The decision gave the du Pont firm a controlling stake in the automaker, and Pierre gained the chairmanship. Soon, General Motors was booming. Du Pont installed Raskob as vice president and finance chief, and Raskob devised a scheme of installment buying that transformed the auto industry. Raskob moved his growing family, which would eventually number 15, into an opulent mansion.

When he met Al Smith, Raskob took to the politician so wholeheartedly that when Smith asked for his help on his 1928 presidential run, Raskob resigned from General Motors to become chairman of the Democratic National Committee. Some said Raskob dreamed of putting the first Catholic in the White House. Smith's crushing defeat left Raskob, like Smith, adrift and in need of something to do.

It isn't clear what possessed Raskob to attempt to rebound from his misadventure in national politics with a $50 million roll of the dice on real estate. In 1929, as the stock market frothed to record heights, Raskob soured on stocks. Bricks and mortar might have seemed less ephemeral. Raskob needed only to crane his neck in the streets of Manhattan to see a thrilling new era being ushered in by the real estate men.

The bull market, coupled with engineering advances, had sparked a skyscraper boom. Twenty- and thirty-story buildings no longer even turned the heads of jaded locals. Publicity-hungry real estate developers regularly announced record-breaking skyscrapers, although many projects got no further than a press conference. By 1929, Manhattan had nearly 200 skyscrapers, about half the nation's total. New York's skyline had become its signature.

But like the stock market, real estate had always been whipsawed by booms and busts. It is difficult to imagine that an investor as astute as Raskob would not have considered the possibility that he was buying in near the top of the market. But Raskob also would have known that Walter P. Chrysler, a friend and business rival from the automobile industry, was planning his own Manhattan skyscraper. Chrysler wasn't saying how tall. That Raskob, a man with no experience in real estate, would choose as his inaugural project to erect the tallest building in the world is testament to either a supreme confidence, a blooming arrogance, a fierce competitive drive, or, in all likelihood, all three. Whatever their motivations, Raskob and his partners were drawn into a contest for skyline supremacy, the financial rewards of which were anyone's guess. Over the coming months, the construction of office buildings in New York would veer into the realm of monument building.

Together, Raskob and du Pont sank about $8 million into the project to get it going. Bethlehem Engineering Corporation, the site's previous owner, had already scrapped plans to erect a 55-story office and loft building. There was scant economic justification for Raskob and his partners to erect anything much higher. But Raskob wanted to create a real stir. He yearned for something taller—the tallest, in fact. At a meeting with his architect, William F. Lamb, he stood a pencil on end and challenged Lamb, "How high can you make it so it won't fall down?"

Raskob suggested 100 stories. After working through more than a dozen schemes, Lamb and his associates at Shreve, Lamb & Harmon concluded that 80 stories would be optimal. Starrett Brothers, Raskob's contractor, estimated the Empire State Building would cost $30.4 million to build, not counting the $16.5 million spent on the land. On its face, it seemed laughably expensive for a single office building. But an appraiser hired by Raskob estimated that when fully rented, the tower would be worth $55 million. To Raskob and Smith, the project looked plenty solid on paper.

On October 1, 1929, Smith and Raskob climbed to the roof of the Waldorf-Astoria and theatrically raised a handsaw and hammer for the assembled photographers. "Gentlemen, stand back," Smith warned. With that, he tugged on a rope, toppling a weather-beaten section of cornice onto the roof. "This historic building, known all over the world, must come down in the northward march of progress," he proclaimed. With that began a whirlwind of activity unlike anything ever before seen in New York.

The advent of the skyscraper, a wholly American invention, was as much a testament to rampant self-promotion by builders as it was a reaction to the scarcity of land in New York City. Corporations had begun to view their buildings as advertisements. Was there a more attention-grabbing billboard than the top of the Manhattan skyline? As an exercise in gaining recognition, however, it was a nearly zero-sum game. There could be only one king of the skyline, one focal point for visitors craning their necks to pick out the tallest building. Builders like Smith and Raskob could do no more than guess at the economic payoff such a distinction would yield. Only the future would tell to what extent ego had begun to cloud the business judgments of otherwise shrewd men.

Within weeks of Smith's announcement, the Chrysler Building rose past the Woolworth Building, then the world's tallest. Bank of Manhattan's new tower on Wall Street, slated for 925 feet, was keeping pace with it floor for floor. Both were intent on bagging the record. Raskob and Smith must have sighed with relief when they learned that Walter Chrysler intended to top out his streamlined tower at 78 stories. But Raskob underestimated his old foe. The Bank of Manhattan building had crested an irritating two feet higher than Chrysler planned to go. Chrysler ordered his architect, William Van Alen, to reach higher. Van Alen reexamined his plans. His building's metallic dome was really nothing more than a fire tower. He suggested building something inside this tower, in secret, then hoisting it into place in the final hour. Together with his steel engineer, Van Alen designed a modernistic flagpole of latticed steel, 180 feet tall and eight feet seven inches wide at its base. Workers fabricated the javelin-like spire in pieces, lifted it into the tower, and riveted it together. A 30-ton crane stood ready. Van Alen waited for a perfectly calm morning. When it came, as the architect watched nervously from the street, the crane lifted the 28-ton needle into place. It took just 30 minutes. With that, Walter Chrysler's skyscraper topped out at 1,048 feet, taller than the 986-foot Eiffel Tower, then the world's tallest structure, and more important, taller than anything yet proposed by John Raskob.

Not to be outdone, Raskob ordered his architects back to the drafting table. One month later, at a luncheon of the Fifth Avenue Association, Smith announced that the Empire State Building had grown from 80 to 85 stories, or 1,050 feet. It would rise beyond Walter Chrysler's creation by two lengths of Smith's shoe. Smith, as it happened, was only warming to the contest. Weeks later, Smith announced that he and his partners expected that in the near future passenger zeppelins would establish "trans-Atlantic, transcontinental, and trans-Pacific lines, and possibly a route to South America from the port of New York." With "an eye to the future," Smith continued, he and his partners had decided to mount on the Empire State Building a 200-foot "mooring tower." Elevators would whisk zeppelin passengers down to Fifth Avenue within seven minutes of tying up, he promised. As for the potentially knotty details, Smith offered none.

The board of Metropolitan Life Insurance Company, from which Smith had only recently resigned, had approved a loan of $27.5 million to fund the building's construction. Terms of the loan called for the building to be enclosed within a year and completed by April 1, 1931. When Franklin D. Roosevelt, who had followed Smith into the governor's mansion, asked Smith when the building was to open, Smith told him May 1, 1931.

"I suppose that means the following October," replied Roosevelt.

"No," promised Smith. "Put that down on your calendar."

By February 1930, all that was left of the old Waldorf was a few chunks of mortar and pieces of the old walls. A long curving truck ramp descended into a massive hole. On Saint Patrick's Day, which Smith regarded as an auspicious day, he set into motion the symphony of planning that Lamb and the contractor had labored over for months. An army of workers that would soon swell to more than 3,000 descended on the site. Derricks swung steel girders into place 18 hours after they left the furnaces in Pittsburgh and just hours after they had been numbered for assembly in an empty lot in New Jersey. The building's skeleton marched upward at a rate of four and a half floors a week. In June, 290 bricklayers and 384 carriers left the ground, chasing the steelworkers into the sky as they ate into a lode of 10 million bricks. Following them, stoneworkers clad the building in a thin layer of Indiana limestone, 200,000 cubic feet in all. Onto this gray skin workers bolted 300 tons of polished chrome-nickel alloy fashioned into shining vertical spandrels. Red metal window frames were laid into 6,400 holes in the tower.

Groaning trucks clogged the nearby streets, waiting to dump their payloads. Elevators whisked steel, tiles, sheet iron, bales of wire, lumber, and pipe to the upper reaches, where miniature railcars moved it to the tradesmen. The skeleton crawled with workers. Four restaurants were set up to serve hot noon meals, and water boys roamed the structure with milk and cigarettes. Crowds gathered on the sidewalks to marvel at the spectacle. Cranes high above swung bundles of girders to the 285 steelworkers. The air rang with the hammerblows of the riveters, who perched precariously on the girders they joined together with cherry-hot rivets. Smith could only shake his head in disbelief. "I made one trip up," he marveled to a reporter for the *New York Sun*. "And once was enough. When I saw some of those kids—steelriggers and stone masons—go toe-dancing over steel beams or maybe along a foot-wide strip of stone work, with not a thing under them but air, it made me kind of sick. I don't see how they did it. Honest, I don't."

On September 9, a bow-tied Smith joined Raskob, du Pont, and Lamb at the building's Fifth Avenue entrance, a silver trowel in hand. A crowd of 5,000 had gathered to watch Smith cement in the building's cornerstone, a 4,500-pound block of Swedish granite. Behind the stone Smith placed a copper box containing a history of the building, photographs of himself, his partners, and the architects, samples of coins and paper currency up to $100, and a rag-paper edition of the day's *New York Times*. "If this building is ever demolished to make way for a greater building, the people of that day can read pretty accurately the history of the day," Smith intoned, reflecting the widely held belief that buildings would eventually soar far higher.

During the previous decade alone, the city's population had grown by 2 million, reaching nearly 7 million. With 1930 only two-thirds over, New York was on its way to demolishing a record number of buildings, with 1,598 already razed and at least 1,265 more expected to fall. The skyscraper was still a novelty, and real estate experts could only guess how high buildings would eventually go. That September, one engineer told the American Welding Society that a mile-high tower— the equivalent of four Empire State Buildings stacked atop one another—was perfectly feasible. Professor Clyde Morris of Ohio State University predicted that when high winds buffeted these ultrahigh structures, occupants would occasionally become ill with "a malady akin to sea sickness."

In late September 1930, steelworkers riveted the last piece of structural steel into place on the Empire State Building. An

American flag was unfurled at 1,058 feet, to the cheers of more than a dozen workers who stood precariously on the top beam waving their hats. By now, the simple elegance of William Lamb's design was apparent to anyone who frequented the midtown streets. Gone was the classical ornamentation, the terraced bulk, of early skyscrapers. The Empire State Building was all vertical lines. No cornices or ornaments interrupted the soaring expanse of limestone. Lamb had forsaken the tradition of setting windows back into a building's facade, a visual trick used to reassure occupants of a building's strength. The effect, Lamb reasoned, would be lost on a wall 1,000 feet high and 200 feet wide. Window setbacks would visually perforate it into a monotonous grid. Lamb set the windows nearly flush with the limestone. The tower was sleek, Machine Age, its spandrels stamped with lightning bolts, the gently sloping setbacks of its apex making it appear even taller than it was.

In all of the breathless newspaper coverage of Smith's new building, in all of Smith's ruminations on the tides of change, a potentially serious problem remained virtually unmentioned. On October 29, 1929, weeks after the demolition of the Waldorf had begun, the stock market crashed. Sixteen million shares traded on a single day, and the greatest economic depression in the nation's history began. Privately, Smith was gravely concerned. Almost overnight, it had become untenable for Raskob to assert that it made economic sense for his building to rise to the top of the skyline. It probably would not have been too late to reverse course, had Raskob's pride allowed it. There is no evidence that the partners seriously considered it.

If Smith had ever believed the Empire State Building would reap big returns for little personal effort, he had been sorely mistaken. Smith had to find tenants quickly. Yet businesses were shedding offices, not leasing new ones. He had hoped the venture would be a pleasant distraction from his political woes. But the job quickly became full-time—and a pressure cooker, at that. Smith put up an increasingly unconvincing front about the building's prospects. "We have reason to believe it will be fully rented from the start of occupancy," insisted Smith more than two months after the market plunged. As construction forged ahead, more and more people on the street below began wondering aloud, "How can they fill it?"

The Great Depression affected people of every economic station, but was particularly devastating to the newer Americans, the Irish, Italian, and Jewish immigrants, Al Smith's people, who had ridden the economic boom out of the tenements. To the thousands of workers toiling on the project, the Empire State Building was a godsend. They clung to their jobs like a lifeline. In early April 1931, as the building neared completion, a 30-year-old Italian carpenter's helper in a blue work shirt and gray pants arrived at the site at 8 A.M., saying he was looking for work. He appeared despondent. He rode an elevator toward the top, then leaped from a window, striking a roof on the twenty-first floor, where workers found his broken and lifeless body. Police discovered that the man, who left behind a wife and child, had once worked on the building.

As if the economic news wasn't bad enough, Smith and his partners faced formidable technical challenges to their dirigible-mooring scheme. Anyone who bothered to ponder the mechanics of unloading passengers at such heights came away skeptical. Tall buildings break breezes into incalculable currents. City streets act like chimneys. Roofs reflect the sun and generate minisqualls, turning the air turbulent and untrustworthy. How would the enormous craft, devilishly difficult to steer, reach the spearlike mast of the Empire State Building in the erratic winds? Did Smith really expect passengers to step out of a wind-buffeted dirigible onto a long, sway-ing gangplank a quarter mile above the pavement? The world's most experienced pilot, Hugo Eckener, who had piloted the *Graf Zeppelin* on the first around-the-world flight, offered an embarrassing assessment. "I would never try it with the *Graf Zeppelin*," he told an *Evening Post* reporter. Nonethe-less, on November 21, 1930, steelworkers toiling unseen in the fog installed the last pieces of the 200-foot mooring mast.

When the scaffolding finally came down off the mooring mast, the growing reservations about the zeppelin scheme seemed to matter a little less. The plan had spurred architect Lamb to his crowning achievement. The mast, a glinting, chrome-nickel shaft, was lined with vertical bands of light, seemingly held up by winged buttresses in cast aluminum. He had given Manhattan a monument to the future itself.

☐ne year and 45 days after construction began, the build-ing was finished. It had cost less than $42 million, well under budget, thanks to the Depression. If Smith and his partners were filled with foreboding about the building's economic prospects, they weren't about to let it spoil their party.

On May 1, 1931, a cool, cloudless day dusted with haze, Mary Warner and Arthur Smith, Smith's two grandchildren, struggled to snip a ribbon stretched in front of the building's Fifth Avenue entrance. Their grandfather stepped forward, yanked it down, and several hundred invited guests surged into the lobby. Mounted police held back thousands of spec-tators. At precisely 11:45 A.M., the man who had ended Smith's political career, President Herbert Hoover, walked into the telegraph room at the White House and pressed a button. The marble lobby of the Empire State Building was flooded with light. Smith invited his guests to take in the view from the eighty-sixth-floor observation deck.

Men and women pressed to the parapets, transfixed by the

sight of the sprawling city laid out like a blanket below them: the factories of Brooklyn, the green hills of Staten Island, the apartments of the Bronx, the tree-lined streets of Queens. Steamers and tugs crawled across the waterways like bugs. To the south, they could see down through the bay, the Verrazano Narrows, and all the way out to sea. Seemingly at their feet, tiny cars and trucks inched up the ribbons of Fifth Avenue and Broadway. The city's other skyscrapers seemed less awe-inspiring when viewed from above. "Few failed to exclaim at the smallness of man and his handiwork as seen at this great distance," noted one reporter.

That night, after darkness blanketed the city, turning the vista into a field of a million lights, Smith offered over the radio airwaves his sentimental perspective on the changes transforming the city. "The ground upon which this building stands was farm land when my own mother was born," Smith said. "The present value of this land is twenty million dollars, but from the top of this building you can see cabbages growing in the fields of the few truck gardens that remain on Long Island. It is truly wonderful to look back on little old New York with its three-story brownstone private houses and the subdued quiet of its gaslamps, and the music of the bells on the collars of the horses that pulled the street cars, and look upon it tonight with its great towering structures—the Empire State Building, the tallest building in the world. The flood of light that surrounds the island and the swiftly passing automobiles below almost makes one feel that he has been suddenly carried from old New York to the fairyland of new New York—the center of the world and of industrial activity."

For Smith, it may have been his most satisfying moment as a developer, when the triumph of bringing something new and exciting to the city was fresh. But real estate history is filled with the hard-luck stories of developers who were blinded by the magnificence of their own buildings. Smith and his partners had not only altered the skyline of the nation's largest city, they had defined it. Yet the hardest part was yet to come. They had to prove that the Empire State Building was more than just a monument to their own unbridled ambitions. They had to make it pay off.

To the general public, the Empire State Building swiftly proved magnetic. In part, in a day in which few people had ever flown in an airplane, it was the utter newness of looking down at the world from a quarter mile high. Like a midway barker, Al Smith boasted that the tower's eighty-sixth-floor observatory and its tiny, glass-enclosed one-hundred-and-second-floor gallery offered "a view unsurpassable without actually flying." Although Walter Chrysler ignored a special invitation from Smith, during the first four days of May 17,000 others paid one dollar a head to ride to the top. Within a month, despite the Depression's squeeze on people in every walk of life, nearly 100,000 had paid for the trip.

Few people from America's hinterlands had ever set foot on an elevator, let alone stood 86 stories above a city street. On the open-air terrace of the observatory, a four-and-a-half-foot parapet was all that separated visitors from the gut-wrenching void. Gripping the rail tightly, visitors would peer warily over the edge, stiffening their legs against the knee-weakening effects of vertigo. "That's a long way down," is all many could manage.

Guard Pete Aloysius, a husky redhead who began patrolling the observatory on opening day, saw an astonishing range of reactions to the high exposure. The wife of an airline pilot, herself scared to death of flying, walked right over to the wall and gazed down. Her husband the pilot scurried back to the enclosed section, stuck his head out a window, and hollered for her to back away from the edge. One day, five sailors from a ship anchored in the East River decided to walk on their hands and knees around the wall encircling the observatory.

Parents set their children up on the wall to photograph, then berated guards who plucked them off.

For many native New Yorkers, it was as if they were seeing their city for the first time. Guards chuckled as locals confused Brooklyn with New Jersey. In July came tantalizing newspaper reports that binocular- and telescope-toting men had spotted nude sunbathers on the roof of an apartment complex near the East River. "This afternoon, for instance, the prize peek was a nude young lady who sat upon a cot in a nearby building's penthouse yard and painted her toe nails a blood red," one paper breathlessly reported. It is unclear what role the building's press agents played in such pulse-quickening reports, which doubtless did no harm to the building's attendance figures. To Smith and his partners, the numbers rolling in were cause for celebration. Visits to the observatory were double what they had expected, and it seemed possible that 1 million people might make the trip in the first year.

The building swiftly proved seductive to legions of thrill seekers and kooks, who reacted as if the Matterhorn had been dropped into midtown Manhattan. America was gripped by an epidemic of flagpole sitting and tree perching, marathon dancing, nonstop bicycle riding, eating and drinking contests, and other attention-getting feats. Alvin "Shipwreck" Kelly, the patron saint of flagpole sitters, requested permission to ply his trade atop the mooring mast. Smith said no. A group of radio engineers at the building formed the Top Nut Club, admitting colleagues willing to clamber up an iron ladder, pass through a trapdoor, climb the iron spikes on the pole holding a radio antenna and weather instruments, and touch the top nut of the weather vane. Five members of the Polish Olympic ski team, in town for the 1932 Winter Olympics at Lake Placid, bounded up the building's stairwell, two stairs per stride. When they emerged 21 minutes later on the one hundred and second floor, they found the Czechoslovakian ski team. An attaché of the Czech consulate immediately challenged the Poles to a race. Building managers scotched the idea. (Forty-three years later, a former New York City fireman won the New York Road Runners club's first annual footrace up the stairs, reaching the top in just 12 minutes, 32 seconds. At the time, he was drawing a tax-free disability pension of $11,822 a year from the fire department for a back injury.)

Smith and his partners, desperate to fill the building with paying tenants, welcomed almost any publicity they could get. Characters like A.W. Aldrich were a publicist's dream. One February afternoon, the short, bald, 49-year-old Vermont farmer loosened his tie and took to the stairs, carrying his coat over one arm and his hat in hand. He plodded flat-footed, "like an Indian," to save his leg muscles, he later said. He reached the one hundred and second floor 37 minutes and 1,860 stairs later. "It was sort of monotonous, but there's some good masonry," he told reporters. "We don't call this high in Vermont." The newspapers gleefully pumped his climb into an Olympian feat. The 1933 release of *King Kong*, with its climactic scene of a great ape making its last stand on the building's crown, turned its dramatic silhouette into an indelible image to millions of moviegoers across the nation.

Yet there was also a dark side to the building's growing allure. Six months after the building opened, a blond, blue-eyed man boarded the elevator to the one hundred and second floor, nervously fingering five cigars in a small box he held. When the doors opened at the enclosed uppermost observatory, he bolted out, vaulted a metal gate, bounded up a stairwell to the dirigible-landing balcony, and threw himself over the breast-high parapet. He struck the base of mooring mast, breaking some glass, dropped past 20 visitors on the eighty-sixth-floor observatory, and landed on a narrow roof. In the pocket of his gray suit was a picture postcard of a group of German schoolboys and a priest. On the back, he had written in German: "My darling: This is a picture of my son,

Arnim, which was taken in Astoria, L.I. on June 4, 1930."
Police identified the man as Friedrich Eckert, a 32-year-old
shopkeeper from Queens.

To Smith's horror, Eckert was not to be the last lost soul
who looked to the building as a way out of the world. Occasionally, luck intervened. The following September, 37-year-
old C. Cass Lawler rode the elevator to the observation deck
and placed his topcoat and briefcase on the terrace. In his
coat pocket, he left a note to a Mrs. P. J. Lawler that read:
"Have been sickly. Bad Rheumatism." He waited until only
two women stood near him, then climbed onto the parapet
and jumped. The women screamed. The observatory manager ran to the wall and looked over in horror. On a three-
foot ledge three stories below he saw Lawler, very much
alive.

But more often, fate played the other way. Two winters
later, 20-year-old Irma Eberhardt phoned her boyfriend at the
Manhattan restaurant where she had left him after a quarrel.
"I'm going to kill myself," she told him, then hung up. As he
raced to a nearby police station, she rode the elevator to the
observatory and jumped into the darkness. The wind carried
her over ledges and roofs. She struck a sixth-floor setback,
then crashed into a frosted glass and metal marquee above
the street with the violence of an explosion. In her black
handbag, still clutched tightly in her hand, police found a
YMCA membership card, 83 cents in change, and a compact
carrying lipstick and rouge.

The owners were baffled by the dark allure their building
had cast over the suicide-prone, and felt powerless to stop
them. Suicides, at the time, were viewed as a police matter.
Only later would psychiatrists come to understand that some
people bent on ending their lives were determined to make a
dramatic display of it. It was their last statement. In the distorted logic of the suicide-prone, the Empire State Building
offered an incomparable platform for telling the world, "You

failed me." A leap off the observation deck was not something loved ones could hide from the world.

Guards had been trained to keep their eyes peeled for the wild-eyed. But too many jumpers had been able to conjure up an almost preternatural calm before their lonely dives. It would take nearly 16 years for Raskob and his partners to be shamed into making a serious effort to deal with the problem. On January 26, 1947, Frances Coover of Ames, Iowa, was walking along the sidewalk in front of the building when she was struck and injured by a man hurtling to his death. His was the ninth suicide leap from the observation tower. (Six others had jumped from office windows.) On May 10, after a melancholy salesman threw himself off the observation deck, the owners took action. "Although the problem of suicide is primarily a police matter," a building manager said, "the building desires to render every possible assistance in curbing those bent on ending their own lives as well as preventing any possible injury to people on the street." He announced that a steel fence would be erected on top of the observation deck's four-foot six-inch parapet.

Bracing for a final rush, the observatory manager added guards and instructed them to watch for people who were alone and acting agitated or morose. In June, after a noticeably nervous elderly woman bought a ticket, a manager rushed to the terrace to stay with her. He eventually guided her all the way to the street, where she admitted she was contemplating suicide. Two weeks later, a jittery 29-year-old man stood at the edge of the deck staring out at the lights of the city. A guard moved close and struck up a conversation. The man confided that his head was spinning and his life was a mess. He wanted to end it, the man said. The guard called an ambulance, and persuaded the troubled man to ride to Bellevue Hospital.

But that wasn't always possible. The 22-year-old man in the loud plaid sport coat standing before the parapet on July 14 and gazing at the Hudson River appeared calm and in good spirits. He removed the wallet from his pocket. A quarter dropped to the terrace and rolled toward a 12-year-old boy. The boy retrieved it and offered it to the man. "You keep it," the man replied. "I won't need it." The boy plugged the quarter into a telescope. The man laid his wallet on the terrace and climbed the wall. A guard rushed toward him. The man jumped to his death. Between October 20 and November 9, guards intercepted five more people bent on jumping. Finally, on December 4, 1947, a seven-foot-tall fence with diamond-shaped mesh slightly bigger than a human head was in place. At its top, steel rails curved inward. It left building managers with the impression—mistaken, it would prove—that the only way down now was the elevators or stairs.

The men who erected the Empire State Building had succeeded in creating a nearly universal totem of New York. Yet their late, great entry in the first wave of skyscrapers was meting out a painful lesson. Their stated intention had been to make money. But the real estate business, they were learning, seldom rewarded monument builders. Trying to outdo your next-door neighbor was not a sound formula for making money. More often, it was a recipe for ruin. Developers overcome by the impulse to possess a piece of the skyline were said to suffer from "edifice complex." It was a shorthand way to say that ego or raw ambition had gotten in the way of business sense.

Shortly after the building opened, Al Smith received a gift in the mail from an admirer. It was a model of the Empire State Building, more than two feet tall, carved entirely from a block of anthracite coal. There is no record of whether Smith regarded the gift as any kind of an omen. But by then, in spite of the public acclaim for the building, despite the crowds of paying visitors, in spite of the financial might of his partners, it was dawning on Smith that the project could go down as one of the biggest blunders of his life. Smith was now the public face of a venture that embodied the yawning disconnect between the speculative excess of the 1920s and the grim economic reality of the 1930s. The Empire State Building became a symbol of its time, but not the kind that Smith and his partners had anticipated.

Raskob and du Pont, now snug in an eightieth-floor office decorated with imported, hand-carved, Georgian paneling and working marble fireplaces, had felt the logic of the project was unassailable. Yet below them, for floor after floor after floor, there was not a single tenant. Although Smith had boasted that a sizable portion of the tower had been preleased from plans, it was 80 percent vacant. The Model Brassiere Company's outpost on the forty-first floor was Raskob's nearest neighbor. Within months, the word "folly" was on the lips of New Yorkers. The building's woes cropped up in vaudeville gags and songs. Acid-penned cartoonists lampooned it. The "Empty State Building," it was called. Smith ordered 60-watt bulbs to be left burning on the cavernous empty floors above the forty-first so it didn't appear that the building's spire was floating on air. Each night, a watchman trudged down from the eighty-sixth to the fiftieth floor, punching time clocks and making sure the mail chute below Raskob's office had not clogged. A year and a half after the gala opening, rental reports show, only 25 percent of the building's available space had been leased, and 56 of its 86 floors were vacant.

The zeppelin-mooring plan was merely the most visible embarrassment. In September 1931, a small dirigible circled the mooring mast, jockeying in a 40-mile-per-hour wind. On the one-hundred-and-fifth-floor balcony, three men from its crew waited to grab a rope trailed by the aircraft. A steeplejack was poised with a sharp knife to sever the line if it got tangled. At 9:10 A.M., with considerable difficulty, the crew secured the craft for a scant three minutes. Several weeks later, the far larger Goodyear blimp *Columbia* motored in, trailing from a 100-foot rope a bundle of *Evening Journals* that had been plucked from the roof of the newspaper's plant across town. After several misses, the bundle hit the parapet, and the rigger cut it loose and passed it to Smith. No one dared remark that the chore would have been far simpler on the ground. With that, Smith and his partners, as quietly as they possibly could, simply dropped their plan to make their skyscraper into the transportation hub of the future.

To keep the building in the news, publicity agents resorted to a string of increasingly hokey antics, repeatedly summoning a depressed Smith to serve as ringmaster. A bronco rider passing through town with a traveling rodeo was invited to ride his horse into the lobby and take it up the elevator to the top. Circus giant Robert Wadlow, an eight-foot five-inch 19-year-old, posed for a publicity photo with Smith peering at him through a telescope. There were bicycle riders from Holland, cowboys from the Ozarks, chorus girls from Times Square, and spelling bee champions from the New Hampshire hills. Dr. Alfred Warsaw, an 80-year-old former opera singer from Washington, was allowed to test whether he could make himself heard on the streets below. (A reporter down below said all he could hear was taxi horns.)

The Empire State Building, it was now obvious, was lurching toward bankruptcy, saved only by the deep pockets of Raskob and du Pont. In its first 19 months, the building lost a whopping $4.2 million. Raskob and du Pont restructured their financing, giving up some of their ownership stake to the holders of the second mortgage bonds in exchange for more favorable repayment terms. Metropolitan Life, which held the $27.5 million mortgage, agreed to defer some of the interest payments. The emergency measures gave the owners only the slimmest breathing room.

In January 1933, Smith's treasurer wrote a gloomy letter to

the Board of Commissioners of New York City Department of Taxes and Assessments. The owners had received "no return whatever on their investment of $23,500,000," he wrote, and more losses were likely. "Manifestly it is impossible for any property, no matter how well financed, to carry a burden of this kind without relief. We are exhausting every effort to provide the relief needed in order to prevent the failure of this great enterprise which would be a great blow, not only to the owners, but to the City of New York and its property owners everywhere." The city had already shaved the building's assessed value from $42 million to $40 million. Smith's treasurer pleaded with the city to reduce the value, and thus the tax bill, once more. The city slashed the assessment to $34 million. Later that year, Metropolitan Life agreed to postpone all interest payments. More important, the insurer agreed not to try to foreclose on the building before March 1, 1935.

Metropolitan Life, in fact, had no desire to own a nearly empty skyscraper whose woes were intensifying as the Depression dragged on. In March 1935, Smith wrote to a vacationing Raskob about the bleak outlook: "I can sum it up in a few words and say that it could scarcely be worse than it is." Smith begged and pleaded, gaining another reprieve from Metropolitan Life, this time from the beginning of scheduled principal payments. By 1936, the city had cut the building's assessment to just $28 million, more than $12 million less than the construction cost. Raskob and du Pont mulled over the prospects for selling the building, which was still vacant between floors 42 and 80. They weren't good. On the final day of 1937, the building's worst year ever, Smith concluded another restructuring with Metropolitan Life, the building's third. Raskob's decision to press ahead with construction of the Empire State Building in the teeth of an economic depression was proving an epic business blunder.

What Smith and his partners really longed for was to be rid of their albatross altogether. In 1942, they secretly began looking for a buyer, a formidable task given the building's still-shaky finances. It was hardly a time when wealthy men were of a mind to gamble on the future. America had entered World War II. Who but the federal government had that kind of money to throw around during wartime?

Smith and his partners pressed the government to buy it. On May 26, 1943, Smith delivered his pitch in a letter to Harold Smith, the government's Director of Budget. "In our initial meeting to discuss the purchase of the Empire State Building by the Federal Government I purposely avoided discussing the question of price and terms in order to have opportunity to study these questions more carefully," Smith wrote. "I think you will find the two statements enclosed herewith most interesting in support of the $38,000,000 price now submitted." If the government bought the skyscraper and filled it with the federal employees then scattered across the city, Smith argued, it would save $1.5 million a year. The $38 million purchase price, he wrote, would be worked off in 14 years. The government didn't bite, nor did anyone else. In early 1944, a dejected Smith wrote to du Pont: "As you know for the past two years we have been engaged in an effort to dispose of our building which, so far, has not been successful, but we are continuing our effort with the hope of eventual success."

That May, Smith's wife of 44 years died of pneumonia, and he retreated to the seclusion of his apartment, a broken man. In August the 70-year-old Smith entered the hospital suffering from heat exhaustion. Weeks later, Smith passed away of lung congestion and heart failure, and was laid to rest beside his wife under a plain stone marker on the side of a hill in the Old Calvary Cemetery in Long Island City.

Bad luck continued to dog Smith's surviving partners. It must have seemed, in fact, as if the building was cursed.

Jack Wernli, a staff photographer who snapped celebrities on the observation deck, was late again for work on the morning of Saturday, July 28, 1945. He got off the elevator on the eighty-fifth floor and tiptoed up the stairs to 86, intent on avoiding his boss. At 9:49 A.M., as he pulled the lever on the time clock, there was a deafening explosion. He figured his boss had rigged a booby trap.

Army Lieutenant Colonel William Smith Jr., a 27-year-old veteran of 34 bombing missions over Germany, had been flying a twin-engine B-25 bomber from Bedford, Massachusetts, to New York's LaGuardia Airport, and had secured permission to continue to Newark, New Jersey. The fog was blinding. When he dropped down out of the clouds, he found himself approaching a forest of skyscrapers. In a panic, he banked away from the Grand Central Building, then from another tower on Fifth Avenue, only to find himself bearing down on the biggest one of all. In desperation, he pulled up hard, twisting. The 10-ton bomber plowed into the office of War Relief Services of the National Catholic Welfare Conference on the seventy-eighth and seventy-ninth floors, 913 feet off the street, tearing a gaping hole in the Empire State Building's north side. The aircraft's wings sheared off. Its fuselage hammered into an I-beam between elevator shafts, bending it 18 inches inward. The building shuddered. The bomber's fuel tanks exploded, sending brilliant orange flames leaping as high as the observatory and flaming fuel blowing through the offices and cascading down the stairwells. One of the aircraft's engines torpedoed out the south wall of the building, falling to the roof of a 12-story building on Thirty-second Street, where it started a fire that demolished the penthouse of noted sculptor Henry Hering, destroying much of his life's work. Fortunately, the artist was playing golf at Scarsdale Golf Club. The other engine crashed onto the roof of an empty elevator, sending it plunging to the basement 1,000 feet below.

Fifteen to twenty female clerical workers for the War Relief Services fled their desks in terror. Only a few reached the safety of the fireproof stairwell. A male coworker either jumped or was blown from a window, landing on a ledge six floors down, where his body was later found. An elevator operator was blasted out of her cab and burned severely. Two women found her, administered first aid, and turned her over to another elevator operator to transport to the lobby. When the doors closed on that car, the cable snapped with a crack like a rifle, and the two women plunged to the basement. Firemen cut through its roof, and a 17-year-old Coast Guard apprentice who had dashed into the building carrying a first aid kit crawled in. He was astonished to find the two women alive, thanks to automatic braking devices. "Thank God, the Navy's here," said the burned woman.

Firemen extinguished the flames in 40 minutes and began removing the bodies of 11 building occupants and the bomber's three-man crew. Early that afternoon, Brigadier General C. P. Kane, commanding general of the Atlantic Overseas Air Technical Service Command at Newark, arrived to take charge of the Army investigation. He refused to take questions, or even give his name. A colonel accompanying him barked to the swarm of reporters: "The Army wants no publicity on this."

After 15 years of adversity, Raskob was now hardened to it. He declared the building sound, and reopened it for business on Monday morning, two days after the accident. The spectacular crash—which seemed like a lost scene from *King Kong*—cemented the building's mystique as more than an office tower. The towering sentinel on New York's skyline had absorbed the blow, from a bomber no less, like a giant sequoia, quivering only momentarily.

Just what Raskob and his partners had given to the city of New York, however, was still far from certain. Was it the largest architectural folly ever built, a rich man's version of the quirky stone castles erected in faraway places by eccentric builders intent on glorifying themselves? Or was it a sane business venture? Oddly enough, those were the very same questions that would rear up 46 years later when one of the strangest hunting parties ever to roam the planet in search of real estate trophies made the Empire State Building a singular obsession.

Trophy Hunting

I n October 1983, decades after the disastrous early years of
the Empire State Building had slipped from the city's col-
lective memory, an Asian woman crossing a street in London caught the eye of Jean-Paul Renoir, the French-American
investment banker who would eventually find himself at the
center of the intrigue over the skyscraper. She's attractive, he
thought. She looks like she has class. The following day, to
Renoir's astonishment, the very same woman appeared in the
office of his boss, Duke Chapman. Kiiko Nakahara had come
to tell Chapman, then an American Express executive in London, of her desire to acquire overseas assets for her father, a
wealthy Tokyo businessman. To Chapman, who was more
accustomed to seeing Greek shipping magnates or Middle
Eastern tycoons, Kiiko's mission struck him as odd. The meeting yielded no business at all for Chapman. But Renoir, who
worked for Chapman, was smitten. Renoir, then 36, liked
Kiiko's style. She seemed charming and exotic. Renoir spent
the next week with her in London. To Renoir, she seemed

more supportive of him and frugal in her ways than his American second wife had been. "I can understand why John Lennon broke up the Beatles to be with Yoko Ono," he would later remark. "There is something so refreshing about a Japanese woman after you've been with these American bitches." It was Renoir's nature to speak bluntly about such matters, not in a ribald or elbow-ribbing manner, but with stone-cold seriousness. He was, it would seem, an unflinchingly judgmental man.

Renoir, who had been dividing his time between London and Bahrain for American Express's Lehman Brothers unit, was regarded by his peers as a smart businessman, a tireless worker, and a good salesman who knew his product cold. Yet he had always struck colleagues as alarmingly intense, impatient, and more than a little angry at the world. He wore his hair military-short, wasted little time on small talk, and peppered his speech with profanity. He was capable of considerable charm, but could also be curt and abrasive, especially to those he thought disagreed with him. He intimidated people, put them on the defensive, came across like a tough guy in a suit. "He kind of scares some people," one longtime associate later recalled. "The way he talks. He looks like a gangster. I don't know if he still has that haircut. He could be a lumberjack, or in the French foreign legion. People always said, 'You wouldn't want to piss him off.' "

From early on Renoir had been troubled by issues of identity. He was born Jean-Claude Perez Van Neste in Marseille, France, in 1947. His father, a small-time wholesaler, was Jewish, his mother, a Flemish Catholic. A sense of persecution took hold in Renoir early, leavened by his father's stories of being hounded by the World War II Vichy regime and fleeing to the south of France. Although Renoir's mother raised him as a Roman Catholic, he felt the sting of anti-Semitism when other schoolchildren discovered that his father was a Jew. Renoir enrolled in martial arts classes, and after a few dustups, his schoolmates stopped picking on him. By age 11, Renoir was lifting weights, a practice he continued for years, which gave him the broad-shouldered look of a brawler. At age 14, he was sent to school in Scotland, where he perfected his English. Already, Renoir was dreaming of building a business empire, but his parents, he would later claim, denigrated his aspirations. Renoir grew to despise them. (Years later, when his father died, Renoir skipped the funeral, and he has said he intends to do the same with his mother.) His grandmother arranged for him to move to the United States at age 17 to live with his aunt and uncle. Concerned about anti-Semitism, he changed his name to Jean-Paul Renoir. In a decision his detractors would later use to raise suspicions about his honesty, he made no concerted attempt to change his name on official French records for 30 years.

Renoir came away from France viewing his homeland as an appalling country, bigoted and hostile to anyone who managed to accumulate money. "It has a false modesty toward money," he would say, "in the same way that Americans have a false modesty toward sex." In the United States, Renoir flourished. He attended Johns Hopkins University. The counterculture was beginning to flower, but Renoir dressed in French suits and joined the ROTC. He graduated in three years, became a U.S. citizen, was commissioned in the Army, then attended New York University business school, where he married and quickly divorced. Primed on fitness and health food, Renoir viewed himself as an adventurer, the kind of man, he would later say, who in the 1400s would have gone on the Crusades, in the 1600s, to America. In the 1970s, he chose venture capital, working for a small New York firm. He married for a second time, but grew to resent his wife for her spending. Renoir saw himself as a Calvinist about such things. They separated and later divorced. In the early 1980s, he joined Lehman Brothers, moved to London, and began prospecting for institutional clients and wealthy individuals in the Middle

East, spending considerable time in Bahrain. Although the temperature in the desert routinely hit 100 degrees, Renoir would run through the sun-blasted landscape, sometimes in the heat of the afternoon. His colleagues called him "Man of Steel."

Not long after he met Kiiko in London, Renoir moved to Hong Kong, and their relationship blossomed during weekends in the Philippines. Kiiko struggled with her English and spoke no French. Renoir spoke little Japanese. They communicated with one another in a broken hodgepodge of English and Japanese.

It was around this time that Kiiko first appeared at the office of Patricia Hawkes, an affable if slightly eccentric English expatriate in Paris. Patricia and her husband Philip were veteran real estate brokers specializing in the sale of architecturally distinctive properties at least two centuries old. It is a challenging business. As Patricia Hawkes is fond of saying, nobody needs a French château. However historic and regal they may look from the outside, more often than not they are damp, cold, and in need of substantial work on the inside. For rich people accustomed to hot tubs, swimming pools, and tennis courts, they are all but unlivable. And they are sinkholes for money. But to a certain class of buyer that values classical beauty, the centuries-old estates of the French aristocracy hold a unique allure. The Hawkes's challenge is to separate legitimate buyers from the stream of eccentrics chasing fantasies. At first, Patricia didn't know what to make of Kiiko Nakahara. Through her interpreter, Kiiko told Patricia that her father had ordered her to buy 40 of the best châteaux in France. To Philip, such a ludicrously grandiose pronouncement didn't inspire a great degree of confidence.

Yet Kiiko had come recommended by a brokerage firm in London, which had sold her property in Oxfordshire. Patricia inferred that Kiiko must have real money. So she began driving Kiiko from château to château in the countryside around Paris, teaching her about their history. As they canvassed the historic sites, Kiiko took photographs, roll after roll of them. These, she said, were for her father. After her father saw the pictures, Kiiko would always phone back. For month after month, château after château, the answer was the same. Her father was not interested. The properties weren't architecturally striking enough. Gradually, Patricia began to get a feel for the taste of her would-be buyer. Kiiko and her father were developing an eye for classical grandeur.

Kiiko had always described her father to Jean-Paul Renoir as a genius tycoon who was woefully misunderstood by his compatriots, who were jealous and eager to put him down. In the summer of 1985, when she and Renoir began speaking of marriage, Kiiko screwed up the courage to introduce Renoir to her father.

When Renoir entered Hideki Yokoi's office in an expensive district of Tokyo, the old man was sitting behind a messy desk. Renoir offered him a luxury watch he had purchased on a business trip to Geneva. Yokoi handed him a bag filled with Panasonic personal security alarms, the kind women carry to ward off attackers. Renoir looked around him in wonder. To Renoir, it looked like a warehouse of imitation Louis XV furniture. Yokoi spoke to his daughter in Japanese, then thrust a document toward Renoir. Kiiko told Renoir that her father wanted his opinion on a deal. Renoir glanced at the document, which looked like an old prospectus connected to the attempted sale of the assets of an insurance company. Renoir left the office with the impression that Yokoi was a throwback to an earlier time.

Kiiko and Renoir were married in a civil ceremony in August 1986. At first, Renoir remained in Hong Kong, his wife in Japan. In 1987, Renoir was finally able to join her when he transferred to Tokyo to set up an asset management unit for Lehman Brothers to market fixed-income investments to trust companies and life insurers. Renoir adopted Kiiko's son by her first marriage. Kiiko entertained her husband's clients and associates at their Tokyo apartment. She did not bow and scrape in traditional Japanese style, but presented herself more as an equal to her husband. Renoir saw his wife as a Japanese feminist.

In the summer of 1986, the American dollar fell from 260 yen to 150 yen in a matter of months, making Japanese goods more expensive in the United States, a troubling development for Japan's export economy. Japan's Ministry of Finance lowered interest rates to sustain economic growth, and Japanese businesses sucked in the cheap money like oxygen, plowing it back into stocks and real estate. Property values in Japan doubled between 1985 and 1989. In Tokyo, the value of land lost all connection to reality, driven into the stratosphere by speculative frenzy. Economist David Asher calculated that by 1988, Japan's landmass was worth four times all the land in the United States, which was 25 times larger. The grounds of the Imperial Palace in central Tokyo, which were categorically not for sale, were nonetheless worth as much as the entire state of California. Cramped two-bedroom Tokyo apartments were selling for $1 million, prompting one lender to introduce a 100-year mortgage, to be repaid by a borrower's grandchildren. In a triumph of myopic thinking typical of economic bubbles through the ages, experts predicted land prices would hold up.

Japan's "bubble economy," as it was later called, made Hideki Yokoi a billionaire. His most valuable holding, the Hotel New Japan, sat squarely in the heart of the Akasaka district, home to parliament, the prime minister, and the crown prince. The value of the land under it swelled tenfold to nearly $1 billion. It became the bedrock of Yokoi's fortune, which by his own estimate, peaked at $4 billion, although some media reports pegged it as high as $7 billion.

Like many of Tokyo's land-rich property moguls, Yokoi realized that runaway Japanese land prices had given him formidable buying power overseas, where property prices, in comparison, now seemed absurdly cheap. Buying cheaply had always been a bedrock business principal for Yokoi. Castles in England and France could be had for a few million dollars. It seemed to Yokoi as if he had little to lose. So he set out on a trophy-hunting spree like no other.

Yokoi recruited Kiiko—who, unlike him, had traveled widely in the Western world—to be his eyes and cars outside of Japan. She visited dozens of British castles and shipped Yokoi hundreds of photographs. The first castle to catch Kiiko's eye was called Thame Park, located in the countryside outside London. She told her father how lovely it was, how much she was impressed with it.

Yokoi examined the pictures. The castle indeed possessed a classical magnificence. It was as if it had been lifted from the pages of a fairy tale. He phoned his daughter. "Oh, it's so beautiful," he told her. "Compared to properties in Japan, it is cheap. So why don't you buy it."

Kiiko did just that, using money wired by her father. Yokoi told her to buy it for herself, Kiiko later maintained. He said he would visit and work the farmlands. "He wanted to live with me in England," she said. "He wanted to be a farmer in England." Kiiko eventually created a suite of rooms there for her father.

A few months later, while traveling through Surrey County in southeastern England, Kiiko fell in love with a second castle called Juniper Hill. She phoned her father. It's charming, she told him. When Yokoi saw photographs, he agreed. He told Kiiko to buy it. She bought it for 1.6 million pounds sterling. His appetite whetted, Yokoi began to collect castles in earnest. He bought 90-room Glenapp Castle, considered one of Scotland's most important landmarks, and Coopersale House, another historic British property. In Spain, outside Barcelona, Yokoi purchased Falguera Palace, once home to Spanish nobility.

It was in France, however, that the father-daughter team hit their stride. In January 1985, they purchased the regal château de Sully, which sits alongside the Seine River in the sleepy village of Rosny-sur-Seine, just a short drive from Paris. That spring, they bought a château hotel, and months later, another château. In 1987, they bought two more, and in 1988 they added a villa in the south of France and a magnificent restored château in Champigny-sur-Veude with its own stud farm and sixteenth-century gothic chapel. In 1989, they bought another two, capping off the portfolio with a small eighteenth-century château in Louveciennes, where Madame du Barry had once entertained her royal lover, Louis XV. All told, between 1985 and 1989, Nippon Sangyo, Yokoi's holding company, spent 154 million francs, or about $25 million, on nine châteaux.

Renoir, who was arguably the one best equipped to weigh the investment potential of the French properties, didn't share his wife's enthusiasm for the growing French portfolio. "He bought stupid properties in the boondocks of France," Renoir would later say. "He'd say, 'How can I lose? You can't buy an apartment in Tokyo for this.' "

Yokoi and his daughter were after more than a storybook kingdom in the French countryside. By 1988, America had begun to resemble one giant Wal-Mart to Japanese investors. Real estate, in particular, seemed ridiculously inexpensive. With the yen having doubled in value against the dollar, it was as if America was holding a half-price sale on its buildings. Japanese investors, emboldened by borrowing costs that were one-third of what they were in America, began snapping up hotels in Hawaii, office buildings in Los Angeles, golf courses in Florida. In 1988 alone, Japanese investors bought $10 billion worth of U.S. real estate, double what they had five years earlier. By 1991, this tidal wave of property purchases had hit $77 billion.

Sensing an opportunity that might never be repeated, Japanese buyers gravitated toward Tiffany-class buildings. They bought them for top dollar. They built them lavishly from scratch. Many American real estate veterans, whistling through their teeth, were only too willing to cash out. Number crunchers couldn't comprehend how Japanese trophy hunters could justify such spending. In 1989, the Sazale Group, a Tokyo hotel company, bought the 92-room Hotel Bel-Air in Los Angeles—a notorious playground for Hollywood royalty—for $110 million, a record $1.2 million a room. Japanese developer Takeshi Sekiguchi spent $600 million erecting the Grand Hyatt Wailea hotel in Maui, Hawaii. He built a fake volcano rigged to erupt twice a night, a 2,000-foot string of swimming pools, grottoes, and waterfalls connected by canal-like locks, and hot tubs bubbling with milk, minerals, fruits, and soda mix. His brochure anointed it the "ultimate creation by mankind on earth during this century." An American real estate economist calculated that to pay for such extravagance, the hotel needed to charge guests $700 a night. Japanese buyers shrugged off such skeptics. They weren't investing for the short term, they explained. In the long run, trophy properties would hold their value better than pedestrian ones, the buyers maintained. Many Americans figured they were right.

Yokoi was eager to join in the Japanese trophy-hunting binge in America. Kiiko contacted Naomi Okada, a Japanese native who had moved to New York years earlier to sell real estate. Yokoi's name sounded familiar to Okada. When he found Yokoi listed in *Forbes* magazine as one of the richest men in Japan, Okada realized that Yokoi could become a very lucrative client. Okada suggested to Kiiko a number of potential property investments in New York. Kiiko would relay the information to her father. Invariably, Yokoi sent word that he wasn't interested. Okada flew to Tokyo. Kiiko escorted him to see her father. "Maybe one day I'd like to live in America," Yokoi told Okada. After Okada returned to New York, Yokoi phoned him to inquire about the Biltmore, a mansion Yokoi had heard was the largest private residence in America. Yokoi instructed Okada to bid on it. Okada called around. The Asheville, North Carolina, landmark, built by the Vanderbilts, wasn't even for sale.

Yet not far from Manhattan, in Cold Spring Harbor on Long Island, sat a dilapidated 109,000-square-foot white elephant called Oheka Castle. Banker Otto Kahn had erected the home in 1919, borrowing its style directly from French châteaux he admired. It was a Gatsbyesque creation, nearly twice the size of William Randolph Hearst's San Simeon, surrounded by formal gardens and lawns as flat as billiard tables, with a dining room that comfortably sat more than 200. Orson Welles, in fact, had used its exterior in the filming of *Citizen Kane,* his film about Hearst. By the early 1980s, however, Oheka Castle had fallen into ruin. It had been vacant for seven years. There were no windows, doors, or gutters. Dozens of fires had consumed much of the roof. It had become a gothic magnet for local delinquents.

In 1984, just 15 minutes after first laying eyes on it, Gary Melius, a Queens-born real estate developer, offered $1.45 million for the derelict mansion and its 22 acres. His bid was accepted. Melius, a short, potbellied, onetime plumber who wears his hair combed straight back from his forehead, set out to carve the building into condominiums. Within a few years, Melius had poured $14 million into the effort, but was still well short of completing the job. With his money running dry, Melius put the castle on the market for $52 million.

When he heard about the property, Naomi Okada called Yokoi immediately.

"There's a 170-room castle for sale," Okada told him.

"Get me the information," said Yokoi. "Take lots of pictures. Express mail the rolls. We'll develop them here."

Okada shot 10 rolls of film while touring the property. He sent them off to Yokoi. A week later, his home telephone rang at 4 A.M.

"I just developed them," Yokoi told the groggy broker. He peppered Okada with additional questions.

Okada gathered answers and sent them to Japan. Yokoi instructed him to bid $10 million. Melius flatly rejected the offer. In the middle of the night, Melius and Yokoi hammered out a deal. Yokoi agreed to pay $22.5 million for the partially renovated mansion. On August 3, 1988, Kiiko and Melius closed the deal. After the paperwork was complete, Melius asked Kiiko whether she had made arrangements for security and maintenance. She admitted she hadn't. So Melius offered to manage the property, and Kiiko accepted. They cemented the deal over veal Parmesan at a local diner. Melius's first order from Yokoi was to erect a concrete wall around the entire 22-acre estate.

Still, this wasn't the kind of splash Yokoi wanted to make in America. He was after a bigger trophy. He sent his daughter ricocheting from one grandiose target to another. He dispatched her to New York to figure out how to buy the World Trade Center. She approached the owner of the *Queen Elizabeth II* ocean liner. She inquired about New York's Plaza Hotel and Rockefeller Center, and the Hearst Castle in California. She negotiated with bankers in an unsuccessful bid to buy Hilton Hotels Corporation. Many of Yokoi's targets were not even for sale. Kiiko struck out across the board.

Okada flew to Tokyo once again. The diminutive billionaire escorted him to a chauffeured limousine, which whisked the two men to Yokoi's bank. Yokoi walked the New York broker into a vault, opened a safe-deposit box, and pulled out bundles of stock certificates wrapped in string. Okada was unsure of what to make of the gesture. It seemed as if Yokoi wanted to prove to him that he was rich and important. Or maybe this was no more than a billionaire's idea of entertainment.

By now, it was dawning on Okada that Yokoi wasn't especially astute at buying real estate. Yokoi seemed to think that the only direction property values could move was up. Okada sensed that Yokoi might be more decisive about buying beaten-down companies. Okada decided to pitch him a whale: Cadillac Fairview, a troubled Canadian real estate giant. Okada flew to Toronto to tour the properties. He returned with Kiiko for another look. Okada figured Yokoi would need to bid $1.5 billion. On the day of the deadline, Okada and Kiiko waited in Toronto for a call from Yokoi. And waited. And waited. Yokoi never phoned. Another potential deal was dead. Yokoi seemed be losing focus. He ordered Okada to meet with Macy's executives about a bid, to contact a New York bank that was in play. Okada began to despair that Yokoi was more talk than action.

By 1989, New York developer Donald Trump was quietly shopping for a buyer for a vast parcel of undeveloped railroad yards he controlled on Manhattan's Upper West Side. Trump wanted $800 million for the land. Okada figured he'd try hooking Yokoi into the deal. Okada told Trump the Japanese billionaire might be interested. Okada collected piles of plans and pictures and carried them to Japan. Yokoi seemed intrigued. His daughter was coming to New York, he told Okada. Introduce her to Trump, Yokoi said.

Kiiko's first meeting with Trump was brief. She presented Trump with a gift from her father, a makeup kit for his wife. Trump asked about her father. He had never heard of Yokoi. Kiiko told Trump she would get back to him about the property. "We look forward to the honor of doing business with you and your esteemed family, and to the pleasure of your next visit," a Trump Organization official wrote days later in a letter to Kiiko. It is unclear whether Trump ever regarded the

Japanese tycoon as a promising buyer. "It was a great pleasure to meet you last week," Trump wrote to Kiiko. "Mrs. Trump is most grateful for the make-up kit. It is a handsome and beautiful kit that she will enjoy using during our travels." Yokoi never bid on Trump's land.

Yokoi lurched from one half-baked idea to another, relying for advice on an unlikely circle of small-time businessmen. One day, Kiiko told Melius that her father wanted to meet him. He might want to do more business with you, she explained. Melius had a four- by six-foot model of Oheka Castle built and shipped to Japan at a cost of $10,000. He flew to Tokyo and reported to Yokoi's office. The model was sitting on the floor. Yokoi gave Melius a clock. Through an interpreter, the two men attempted to talk. The conversation was stilted. Over lunch, Yokoi asked Melius if he wanted to buy Bloomingdale's department store. Yokoi told Melius to offer $1 billion for it on his behalf. After lunch, Yokoi bid him good-bye. Melius was dumbfounded. "What am I doing here," he asked himself. "I came to Japan to have lunch?" When he returned to New York, Melius conveyed Yokoi's offer to Bloomingdale's. The company declined it.

Saks Fifth Avenue, at least, was available. Merrill Lynch & Co. was looking for a joint-venture partner for the purchase of the upscale retailer. Kiiko flew to New York several times to negotiate a deal. In the end, Yokoi's financing in Japan fell through. The deal collapsed. Kiiko was depressed for days, literally unable to get out of bed, unwilling even to pick up the phone. Yokoi grew concerned. He visited Kiiko. "I'll do something to make up for this loss," he said. "This next deal that we have, we will make sure that it goes through."

Japanese government officials, worried about the outcry over Japanese speculators hitting America's beaches with suitcases of yen, had warned their citizens to avoid conspicuous purchases. Already, nearly every four- and five-star resort in Hawaii was either owned by the Japanese or built with their money. Buying national landmarks was another matter. One Japanese real estate firm had already been warned off bidding on Chicago's Sears Tower, the world's tallest building.

In the fall of 1989, two stunning acquisitions rocked the American business world, leading some Americans to conclude that the Japanese were well and truly taking over. In October, Sony Corporation bought Columbia Pictures for $5 billion. Weeks later, Mitsubishi Estate Company bought a majority stake in Rockefeller Center for $846 million. "We can easily see an emotional wave coming out as a result of this deal," worried one Japanese official about the takeover of the landmark 19-building Art Deco complex. The two acquisitions fulfilled the worst fears of the Tokyo bureaucrats. American politicians began banging the drums for Japan to lower barriers to foreign investment in Japan. "Unless we do more than just say, 'Isn't that too bad,' we may be greasing the slide of America to a second-rate economic power in the 21st century," grumbled Senator James Exon of Nebraska, who joined in sponsoring legislation that would give the president power to block certain foreign acquisitions.

On Main Street, the news kicked off a nationwide sulk about the rise of Japan, exposing a growing American inferiority complex. Books like Michael Crichton's novel, *Rising Sun,* which portrayed the Japanese as omniscient and infallible, fanned popular concerns about an America in decline. At a minimum, the budding resentment of Japan merely reflected fears about Japan's enormous economic power. But privately, Japanese officials and real estate executives complained of an uglier force at work, racism dating back to World War II.

American property owners had an altogether different outlook. Real estate markets in the United States had been sizzling for half a decade. Drunk on easy money from thrifts, developers put up far too many buildings during the 1980s. They had filled America's cities with half-empty new towers. Developers had already begun sending back keys to their panicked bankers. By 1990, as Japanese investment money coursed in, the U.S. real estate economy was already imploding. The glory days of the celebrity real estate developer were over. Donald Trump, the paragon of American real estate in the eyes of many Japanese, began missing payments on more than $1 billion of debt that supported his casino and real estate empire. With his lenders turning cold eyes on his finances, Trump launched a desperate campaign to raise cash.

To many real estate pros, the Japanese, quite simply, looked like dumb money, the last into a market teetering on the brink of collapse. Investors from Germany and elsewhere in Europe were buying, too, but the Japanese showed a startling lack of concern about how overbuilt American markets had become. In 1991, a partnership headed by U.S. investment magnate Marvin Davis sold California's famed Pebble Beach golf resort to Japanese developer Minoru Isutani for $841 million, reportedly collecting a profit of about a half billion dollars. The notion that David Rockefeller or Marvin Davis may have pulled a fast one on the Japanese seems to have occurred to no one except the real estate pros who rolled their eyes at the astonishing prices being paid. To the American public, the Japanese takeover of Pebble Beach seemed like one more nail in America's coffin.

In the spring of 1991, Yokoi happened upon an intriguing article in a Japanese newspaper. The Empire State Building was on the block. Now here was a property that suited his tastes. He phoned Kiiko early one morning and asked if she had seen the news. She told her father she hadn't. Yokoi said he would fax the article to her office. After you've read it, he told her, call me. When she arrived at her office, her father called once again. "Did you see the article?" Yokoi asked. Kiiko said she had. "Would you come and see me?" he instructed.

Kiiko hurried to her father's office. The article reported that Salomon Brothers planned to auction the famed sky-scraper on behalf of its owner, Prudential Insurance. The owner was looking for at least $40 million, it said. That was far lower than the values reported to Yokoi for the World Trade Center and Rockefeller Center.

"It's cheap," Yokoi told her. "It looks good. It looks inter-esting."

Yokoi told his daughter to contact Salomon Brothers. Kiiko spoke to a man in the investment bank's Tokyo office. She picked up a written prospectus on the building, which had been translated into Japanese, and brought it to her father. Yokoi paged through the material.

"There's some kind of lease agreement. It looks like it's not going to be a simple deal," he told her. "But it still looks like a good deal." He told Kiiko to check on the pricing level.

She met again with the Salomon broker. No sooner had she returned to her office than her father called again. He told her to hurry over to see him.

"Salomon said it is $40 million, just like the newspaper said," said Kiiko.

"If that's the price level, let's try for it," he said. He told her to get in touch with an accounting firm to figure out how to structure a bid.

What Hideki Yokoi said to his daughter next—or didn't say—will forever be open to dispute. Kiiko would later swear that her father told her, "Omae ni yaru." Translated literally, the words mean "To give to you." (In Japanese, the subject "I" is not used). A less wooden translation: "You can have it." Did Yokoi really intend to give his daughter the Empire State Building? The world's most famous skyscraper, a bauble for a

Japanese billionaire's daughter? Now that would speak volumes about Japanese supremacy in the global economy. Later, after the ensuing events had torn his family apart, Yokoi would insist that he had made no such promise. Only one thing was certain: Yokoi never put his intentions for the Empire State Building into writing.

Yokoi and his daughter met with Prudential's bankers in Tokyo. They consulted a lawyer from the Tokyo office of the New York law firm, Skadden, Arps, Slate, Meagher & Flom, as well as representatives of the Coopers & Lybrand accounting firm, about structuring a bid.

Renoir was away in Chicago that summer taking a course in derivatives at the Chicago Mercantile Exchange. Kiiko reached him by telephone. She told him she and her father wanted to try to buy the Empire State Building and asked him to help figure out how much she should bid.

"Are you sure?" responded Renoir.

Kiiko assured him they were.

"This is crazy," Renoir told her. "What are you going to do with it?"

"This is more important than what you do at Lehman," Kiiko snapped. "My father is buying it for me."

Renoir phoned Gregory White, the Salomon Brothers banker in New York who was running the auction. White already had several bids in hand, including a $32 million bid from a partnership controlled by Peter Malkin, who with Leona Helmsley, controlled the building's long-term lease. White explained the bidding process to Renoir. A number of bids had already come in, White told him. Renoir grew concerned that his wife was too late. White suggested a bidding bracket to Renoir that would make him the top bidder. Renoir phoned Kiiko and told her if she and her father wanted the building, they would have to bid at least $41 million. Yokoi agreed. Renoir reached White on his cellular phone and offered $41 million.

With Renoir's bid in hand, Salomon Brothers tried to squeeze a higher one from Peter Malkin. As the longtime lessee of the Empire State Building, Malkin had built-in credibility with the Prudential brass. That was hardly the case for Renoir. But unbeknownst to Prudential, Malkin was boxed in. Leona Helmsley had already rebuffed his proposal to bid on the building together, reasoning that given their lease lockhold on the building until 2076, she and Malkin already owned the building in all but name. Through a time-consuming solicitation process, Malkin had secured permission from hundreds of small investors in a separate partnership to bid $32 million. But he had no authority to raise the bid. Malkin had to tell Salomon he couldn't match the high bid.

It wasn't even close, White thought. After consulting with Prudential, he reached for the phone and called Renoir. You won the auction, he told him. Renoir immediately phoned his wife and father-in-law with the good news. "Thank you very much," said Yokoi, in English. On August 21, 1991, the day after Kiiko's forty-sixth birthday, her father wired her the money for the down payment. To Kiiko, this constituted evidence that her father intended to buy the building for her as a birthday gift. "My father is the kind of person who does nice things," she would later explain. Two days later, Kiiko's lawyer signed a formal contract to buy the Empire State Building for $41 million.

Kiiko joined Renoir in New York to grind through the complex process of completing the deal. Years later, Renoir would scarcely remember his fateful meeting in Rockefeller Center with Prudential executive Kurt Reich, who was supervising the sale for the insurer. When he walked into Reich's office, Renoir was unimpressed. Reich seemed too young to be important. Renoir figured he was some middle-level bureaucrat. Perhaps that explains the poor impression Renoir made on Reich, his less-than-forthcoming summary of his father-in-law's career, his unwillingness to even provide Reich with the name of Hideki Yokoi. Renoir left Reich's office oblivious to the alarm bells he had set ringing.

Renoir would later maintain that he was not the least bit surprised that Prudential had gone into a panic when it discovered that it had agreed to sell the Empire State Building to the family of Hideki Yokoi. "If I were Prudential, I wouldn't want to sell to Yokoi or his family either," said Renoir.

Kiiko called her father with the news that Prudential had backed out of the deal. Yokoi was furious. "Why is it that you couldn't buy it?" he snarled. "Don't ever come back to Japan until you buy it."

Kiiko called Renoir in a panic. "You have to get it!" she shouted. "You have to get it! My father wants it!"

Kiiko spoke to her father about the situation again and again. Yokoi's anger didn't subside. "You cannot do it by yourself," Yokoi eventually scolded her. "So ask your husband, Jean-Paul."

Renoir would later insist he had been leery of tarnishing his own career by getting involved with his father-in-law. But he thought his wife would never forgive him if he didn't help her buy the Empire State Building. Renoir thought the building was a stupid investment by almost any measure. At $41 million, it offered a minuscule return. And the long-term lease to Helmsley and Malkin would keep it that way. But Yokoi didn't care. In Japan, inflation had erased returns on most investments. As for the lease, Yokoi had never respected leases. Leases were meant to be broken.

Renoir turned to a friend, investment adviser Charles Lindsay. Lindsay, a displaced Wall Streeter who had set up an investment boutique in Greenwich, Connecticut, tried to steer Renoir in a different direction. If Yokoi wants to put $41 million into real estate, Lindsay told Renoir, he should put it into an investment that would actually make money. Lindsay showed Renoir a prospectus on a pool of properties being sold by the federal thrift bailout agency. The Resolution Trust Corporation, created to clean up after dozens of failed savings and loan associations, was peddling billions of dollars worth of buildings and defaulted commercial mortgages at a fraction of their face values. Lindsay had set up an investment fund to buy into the deals. As Lindsay saw it, a 20 percent return was as good as guaranteed. "You could take the toilet bowls out and sell them on the street and probably cover your costs," Lindsay would say. Renoir sent the material to Yokoi, who thumbed through the pictures of the property. Forget it, Yokoi told Renoir. These weren't beautiful buildings.

Renoir contacted New York lawyer Tom Berner, who represented a maverick investor named Oliver Grace Jr. As a young man, Grace had decided to follow in the footsteps of his father, an unconventional businessman who wore a patch over one eye, looked like a pirate, and had made considerable money investing in Japanese and German bonds during World War II. In the late 1980s, Oliver—along with his brother, John Grace, and T. Boone Pickens III, son of the famed corporate raider—had launched a controversial string of attacks on mutual funds with investments in Japan. In 1987, they forced one fund, Japan Fund Incorporated, to convert from a closed-end to an open-end mutual fund. A year later, they forced Crescent Japan Investment Trust PLC to do the same. Investment partnerships controlled by Grace and his brother made considerable money on the battles. Berner arranged a meeting between Renoir and Grace.

Just weeks after Prudential had pulled the plug on Yokoi's bid, Renoir and Kiiko sat down with Grace. Kiiko told Grace her father wanted to buy her the Empire State Building as a gift. Renoir proposed a deal under which Grace would buy the skyscraper for Kiiko with money supplied by Yokoi. Renoir would pay Grace for his trouble. Grace worried that if the identity of the true owner leaked out, Prudential might sue him. He would need an indemnity, Grace said. After a string of additional meetings, Grace agreed to place a bid. Years later, Grace would insist that money had not been his only motivation. "My family had been successful in Japanese investments," he said. "I felt that just because someone is Japanese, they shouldn't be denied the opportunity to own the Empire State Building."

Another New York lawyer, Henry Bubel of Patterson, Belknap, Webb & Tyler, set to work devising a corporate structure. He tried to mention the Empire State Building to others as little as possible, lest Prudential catch wind that Yokoi was making a secret second run at the skyscraper. A deal took shape. Grace would create a new company called E. G. Holding Company to make the bid. Yokoi's Nippon Sangyo holding company would lend E. G. Holding $4 million to make the offer. If Grace won the auction, Yokoi would lend E. G. Holding the rest. E. G. Holding would take title to the skyscraper. But Grace would be, in essence, no more than a straw man. After a waiting period of about a year, Grace would pay off the loans from Yokoi by merging E. G. Holding into another new company, NS 1991 American Trust, which would be controlled by Kiiko and Renoir.

Grace thought that if he took his time negotiating the deal, he could bag the property for a lot less than the $41 million Yokoi had previously agreed to pay. But Renoir seemed uninterested in bargaining and impatient to close the deal. So Grace placed a bid of $39 million. Kurt Reich, the Prudential executive in charge of the sale, asked to meet with him. Just seal the deal, Renoir told Grace.

Reich had not caught a single whiff of the unfolding subterfuge when Grace strolled into his office. When Reich asked Grace why he wanted to buy the building, Grace, amazingly, was completely unprepared to answer, and found himself at a momentary loss for what to say. He could hardly imply that at $39 million, he thought it was a good deal. Grace thought quickly. Estate planning seemed like a plausible answer. So he told Reich that he wanted to put the building into a trust for his children, as a long-term inve stment. Reich appeared to swallow the fib. When Reich pressed him for another million, Grace readily agreed. Grace pleaded with Reich to keep the deal a secret, he would later say, simply because he didn't want word to get out that he had so overpaid for anything, even the Empire State Building. Grace left Reich's office with an agreement to buy the landmark for $40 million.

Kiiko's lawyer, Henry Bubel, told her it was time to get the money from her father. Bubel dialed Yokoi from his office. Kiiko spoke to her father in Japanese. Bubel understood not a word. Several days later, $36 million was sitting in an E. G. Holding account, and on November 27, 1991, E. G. Holding took title to the Empire State Building.

Yokoi had every reason to feel triumphant. He had managed to buy a quintessential piece of America. He had outsmarted the Americans, snatching the defining point of New York's skyline from an owner who had deemed him unworthy. Granted, the onerous long-term lease to Helmsley and Malkin all but guaranteed that that his yearly return would never reach 5 percent. ("It was the most stupid investment you could possibly imagine," Renoir would later snort.) But this wasn't about making money. The fancy ownership ruse aside, Yokoi and his daughter now owned the world's most famous skyscraper. Or so he thought.

For Peter Malkin, the bizarre auction had been an exercise in frustration. He had been rebuffed by Leona Helmsley, outbid by an irrational bidder from overseas, then given a second chance. A final call from Salomon Brothers had dashed his hopes for good.

"You'll find this hard to believe, but we have another buyer at $40 million," a banker told Malkin.

"Is this one real?" asked Malkin.

The banker assured him it was. Even more frustrating, Malkin didn't even know who had bested him. Salomon refused to identify the person or persons who were behind E. G. Holding. A banker told Malkin to begin sending the Empire State Building rent check to an accounting firm in Long Island. His new landlord was an utter mystery.

Unwilling to live with the uncertainty, Malkin phoned the accounting firm, affected a casual indifference, and began questioning the receptionist. In no time, Malkin had the name of Oliver Grace. The name meant nothing to Malkin. He left a message for Grace. When Grace phoned back, Malkin introduced himself. "I'd like to meet you and find out what your thoughts are about your investment in the Empire State Building," Malkin said. Grace, making no effort to play coy, agreed. Malkin invited Grace to lunch at the 60 East Club, an old-fashioned businessman's club.

Over lunch, Grace launched into a rambling tale about a recent investment in a geothermal deal in California. He had gotten control of an underground source of tremendous heat, he told Malkin, which could be used to generate power. The utility company wanted to prevent that from happening, he said. So the utility bought him out at a huge profit, he informed Malkin. Malkin glanced at his watch. He was growing perplexed. Nearly an hour had passed without a word about the Empire State Building. As the two men were finishing their lunches, Malkin could wait no longer.

"Do you have any questions about the Empire State Building?" he asked Grace. "Do you have any thoughts or ideas?"

Well, yes, said Grace, he had one thought. He'd like to create a nightclub on the top of the Empire State Building where he could entertain people.

The usually unflappable Malkin was momentarily speechless. "Oh, really," he finally uttered. Collecting himself, Malkin told Grace that with the public observatory, that would be difficult. It would require special permits, which would be difficult to obtain. Grace suggested to Malkin that it would benefit them both to make the building more of an entertainment attraction for tourists. After lunch, the two men exchanged cordial good-byes, and Grace boarded the elevator. Malkin never heard from the young man again.

For nearly everyone involved, the odd events of the fall of 1991 had turned the Empire State Building into a hall of smoke and mirrors. Little about the sale of the building was as it appeared. Unbeknownst to Oliver Grace, Yokoi's hunger for the Empire State Building had little in common with the motives of the other Japanese investors who were buying up America. His desire for the landmark lay in his troubled past, a past shot through with dark secrets. In due course, Yokoi's messy life and bewildering moral compass would engulf the skyscraper in precisely the sort of unseemly chaos that had earned him such notoriety in his homeland.

Yokoi's Secret

I n the years after World War II, America's burgeoning prosperity had become the envy of much of the world. The nation's army of upwardly mobile men in suits and fedoras, its cigar-puffing businessmen who had become millionaires in a single generation, its movie stars and long cars and towering skyscrapers, all became the yardstick by which ambitious people the world over measured their accomplishments. The American influence was no more pronounced than in postwar Tokyo, which in the closing months of the war had been reduced to a lunar landscape of cinder and rubble.

General Douglas MacArthur and his occupation army had set out to remake Japan in the image of America, to create a new nation where one's station in life would matter far less than one's ambition and capacity to work. A rigid moral code that had been generations in the making swiftly unraveled. The American occupation brought homegrown strip shows, pulp magazines, speed-popping bohemian writers, and capitalist greed. *Yakuza* gangsters took fashion cues from American gangster movies, donning sharp suits, dark shirts, and loud ties. It was a world that seemed tailor-made for Hideki Yokoi, a wily young businessman who had made a small fortune in the chaotic years of wartime disorder.

Yokoi was guided, it would appear, by his own notion of what it meant to be rich and powerful in America. He glided about town in a long Cadillac, the pride of a fleet that would eventually include Buicks, Thunderbirds, and Chryslers. He became a fixture in swank nightclubs that had arisen to cater to Tokyo's nouveaux riches. He was a handsome man, and he carried himself as though he knew it. There was an element to Yokoi's rise, in fact, that seemed quintessentially American. He yearned to have it all and, even more important, it would seem, to lord it over his countrymen. To those who knew him, it would come as no surprise that Yokoi would one day find himself drawn to New York's most famous skyscraper.

Like many New York real estate men who had bootstrapped their way to fortunes, Yokoi took a particular interest in the kind of glorious old buildings into which he would never have been permitted to set foot as a boy. MacArthur was making good on a promise to bust up the feudal system under which rich landowners controlled vast tracts of land. Historic estates were available to anyone with enough yen, whatever their class background. Yokoi had saved some 100 million yen during the war, a considerable fortune in those days of deprivation. Operating out of an office in Tokyo's elite Ginza district, Yokoi moved in on cash-strapped nobility like a barracuda, snapping up their estates on the cheap. He preferred the big stuff, the mansions. Some of them he resold, finding the profits far superior to those available in the textile business where he got his start. The gems, several palaces purchased from the royal family, including the magnificent villa of former Prince Nashimoto in Atami, Yokoi kept for himself. For the most part, they sat vacant. It was as if Yokoi simply wanted to assert his power over Japan's disgraced nobility. Renoir would later come to view Yokoi's desire to assemble a portfolio of similarly venerable properties around the globe as rooted in his need to bury his impoverished childhood, to say, as Renoir would later put it, " 'Fuck you' to the world."

The Japan into which Hideki Yokoi was born in 1913 was a closed, feudal society. Although Yokoi's grandfather had been successful in the textile business, his father had developed an abiding love of the bottle and had allowed his family to descend into poverty. By the time he was 11, Yokoi was pushing a wheelbarrow to distant rural villages to buy vegetables from farmers, then wheeling them back to the market to sell. He developed a knack for commerce, learning to buy cheaply when the weather was bad and to sell high when the market was crowded with buyers. Years later, Yokoi would vividly recall the sting of shame he felt as a young boy when he arrived at a family wedding to visit his mother, only to discover that she wasn't a guest at all, but was working in the kitchen as a servant. He pulled his mother out of the kitchen, he would later tell his own daughter, and vowed to her that he would become a wealthy man.

In 1928, at the age of 15, Yokoi moved to Tokyo to apprentice as a textile wholesaler. The older apprentices bullied him mercilessly, forcing on him miserable jobs like cleaning toilets. When his employer finally gave him the opportunity to sell merchandise, Yokoi quickly distinguished himself. At age 17, he moved in with an aunt, bought a bicycle, and set up his own shop. Yokoi would rise early, ride to the underwear manufacturers, buy merchandise, then cart it to kimono shops and department stores for resale. In the trenches of the textile industry, Yokoi discovered a formula that he would cling to for life: buy low, sell high, and delay paying your bills for as long as humanly possible.

It is impossible to know how much the disorder of wartime Japan and the distortions of the market economy shaped Yokoi's sense of business ethics. It is distinctly possible that Japan's increasingly desperate imperial drive, and the economic instability it brought, convinced Yokoi that there was nothing immoral about grabbing as much as he could, with little thought to right and wrong. Perhaps, at the time, much of his world seemed ethically gray. Whatever the reasons, Yokoi's rise did not inspire the kind of admiration enjoyed by many self-made American tycoons. On the contrary, what Yokoi's friends and colleagues would later recall was his greed. Yokoi was said to want it all. And he was, as people in Tokyo would say euphemistically, sly about getting it.

After returning from a stint fighting in Japan's war of conquest in China, Yokoi began supplying the Imperial Army with underwear. As a military supplier, he perfected another business practice: cheating his customers. When the army ordered 10,000 items, Yokoi would ship 20,000, and insist it was the government's mistake. It was a practice that Yokoi employed to similarly profitable effect with nonmilitary customers as well, his brother-in-law, Mitsuo Hishida, who worked for him, would recall years later.

The war turned Yokoi into a wealthy man. He owned four factories that churned out apparel for the army. As the yen poured in, Yokoi sank roots into a walled half-acre family compound in Denenchofu, the hilly neighborhood regarded as one of Tokyo's most exclusive. Michiko, the textile merchant's daughter he married in 1931, bore him a son, Kunihiko, in 1942, a daughter, Chizuko, in 1944, and a second son, Hirohiko, in 1945. Yokoi placed chunks of his residential property under the names of his wife, his sons, and his sister. Like most Japanese men of his era, Yokoi took seriously his duties as a provider. His marriage would endure for many decades, and he tried to share with his children the fruits of his success. But Yokoi's failings as a husband and father would soon become legion, in ways that would eventually unsettle nearly every aspect of his life.

In the leafy sanctuary of his residential compound, Yokoi and his family rode out the final, terrible onslaught by American bombers that preceded Japan's surrender. In the void of his collapsing nation, Yokoi realized, there would be enormous opportunity. Japan's economy had been utterly destroyed, one-third of its wealth wiped out. In the weeks after the war, Japan became a cauldron of profiteering and corruption, teeming with crafty people eager to profit from the suffering of their compatriots. Yokoi moved decisively to grab a share of the spoils. Food and other staples were subject to strict government rationing, and for millions of people, the search for food became a consuming obsession. Black markets sprang up all over Tokyo, where commodities could be had for many times the government-sanctioned prices. For men and women wily enough to secure a role in the trade, the black market offered the promise to earn in a single day what law-abiding laborers toiled for a month to bring home.

Yokoi, a born merchant, jumped in with both feet. He trafficked in food from the provinces. He arranged to buy cotton fabric cheaply from acquaintances of his parents in his home province, then resold it at a steep markup in the black market. One day, Yokoi told his close friend Tsuneji Sato that the police had caught on and were preparing to seize 50 rolls of fabric. Sato concocted a plan. Yokoi unspooled most of the cloth from each roll and hid it. The Tokyo police dutifully carried off 50 nearly empty rolls, and Yokoi sold all of the hidden fabric.

In the black markets, Yokoi learned to navigate a shadow economy dominated by unscrupulous men and women making shady deals. Japan's traditional criminal class, the *yakuza*, emerged as the force of order in the black markets. Unlike the American Mafia, the *yakuza* operated more or less openly, through a welter of legitimate and illegitimate businesses.

Although the leading gangsters cast themselves as the moral descendants of Japan's noble warriors, there was an ugly air of ritual menace and violence that hung over their world. Gang members favored full-body tattoos, and they would amputate their own fingertips to atone for serious violations of duty. The extent to which Yokoi consorted with these denizens of the black market is difficult to determine. It wasn't long, however, before Yokoi's name began being bandied about in discussions about the *yakuza* and business.

In the 1950s, Yokoi turned to the stock market with trading instincts honed in the black markets. He accumulated shares of Tokyo's Shirokiya department store and moved to oust existing management and install himself as president. By then, enterprising gangsters, casting about for new ruses after the demise of the black market, had carved out a specialty in the corporate world. *Sokaiyas,* as they were called, billed themselves as shareholder meeting specialists. For the most part, they practiced extortion, threatening to disrupt annual meetings if they were not paid off. They also moonlighted for other parties interested in "managing" shareholder meetings. To ward off Yokoi, Shirokiya's president turned to a *yakuza* group led by a professional wrestler. Yokoi tapped a university-educated gangster-on-the-rise named Noburu Ando. The thugs apparently rendered one another ineffective. Yokoi could not afford to buy any more stock. He had come up short and lost a considerable sum on the escapade. "I learned a valuable lesson," he told his brother-in-law, Hishida. "The money goes to the most powerful people."

Subsequent runs at oil, shipping, sugar, and hotel companies made Yokoi a feared man in many quarters. Some saw Yokoi as a daring young investor. Most denounced him as a renegade who flouted an unwritten code about how Japanese businessmen should behave. When Yokoi's investments soured, as they often did, he sometimes welshed on his loans, then strung along his lenders in court. Yokoi branched into hotels and bowling, building a 240-lane complex he billed as Asia's largest, and *pachinko* arcades, the noisy Japanese variation on slot machines. Yokoi was intent on becoming one of Japan's wealthiest men.

When he first met Yokoi many years later, Renoir's initial reaction was that Yokoi's devil-may-care approach to business represented a refreshing contrast to what Renoir had experienced in the Japanese banking world. It wasn't that Renoir saw the typical Japanese businessman as a paragon of moral rectitude. "Yokoi was not any worse than the other Japanese," Renoir would explain, "except he was crude about the way he screwed people. He was refreshing, because he was unconventional, in a sickening, hierarchical, fucked up, constipated country."

On August 20, 1945, just days after American bombs stopped falling on Tokyo, a diminutive employee of Yokoi named Tsuya Kosaka gave birth to a daughter. The prospects for an unmarried woman and her child in a Tokyo beset with homelessness and starvation were bleak. But Hideki Yokoi offered to help. It was not an act of charity. Her daughter, Kiiko—born just 19 months after the birth of Yokoi's first daughter and three months before the birth of his second son—was Yokoi's child.

In prewar Japan, having a concubine was seen as evidence that a man had succeeded in business. The war had made it unaffordable for many men, but not for Yokoi. Yokoi bought Tsuya a house. He supplied her with food from the black market. He slipped away regularly from his own household of children, bringing Kiiko one of the rarest of treats in postwar Tokyo, boxes of Sun-Maid raisins, which had found their way into the black market from American troops.

Had Yokoi shown even modest restraint in his amorous adventures he might not have found himself consumed by such family turmoil years later. But Hideki Yokoi, it was clear, had a weakness. Although he forswore booze, cigarettes, and gambling, he could not keep his hands off women. Flush with wealth and power, he seemed incapable of restraint. He would frequently disappear from his home for two or three nights running. Japanese newspapers and magazines chronicled his dalliances with beauty queens and actresses. Yokoi treated women as collectibles, beauty queens as trophies. Associates watched him buy enormous stacks of newspapers, clip out the Miss Tokyo ballots, then stuff ballot boxes with votes for his girlfriends. He was a regular at beauty pageants, larding his office with secretaries hired from their lineups. His mistresses included a former movie actress, a former Miss Yokohama, a onetime Miss Japan, and a former Miss International.

Decades later, Yokoi's almost comically branching family tree would be offered as an explanation for how his acquisition of the Empire State Building could have led to such confusion and distrust. In addition to the two sons and three daughters supposedly sired by Yokoi to his wife Michiko, he eventually added three other children to his official family registry, which he filed with local government officials. Omissions from Yokoi's family registry appear to be legion. For years, Yokoi never officially recognized Kiiko as his child.

Deciphering how many children Yokoi fathered is a dicey business. Years later, Kiiko took a stab at it in a sworn statement that mixes undisputed fact with conjecture, painting a picture of a man seemingly intent on setting a new standard for boorish behavior. "Of my father's 17 or more children, only two appear to have the same mother (Kunihiko and Chizuko), but it also appears that no two have both the same mother and same father." (Kiiko offered no solid evidence that the five children Yokoi claimed his wife had borne had different mothers or fathers. Yokoi's official family registry contradicts her on this point.) Yokoi fathered one child by his wife's younger sister, and he adopted one of his daughter's children as his own, Kiiko said. He bought another of his concubines a lavish apartment in Tokyo where he could visit her once a week, but she sold it and moved to Los Angeles, taking the proceeds with her, Kiiko said.

Yokoi's moral universe is a murky one. There is ample evidence that he willingly supported his growing family. He provided his lovers with homes and apartments. Like a feudal warlord, he dispatched underlings to distribute food and staples to his households. "I know several women other than my wife, and I have not neglected them," he told Japanese journalist Atsushi Mizoguchi. "Once I have a relationship with a woman, I always give her economic protection." To men of an earlier era, such behavior qualified as ethical probity. But in postwar Japan, moral codes had begun to shift. A view was taking hold among the middle and upper classes that keeping a mistress was morally wrong. Yokoi was falling profoundly out of touch with the time.

It is difficult to fathom how confusing it must have been for the children of such a man. Yokoi seemed to be capable of genuine warmth toward his offspring. But merely given the constraints of time, it was difficult for him to lavish much attention on any one child, particularly those, like Kiiko, who grew up in his satellite households.

It is a testament to Yokoi's force of personality that at least some of his illegitimate children didn't grow up to despise him. Yokoi provided Kiiko's mother, who was a sickly woman, with a home and sufficient support that she never again had to work. Yokoi visited frequently, taking his daughter riding in his gleaming American cars. Kiiko grew to adore her father in spite of his shortcomings as a parent and role model. "When we were children," she would recall years later, "my sister and others would say my father is very hard. But he was never hard on me. I was very lucky." She was equally forgiving about his womanizing. "Father is always chasing after young ladies," she conceded, betraying not a trace of disapproval. "My father is like an emperor."

Renoir puzzled over his wife's tolerance of such behavior. "My wife thought he was a cross between the Emperor and the Dali Lama," Renoir said, "and that he was screwing all these people because he was desperate for love." Kiiko, he said, had a cultlike devotion to Yokoi. She perceived her father as a demigod, misunderstood by everyone.

If Kiiko harbored illusions about her father's place in society, they must surely have been dispelled a degree during the summer she turned 13. In June of 1958, Yokoi found himself embroiled in a debacle that still stands as one of the seediest footnotes of Japan's postwar business history. During his Shirokiya department store takeover bid, Yokoi had borrowed 30 million yen from an aristocrat named Duke Takashi Hachisuka, a distant member of the imperial family. Soon afterward, the duke died. Yokoi repaid the duke's heirs 10 million yen, but stalled on returning the rest, prompting a lawsuit by the duke's wife. A court ordered Yokoi to repay the balance. Yokoi appealed, but lost. He claimed he didn't have the money. She discovered—no doubt to her great dismay—that Yokoi had placed all of his valuable residential property, save the drawing room in his house, under the names of various family members, making it difficult for her to seize. It was then, it appears, that she decided she needed some muscle.

On the afternoon of June 11, Noburu Ando, a 32-year-old *yakuza* tough whose face carried the evidence of a 53-stitch slashing received at the hands of a rival gangster, paid Yokoi a visit at his office in the Ginza. Yokoi knew Ando. Ando had backed him during the Shirokiya department store standoff. But Ando hadn't come to reminisce. With him was a debt collection specialist whom Yokoi had been rudely shunning for days. Behind Yokoi's closed office door, shouting was heard.

Various accounts emerged: Yokoi called Ando a "hoodlum." Yokoi told him, "It's not your place to interfere." He referred to Ando as a "yakuza punk." He called him "trash." He told him, "Urchin, I have no business with you." No one disputes that Yokoi did not accord Ando the kind of respect he felt he deserved. Ando left angry. He was not the type of man most people would risk angering.

Three hours later, a young man in a gray suit walked into Yokoi's headquarters. Yokoi's secretary asked his name. "No need to tell my name," he replied, and pushed his way into Yokoi's office. He found Yokoi talking to two men. "Are you the president of Toyo Yusen?" he demanded of Yokoi. The young man pulled out a .32-caliber pistol purchased from an American soldier and fired. The bullet pierced Yokoi's left arm and lodged in his lung. The gunman fled. Yokoi ran after him. Yokoi's brother-in-law, Mitsui Hishida, sprinted up from the floor below. He found Yokoi collapsed in the hallway in a pool of blood. Hishida rushed Yokoi to the hospital. Doctors sliced Yokoi open from neck to belly but couldn't find the bullet. He lost 3,000 cubic centimeters of blood and nearly died. The bullet remained in his lung.

Yokoi told police he had never seen his assailant and had no idea why the man had shot him. But Yokoi was sufficiently despised that the police had no shortage of leads. They swiftly narrowed their investigation to Ando and distributed 100,000 wanted posters with photos of Ando and four members of his gang. They arrested dozens of gang members on the slimmest of pretexts and pressed them for information. Forty-four days after the shooting, acting on a tip from Ando's mistress, armed police broke down the door of a white stucco home in the beach resort of Zushi. Ando and an associate, who were playing chess, offered no resistance. Ando asked to put on a dark suit, a clean shirt, and a striped tie. When he arrived at police headquarters, more than 300 reporters and photographers were waiting. Asked about the shooting, Ando told reporters he knew nothing about it. But he didn't pass up the opportunity to denounce Yokoi's ethics. "A businessman should be more conscientious," he said.

After several days in police custody, Ando confessed that he and seven henchmen had plotted the attack on Yokoi. Ando identified the triggerman as Kazuhiro Chiba, who was arrested days later at the home of a gambler. When he went on trial, Chiba admitted that he fired the pistol, but denied intending to kill Yokoi. Ando told the court he had been indignant at Yokoi, not only for insulting him, but for his various "wrong deeds," including Yokoi's meddling in the management of various companies. Yokoi, who faced the indignity of hearing a gangster denounce his ethics, seemed to elicit little public sympathy.

When he was released from the hospital, Yokoi met his old friend, Tsuneji Sato. "They got me," said Yokoi, laughing.

"They have all gone to prison. You should get on them when they come back," Sato advised Yokoi. "They are urchins and you are a big boss."

Yokoi figured that "what's done is done," Hishida would later recall. Yokoi had always told Hishida: "You shouldn't keep enemies as enemies. You should make them your allies."

Ando served six years in prison. When he was released, he visited Yokoi, presenting him with a fountain pen and ballpoint pen set as a peace offering. Separately, over dinner, Ando apologized to Hishida, who lived two houses away from him, telling Hishida that if he had known Yokoi was his brother-in-law, he never would have ordered him shot. Ando went on to star in a series of gangster movies. The first of them, *Chi To Okite* (Blood and Law), included a scene based on the shooting of Yokoi. Yokoi even lunched with Ando in a publicity stunt to promote the movie.

The December after Yokoi was shot, the Tokyo District Court, acting on a request from Mrs. Hachisuka, declared him bankrupt. The court cited the several hundred million yen he owed to Mrs. Hachisuka and others. But no one who knew Yokoi well believed for a minute that he was finished, or even that he was truly broke. He still lived like a king. He carried the bullet like a badge of honor. He would raise his shirt before family members and business acquaintances alike and ask them to touch his scar, boasting that he had shown no fear. "I've got three balls," he would joke to his daughter Kiiko.

With the benefit of hindsight, it is sometimes possible to spool back to the beginning of a man's undoing, to pinpoint a fateful moment when his life changes irrevocably, forever cleaving into all that came before, and the downhill slide that was to follow. Hideki Yokoi, like many men through the years, was undone by greed. Twenty-four years after he was shot, his life began to unravel with a cataclysmic event that, like many other aspects of his life, Yokoi came to view far differently than the rest of his compatriots. Oddly enough, were it not for the incident that made him one of the most despised businessmen in contemporary Japan, Yokoi might never have enlisted his daughter Kiiko as a close business adviser or emerged from his Tokyo netherworld to make his tumultuous run at the Empire State Building.

Nearly two decades after the notorious incident, sitting in the lounge of a downtown Tokyo hotel clutching the hooked brown head of his cane, Tsuneji Sato, one of Hideki Yokoi's oldest friends, mulled over the enigma of his friend. "Yokoi was greedy and sneaky," said Sato, who at 83 spoke with the brutal frankness that comes with old age. "He was three or four times as greedy as the others." Sato had no trouble remembering the afternoon late in December 1981. Sato was having tea in the lobby of the Tokyo's Imperial Hotel with businessman Hisakazu Honjo when Yokoi approached.

"Sato-san, I am in trouble," Yokoi confided.

Yokoi ushered the two men behind a pillar where they would not be overheard. He complained to Sato that gangsters had installed themselves in some of the rooms and offices of the Hotel New Japan, a first-class hotel Yokoi owned in an expensive district of Tokyo. The gangsters were refusing to leave. For *yakuza* gangsters, it was a common and lucrative scam. The gangsters would occupy commercial space, refuse to pay rent, and demand large payments to clear out. Few businessmen dared challenge them. But Yokoi hated being strong-armed. Yokoi told Sato he had ordered the hoodlums out, but they had refused to budge. Yokoi asked Sato what he should do.

Sato paused in his story, unsettled by the memory of the long-ago conversation. He placed a cigarette between his lips, lit it, took several drags, then stubbed it out. "I've never spoken to anyone about this," he said, before lowering his voice and continuing.

"It's easy," Sato told Yokoi.

"Well, it's not so easy," Yokoi replied. "I don't want any injuries."

"Water and fire are the best," Sato advised him. "You can spray water from the eighth floor. Or if you make smoke with a flare, everybody will think it is a fire. They will run off, but there will be no damage."

Yokoi thanked him and departed.

About six weeks later, Sato was staying with a half dozen friends at a downtown Tokyo hotel. At 3:30 in the morning, the men heard sirens. Sato and his friends piled into a taxi. Soon they were staring up at Yokoi's Hotel New Japan. Flames were licking out of the ninth floor windows. The fire was spreading quickly. Sato's friend Honjo, wearied by a long night of drinking, stood nearby, gazing up in horror at hotel guests driven to the window ledges by the heat and smoke. Sato and Honjo jumped to the same sickening conclusion. Yokoi had done it.

Sato sighed. "I have never said the truth before," he said. "I may have told him to start a fire, a small fire."

Police and fire department investigators spent months trying to piece together what happened at the 513-room Hotel New Japan, once one of Tokyo's plushest, in the predawn hours of February 8, 1982. In the end, they came to a different conclusion than the one arrived at by Tsuneji Sato. They did not accuse Yokoi of starting the fire. But for Hideki Yokoi, the scenario reconstructed by investigators was almost as scandalous.

Steven Dicker, a 24-year-old British toy salesman staying on the ninth floor, had been drinking and smoking in bed. At some point, his cigarette dropped onto the mattress, smoldered for more than an hour, then ignited the wallpaper. A sensor in the room picked up the fire, and an emergency lamp in the night watchman's room on the first floor began flashing. But the hotel had short-circuited the automatic alarm system in order to prevent false alarms from disturbing guests. It was up to the watchman to throw a switch. The man on duty that night, however, had been on the job only two weeks. He had no idea what to do.

Sometime after 3 A.M., a hotel employee saw smoke pouring out from under the door of Dicker's room and heard a man rapping on the inside of the door. In a panic, the employee opened the door with a master key, and Dicker stumbled out in front of a wall of flame. The conflagration belched out the door and ignited the corridor.

Yokoi had been ordered more than once to install a sprinkler system in the hotel. Claiming poverty, he had moved slowly, completing only the first and second floors. Yokoi had also ignored warnings to repair fire doors in the corridors. The doors were designed to spring shut when the temperature hit 120 degrees centigrade to prevent a fire from spreading. That night, some of the doors caught on the carpet. Only one swung closed. As usual, the humidifying system was off, on orders from Yokoi, to save energy. The air was dry, conducive to a vigorous burn. As the flames spread across the ninth floor, they licked up to the tenth floor through ductwork in disrepair and holes left over from shoddy construction.

Because Yokoi had slashed hotel-staffing levels, only nine employees were on duty that night. Just one fire drill had been conducted in the two years Yokoi had owned the hotel. After the fire had been burning for some time, the front-desk clerk rushed to the ninth floor and began activating the alarm bells manually. Employees staggered through the corridor banging on doors and shouting "Fire!" Employees tried in vain to fight the blaze themselves. Finally, a pedestrian who caught sight of the flames and smoke called the fire department.

By then, the inferno was too far along. More than 300 guests were in the hotel, including 63 Taiwanese tourists and a South Korean delegation that had come to learn about Japanese robots. The 108 guests on the ninth and tenth floors awoke to choking smoke and darkness. Disoriented, many lost their way in the smoke-filled corridors and collapsed. Others retreated from the flames and smoke to their window ledges. Cries for help in several languages rang out in the night. Some of those trapped on the ninth floor escaped by lowering themselves on ropes of knotted sheets and curtains and kicking in windows on the eighth floor. Ladders raised by fire trucks arriving on the scene plucked others to safety. The unlucky ones were left crouching in terror on the eight-inch ledges. To the horror of firemen and onlookers, a South Korean businessman jumped to his death. Then another. And another. From the tenth floor, a 25-year-old model and her 40-year-old fiancé jumped. Of the 13 who leaped, only one, an airline stewardess, survived. All told, 33 people died that winter night, including 12 Taiwanese tourists, 6 Korean businessmen, an American, 11 Japanese natives, and the British toy salesman. Their bodies were taken to a nearby temple.

To survive the firestorm of outrage sparked by the disaster, Hideki Yokoi would have had to muster a set of emotions—sorrow, contrition, humility—for which he had never been known. By any measure, Yokoi failed to convincingly conjure them up. When he arrived at the hotel at eight o'clock that morning as firefighters were finally bringing the blaze under control, Yokoi said he was sorry. But his tone was less of contrition than of dismay, and he already seemed to be moving in the direction of self-exculpation. "It was a tragic incident, but I must say it was fortunate that the fire was prevented from spreading no more than to parts of the ninth and tenth floors," Yokoi said. In spite of the hotel losing money, he told reporters, "we have done quite well in efforts to prevent a fire."

As the facts about Yokoi's stewardship of the hotel tumbled out, he seemed taken aback by the rising public indignation. When Yokoi arrived at a temple that evening for a Buddhist wake for the victims, one woman stood up and berated him: "Why did you want to make money so badly at the cost of this?" Yokoi, flummoxed, could think of nothing to say but "I am sorry." Thereafter, he tried to avoid the aggrieved. He sent recently hired employees to visit the injured at the hospital and the relatives of the deceased at their homes. Yokoi had authorized these employees to offer 20 million yen, about $87,000, to each family that had lost a loved one. But the families snubbed Yokoi's men, shouted at them, forced them to prostrate themselves on the ground. They raged against Yokoi for failing to apologize personally. "It was worse than sitting on a needle mat," one employee later recalled.

Increasingly, Yokoi's own behavior reinforced his reputation as selfish, greedy, and untrustworthy. Three weeks after the fire, he angered the crippled hotel's retail tenants by blaming the fire on a curse by evil spirits. In 1936, he said, eight people had died where the hotel stood during an abortive coup by young army officers, and the site had not been purified. Within days, a group of outraged tenants and long-term residents lodged a formal complaint against Yokoi with the police, accusing him of involuntary manslaughter and bodily injury through negligence. At a press conference, Yokoi insisted he bore no criminal responsibility. The hotel had been trying to complete the ordered safety improvements, he maintained. His modest monetary offer to each victim's family, he said, was all he could afford. The public didn't buy that for a minute. Newspapers reported that a private financial research firm, Teikoku Data Bank, estimated that Yokoi's assets were worth more than 100 billion yen, with the Hotel New Japan accounting for nearly half that, although many of the assets were mortgaged.

Yokoi's efforts to diffuse the rage of the victims' families were at best, ham-handed, at worst, downright miserly. Hiroko Hanaoka, who lost her 45-year-old husband in the fire, was given an enormous carton of toilet paper, a large bottle of honey, and then a bagful of eye shadow and lipstick. "Even if he had not been what he was to me, I would have felt uneasy with him," she reflected years later. "There was something about him that made me feel that I should keep away from him. He was a different kind of human being from us."

Two months after the fire, Yokoi was called before a committee of the Japanese legislature. He arrived 10 minutes late. On entering, he bowed deeply in three directions. Hostile legislators jeered at him.

"You are late," admonished one lawmaker. "What were you doing?"

Yokoi stood. "I am very sorry for the inferno that destroyed the top two floors of my hotel," he said. He expressed sorrow for "the inconveniencing of so many people and the loss of the valuable lives of 33 people. I express my deep regret to the deceased and bereaved families." He told the lawmakers his hotel had been running in the red, and he insisted it had been working on installation of sprinklers, although the work had been stopped last year. He said he had already concluded compensation talks with one-third of the Japanese families.

"He is lying," murmured a representative of the families. Later, the families sued Yokoi, demanding 1.6 billion yen in damages. At a court hearing, Yokoi withdrew his offer to pay them, saying in a written statement that his earlier promise had been made under threat. The fire was the fault of employees in charge of fire prevention, not the hotel's management, he said defiantly.

Yokoi's string of crude excuses proved unpersuasive to authorities, who put his whole operation under scrutiny. National tax authorities pored over Yokoi's books. They accused him of underreporting revenue from a valuable tract of land he sold. His companies had exchanged stock with one another at artificially low prices, they said, and Yokoi had taken personal loans from his companies, then treated the payment of interest as optional. Kimonos for his mistresses, wages of maids and caretakers working at his residential compound, and the property taxes on his home all had been treated as business expenses, the tax authorities said. Yokoi had failed to report 600 million yen of income over the prior three years, they said, and five of his companies neglected to report income of 2.6 billion yen. The Tokyo Regional Taxation Bureau ordered Yokoi to pay about 900 million yen in back taxes and penalties.

Fatherly love often prompts men to bear undue hardship to shield their offspring from harm. In Yokoi, that tendency was perversely inverted. All told, six family members had positions at the doomed hotel. Yokoi's eldest son, Kunihiko, 40, was the hotel's vice president and general manager. At times of crisis, family members were the people Yokoi turned to. He expected unswerving loyalty from them. Now, as his world collapsed, he felt he wasn't getting it. Yokoi complained bitterly to his brother-in-law Hishida that his sons had run for cover, leaving their father to face his hostile inquisitors on his own.

But if his eldest son wasn't up to the test, there were others who might be. Kiiko Nakahara, then 37, had never been part of his inner circle. Yokoi had never officially recognized Kiiko as his own. Her half brothers didn't even know her. Yet over the years, Yokoi had demanded the same sort of filial devotion from her that he did of his legitimate children. Years earlier, when Kiiko had impulsively moved to Brazil as an aspiring 20-year-old artist eager to escape her father's orbit, Yokoi had dispatched her mother to bring her back to Tokyo. Yokoi had encouraged his daughter to pursue a career in fashion, eventually helping her to set up her own firm, which designed uniforms for airlines and hotels. He arranged Kiiko's marriage to the son of a friend, a short, unhappy affair that produced a son and a quick separation. Yokoi's sons groused about his stinginess. But to his daughter, Yokoi displayed unflagging generosity.

In the aftermath of the hotel fire, Yokoi's sons began to notice that their father was investing an uncommon degree of trust in this young woman. Yokoi drew his daughter in. He told her he spent more time with her than with any of his other children. He phoned her several times a day, told her his problems with his concubines, asked for her help in caring for his illegitimate children, and complained about his two sons. Father and daughter spent hours behind closed doors discussing business and life. Kiiko was bright enough and worldly enough to realize that her father was more despised than respected. Yet she developed a fierce loyalty to him. Years later, when New York lawyers would be called upon to dissect this father-daughter bond, they would give considerable thought to why it flowered when it did. Kiiko's father clearly loved her, and she him. But to Yokoi, it seemed, Kiiko had something else to offer.

On November 18, 1982, Yokoi discovered the limits of his own power. Nine months had passed since the fire at the Hotel New Japan. Two police officers picked up Yokoi at the home of his mistress, drove him to the Tokyo Metropolitan Police Department, and marched him through a phalanx of photographers. A blue handkerchief covered the handcuffs that shackled his right hand to the hand of a police officer. After several hours of interrogation, Yokoi, his son Kunihiko, and two other executives were arrested. The warrant accused Yokoi of neglecting to install sprinklers and other fire-prevention equipment and failing to draw up a fire-fighting plan. (Charges were never brought against Kunihiko and one of the other executives.) At the age of 69, Yokoi found himself sitting in a Tokyo jail, shivering against the chill of the oncoming winter.

For a man accustomed to doing exactly as he pleased, to be locked up like a common criminal was profoundly unsettling. When Kiiko came to visit, she found her father bundled in layers to ward off a cold that had taken hold of his bones. His nerves seemed shot. Yokoi told his daughter he was disappointed with Japan and wanted to leave the country. He pleaded with her to make him a new life in Europe, to buy him a home. Not just any home, he told her. Yokoi asked her to buy castles, one for each child. Kiiko had heard such talk before. But this time Yokoi was actually weeping. Kiiko had never seen her father reduced to tears. She loved him, she realized. How could she refuse him his wish? "Okay, okay, Papa," she soothed, "I'll do it."

Ninety-five days after he was plucked from the home of his mistress, Yokoi was released on bail. His lawyers met him in front of the jail in two long American limousines. Yokoi climbed in, and the cars nosed through a throng of reporters who had gathered for a glimpse of the disgraced tycoon.

On January 13, 1983, Yokoi stood up in a Tokyo court on the first day of his trial. Reading from a prepared statement, he apologized. He vowed to dedicate his life to compensating the victims. He bowed deeply, then sat down. His lawyer rose and entered a plea of not guilty. Yokoi could not possibly have foreseen that a fire would spread so rapidly, his lawyer told the court. Yokoi thought his manager had taken adequate fire-protection measures, he said. Unfortunately for Yokoi, that manager was also on trial, and evidently not eager to be cast by his boss as the scapegoat. He readily admitted to some of the charges against him, but claimed that he had recommended the installation of improved fire-prevention systems. Yokoi had ignored the recommendation altogether, the manager said. The trial of Hideki Yokoi was to stretch out over 57 separate hearings, scattered over more than four years. Prosecutors were determined to send the billionaire back to jail, for four years, if possible. Yokoi dreaded the possibility. It hung over his head like an anvil.

On the morning of May 20, 1987, Yokoi slipped into a black suit and drove to Tokyo District Court. Four years and four months had passed since he had pleaded innocent to the criminal negligence charge in the Hotel New Japan fire. At the age of 73, his day of reckoning was upon him. It surprised no one that the court brushed aside Yokoi's attempts to blame the fire on the hotel staff and its previous owners. In its long-awaited ruling, the court concluded that Yokoi had brought the disaster on through his single-minded pursuit of profits. The hotel's manager, who had been unable to fulfill his responsibility because of Yokoi's policies, the court said, was given an 18-month suspended sentence. As Yokoi stood to receive his sentence, he looked stiff. He bowed several times to the bereaved families. The court ordered him to prison for three years.

In the ensuing years, as his lawyers fought to overturn the conviction, Yokoi sheltered himself from his nation's scorn inside an anachronistic world of his own making. On the walls of Yokoi's office across from the Imperial Palace hung photographs of his many children, along with a portrait of Yokoi in uniform, a military saber hanging from his belt. Visitors would often find Yokoi seated at his desk, black sleeve covers over his white shirt like some accountant in Dickens's London. His trousers were custom-tailored with a wallet pocket in the front and none in the back, his defense against pickpockets. Beside his desk sat a large black safe, immovable as a piano. From time to time, he would swing open its door, displaying to his gaping visitors brick upon brick of yen, 200 million to 300 million yen in total, he would tell them. His latest mistress, a twenty-something beauty queen for whom he was building a mansion in downtown Tokyo, would often sashay in and help herself to the bundles, he complained one day to Hisakazu Honjo, a local businessman.

Yokoi hoarded things in storage rooms. When Yokoi needed a new shirt, he'd pull one out of a stockpile of 100. One day, Kiiko showed Renoir a warehouse of furniture. A furniture salesman had refused to give Yokoi a discount, she explained to her husband. So her father had bought the whole store. Once, when Renoir was touring one of Yokoi's bowling alleys, he happened upon a room filled with Japanese armor.

Yokoi appeared unaware that the years of postwar deprivation, when he had won gratitude by doling out food and other staples from his private stockpile, were over. Yokoi continued to deliver bags of sugar to his mistresses, apparently believing that to anyone who wasn't as rich as he was, anything was better than nothing. He kept an inventory of fur coats to hand out to daughters and mistresses. He prevailed upon his younger brother to adopt his young mistress so that she would carry the name Yokoi, according to Japanese press reports. In the morning, Yokoi liked to be chauffeured around the city in his stretch limousine with his mistress and their young daughter, and to stop to sip coffee in cafés.

Yokoi must have realized that the odds of escaping prison were becoming exceedingly remote. Each time he lost an appeal, he became more convinced that at least some of his wealth should be transferred offshore. Kiiko came to believe that if Yokoi exhausted his legal options, he was prepared to flee Japan. If his motherland didn't respect him, he would buy prestige elsewhere . . . in a place where he had never set foot, in a place where the horror of recent years would be a distant memory.

Yokoi's motive for assembling his storybook portfolio of castles—a seemingly half-baked plan to flee Japan—was a secret he shared, it appears, only with his beloved daughter. Were the instructions he first gave Kiiko in his Tokyo jail cell known to anyone involved in the sale of the Empire State Building, it is doubtful they would have inspired confidence in the future of the New York landmark.

5

Yokoi Meets His Match

Years later, after Yokoi's empire had collapsed on itself, sending a wave of trouble washing over his daughter, his son-in-law, and the Empire State Building, Renoir would ruminate over a warning he had received from a Japanese colleague at Lehman Brothers. "If you just touch Yokoi once," Renoir's colleague told him, "you will regret it." For years, Renoir had managed to heed the suggestion for the most part, brushing aside requests for advice from Yokoi and his cronies. Despite Yokoi's riches, he seemed to inhabit a different planet than did the investment bankers among whom Renoir was trying to make his mark. To Renoir, the risk of mixing the two parts of his life must have seemed great. But eventually, Renoir, too, was drawn into Yokoi's odd orbit.

In the early 1990s, Hisakazu Honjo began to notice a new set of faces at the headquarters of his friend, Hideki Yokoi. Men in business suits sat silently in Yokoi's offices, like sentinels, from morning until night. Yokoi ignored them. They were his bankers, Yokoi explained to Honjo, representatives of the institutions that had been so eager to lend him money during the bubble economy. But now the economic tide was turning. Real estate investments were becoming shaky in Japan. Men like Yokoi, who kept his financial condition hidden in a fog of obfuscation and deceit, had to be watched very carefully.

Like real estate tycoons across America, Yokoi had built his empire on a simple but risky premise: Buy with borrowed money, and wait for inflation to make you rich. Through three decades of postwar boom, the formula had proven fabulously lucrative for Yokoi, had made him a billionaire. But the unprecedented run-up of real estate values during the 1980s proved no different from any other economic bubble. In May 1989, concerned about speculation, the Bank of Japan announced its first interest rate hike in a decade. Additional rate hikes followed. The bubble popped. During the first nine months of 1990, the Nikkei stock market average fell 44 percent. The average property-related stock plunged 55 percent. Property values seemed to be falling, too, but it was difficult to know for sure. Lenders had shut off the spigot to real estate investors. No one was buying commercial buildings. Once-high-flying real estate companies, like canaries in a toxic mine, began dying.

Before long, Japan's banks ran afoul of regulated capital requirements. Bad real estate loans were pulling them down. By 1993, a full-blown economic bust had set in, evidenced by the skeletons of half-completed buildings that punctuated Tokyo's skyline. Japan's 21 major banks reported $110 billion of nonperforming loans, about one-third of them real estate–related. Eventually, commercial land prices would fall by an average of 50 percent, with major properties in Tokyo down by as much as 80 percent. An avalanche of more than $300 billion of bad real estate loans was bearing down on Japanese banks. Overseas trophy hunting by Japan's property kingpins ended as abruptly as it had begun. Japan's real estate magnates worked full-time to save their hides.

When Tokyo land prices were at their peak, Yokoi had borrowed about $1.8 billion from Chiyoda Mutual Life Insurance Company, a Chiyoda affiliate called Tokyo United Technology, and from Bank of Osaka. The still abandoned Hotel New Japan secured the loans. Yokoi had used the money to buy real estate and stock. Now both markets were in a tailspin. In 1991, Nippon Sangyo, his main holding company, lost 10.3 billion yen, as much as he had paid for all his overseas trophies. Yokoi's lenders turned on him with a vengeance.

Yokoi felt little inclination to shelter his offspring from the impending crisis. Nor was he eager to tighten his belt. In Tokyo, he wasn't yet done with the sprawling mansion he was building for his mistress. He plowed ahead with that. Renoir guaranteed a bank loan of about $1 million for Yokoi, Renoir later said. Yokoi also asked his daughter for about $2 million. Kiiko felt obligated to help. She felt she owed it to her father. She tapped a credit line available to Oriental Kiiko, her uniform design and manufacturing firm. (Renoir later claimed that the loan he guaranteed was never repaid. Yokoi's bookkeeper said Yokoi hadn't borrowed anything from Renoir and that the stock held as collateral on the loan from Kiiko was taken by the bank to cover the debt.) Yokoi sent his son, Hirohiko, and his brother-in-law, Hishida, to plead with executives at Chiyoda Mutual for an extension on the loan on the Hotel New Japan. Chiyoda would have none of it. The insurer threatened to auction off the property. Hirohiko and his older brother, Kunihiko, pledged their houses and cars to secure a $35 million loan to pay Tokyo United Technology, the Chiyoda affiliate that was also pressing for repayment, in a desperate effort to prevent foreclosure.

Yokoi's castles in France—the eye candy that only a few years earlier had seemed to him like an inconsequential expense—now loomed as sinkholes for his dwindling cash. The nine châteaux were costing him more than $1 million a year for upkeep, taxes, maintenance, and salaries for a staff of 50. In 1992, Yokoi abruptly stopped sending any money to

France and asked Kiiko to get rid of the properties. By now, Jean-Paul Renoir recognized the signs of an impending disaster. "You better protect yourself," he warned his wife. "Because your family is going to be completely ruined. Bankrupted."

The orgy of overseas property buying—the European castles, the mansion in Long Island, and above all, the Empire State Building—had cemented the bond between Yokoi and his daughter. Without Kiiko, he would have been lost in the Western world. Kiiko spoke to her father daily. She trusted him. She felt that he trusted her. He had made her a director of Nippon Sangyo, his primary holding company, where she joined Kunihiko and Hirohiko, his two eldest sons, on the board. In 1989, Yokoi had even told her he was adding her to his official family registry, elevating her to the same official status as his legitimate children.

Yet what of the properties they had purchased in such apparent haste? Cautious buyers of real estate examine properties carefully, looking for every cracked tile and faulty outlet, then study market pricing like Wall Street traders. Yokoi had made decisions based on fistfuls of snapshots. It was only a matter of time before Yokoi came to realize that looks can be deceiving, that his precious acquisitions were not all that they had seemed.

Renoir had always kept his distance from Yokoi's investments in France. But by 1992, when Renoir quit Lehman Brothers and moved to Britain with thoughts of launching a mutual fund, serious problems were mounting at the châteaux. Maintenance was overdue. Tax bills were piling up. All the French managers had quit, concerned about being held responsible for unpaid taxes. Kiiko spoke little French. Renoir was a native. Yokoi pleaded with Renoir for assistance. Kiiko was eager to help her father. So Renoir agreed to wade into the mess. He was appalled by what he saw. As far as

Renoir could determine, Yokoi had no business plan for the properties and cared little about their condition. "All he cares about is the image," Renoir would later explain. "All he wants is to show the world, I own this. They were ridiculous investments. Absurd. This was a study in insanity."

Castles are rarely good investments. They simply cost too much to keep up. If an owner doesn't remain vigilant against decay, the properties slide downhill alarmingly fast. That's just what was happening in France and Britain. Kiiko and her husband decided to auction some of the valuable furnishings to raise money to cover overdue bills. Finding buyers for the châteaux, however, was a much taller order. The market was depressed. To longtime brokers, every château sale was considered something of a miracle.

Yokoi had always been a hard-nosed seller. So much so, in fact, that he found it difficult to sell anything. Yokoi would jerk potential buyers around so thoroughly that many would simply walk away in disgust. Kiiko brought her father a number of offers for the châteaux, offers she considered quite attractive. Yokoi routinely sent her back to bidders to ask for more money. Her father's policy, Kiiko told Renoir, was to sell a property for three times what he paid for it. Renoir dismissed the notion as rank stupidity.

Château Millemont, Yokoi's grandest French property, was saddled with a lease to a politically powerful Parisian shooting club. Renoir brazenly moved to oust the club, stirring hostility among the club's elite members. Another château in la Grize, which Yokoi had purchased from an advertisement in the paper, was found to have a huge tax liability that made it a financial drain. Kiiko managed to find a buyer for only one French property, a villa in Helios, which she sold in 1992 for roughly twice what her father had paid.

Elsewhere, the picture was no better. Glenapp Castle in Scotland was consumed by dry rot, and politicians were agitating for something to be done. When Yokoi found out about its horrid condition, he snapped to Renoir: "Let it fall down. I'm fed up with this property." Coopersale, another British castle, drew offers of only half what Yokoi had paid. He took it as an insult. In Spain, authorities were moving to seize Falguera Palace.

When Renoir finally laid eyes on Oheka Castle, the decrepit 127-room mansion outside New York City Yokoi had bought for $22.5 million, he could scarcely believe it. The place was uninhabitable. Gary Melius, the manager and previous owner, was selling furnishings and fixtures to pay bills. "This is a joke," Renoir told his wife. "What do you want to own this for?" Renoir asked Melius if he was interested in buying it back. Melius coolly offered $4 million. Renoir angrily refused.

As the rest of Yokoi's trophy-laden portfolio sank into financial quicksand, the Empire State Building remained the one rock of seeming stability. As an investment, it was hardly lucrative. But it wasn't a sinkhole. And there was every reason to believe it would churn out a savings-account-caliber annual dividend for years to come.

By the spring 1993, there was still only a handful of people who knew that Hideki Yokoi and his daughter had bought the Manhattan landmark. It may have been the best-kept secret in New York. Leona Helmsley didn't know. Peter Malkin hadn't a clue. Nor did Prudential Insurance. Now the time had come for Oliver Grace to retire as the Yokoi family's straw man. He had served his purpose. Prudential was none the wiser. Grace must have been relieved to be done with the ruse. It had been awkward. An article in *The Wall Street Journal* had unmasked Grace as the owner. He had hunkered down and kept his mouth shut. He had arguably earned every dollar of his fee, which has never been disclosed but is believed to be in the hundreds of thousands of dollars.

That April, Henry Bubel, Kiiko and Renoir's New York

lawyer, set to work creating a chain of offshore holding companies. These obscurely named companies would become the new owners of the Empire State Building. For outsiders, it would become next to impossible to decipher who really owned the landmark property. E. G. Holding Company, Grace's front company, merged into NS 1991 American Trust, a Delaware business trust. Renoir and Kiiko were managing directors. A Dutch company was set up to own the Delaware trust. A Netherlands Antilles company was created to own the Dutch company. The end of the ownership chain was a new trust company in the Isle of Man, a tax haven in the Irish Sea. Kiiko Nakahara controlled that trust, called NS 1991 Trust. The beneficiaries of the offshore trust were Kiiko and Nippon Sangyo, Yokoi's holding company. When Yokoi died, however, Kiiko was to become the sole beneficiary of the trust that held title to the Empire State Building.

The convoluted ownership chain, called a *Dutch sandwich*, was designed to get cash from the Empire State Building out of the country with a minimum of taxation. As an added dividend, it made it highly unlikely that Prudential would ever discover the building's true owner. Whether Kiiko and her husband had other reasons for constructing such a complex ownership structure may never be known. Yet already, a kernel of distrust was taking seed back in Tokyo. Yokoi's longtime bookkeeper, Chieko Ohashi, had been nagging Kiiko for months to provide her with a copy of the purchase contract. Kiiko had steadfastly refused. "No matter how many times I asked her for it, she said it was confidential and she couldn't discuss it," Ohashi would later recall. "We were extremely troubled."

Yokoi himself had more pressing matters to attend to. His lenders continued to dog him. Perhaps if he could figure out a way to redevelop the burned-out Hotel New Japan—still his most valuable asset—he might extricate himself from his mess.

That spring, potential help arrived from America in the person of Charles Lindsay, the Greenwich, Connecticut, real estate consultant brought in by Renoir. Lindsay had already gotten an earful about Yokoi from Renoir. His father-in-law was operating in the nineteenth century, Renoir told Lindsay. If Yokoi were left to his own devices, he'd lose everything, Renoir said. When Lindsay arrived at Yokoi's Tokyo office, Yokoi presented him with a desk clock. He began lecturing Lindsay about what a fabulous property the Hotel New Japan still was. He complained to the American that he was being victimized by the government, which was holding him to standards of safety that hadn't existed at the time of the fire. Yokoi was loud and offhanded with his dismissals.

Lindsay recognized right away that he was dealing with a dysfunctional family. Yokoi seemed to have a hair-trigger temper. He would fall into loud shouting matches with his daughter, insulting her business acumen. Animosity between Renoir and Yokoi had been brewing. Kiiko tried to keep the two apart. Renoir avoided meetings with his father-in-law. Lindsay wasn't sure what was happening.

Lindsay knew the Hotel New Japan site was once valued as high as $4 billion. Yokoi told Lindsay it was now worth $2 billion. After looking at it, Lindsay figured $1 billion, which was considerably less than the $1.8 billion Yokoi owed on it. Nonetheless, Lindsay believed it had great potential. If Yokoi could raise $400 million to erect a mixed-use skyscraper on the site, he could pay off his lenders and retain control of the property. What Yokoi needed, Lindsay told him, was a big-name American developer, someone whose name was well known in Japan. Lindsay mentioned Donald Trump. You could model the building on Trump Tower in New York, Lindsay told Yokoi. Trump was a celebrity in Japan. A Trump Tower Tokyo, Lindsay said, could be worth substantially more than Yokoi owed his lenders. Yokoi seemed intrigued.

Depending on one's perspective, Donald Trump was either an inspired choice of candidate to help bail out a struggling Japanese billionaire or a ridiculous one. A couple of years earlier, Trump himself had faced a crisis not dissimilar to Yokoi's. When America's real estate markets soured, Trump found himself in default on more than $1 billion of debt that supported his empire of condominium towers, hotels, casinos, and a commercial airline. His irate lenders had insisted on humbling lifestyle changes. Trump had to get rid of the $30 million yacht, the fleet of helicopters, the corporate jet. In the end, they allowed him to escape bankruptcy. But they forced the sale of such coveted Trump holdings as the Plaza Hotel and Trump Airlines. The crowing of Trump's detractors had been loud and enthusiastic. For America's quintessential 1980s developer, it had been a humiliatingly public denouement.

Yet Trump had emerged from disaster with his brand name intact, if tarnished. He still touted the same self-promoting creed that he had preached in the 1980s: that "Trump" was the ultimate brand name in luxury. Yet he was going about it differently. He was no longer capable—at least not for a while—of borrowing hundreds of millions of dollars to fund his own projects. Trump embarked on a new kind of deal making. He shoehorned his way into deals with deep-pocketed partners, putting up little or no money himself. When his partners got their money back, then Trump would share in the profits. Until then, Trump collected fees to act as project manager and marketer par excellence. General Electric Company had brought Trump in under just such a model to redevelop a prime Manhattan site as Trump International Hotel. Trump festooned the building with bronze and marble and sold out the condominiums in a blaze of publicity, not all of it favorable.

When Lindsay returned from Tokyo, he set up a meeting with Trump. With Renoir by his side, Lindsay extolled to

Trump the virtues of a Trump Tower Tokyo on the site of Yokoi's ruined Hotel New Japan. Trump was noticeably cool. Renoir mentioned that Yokoi and his daughter had bought the Empire State Building. Trump's eyes lit up. Suddenly, he wanted to know everything about the deal and how Yokoi had pulled it off. Trump railed about Leona Helmsley, accused her of destroying the Empire State Building. Something had to be done, Trump said.

Trump asked each of them for their opinion of Yokoi. Renoir told Trump he thought Yokoi's capacities as a businessman had diminished. Yokoi couldn't handle his asset base, Renoir said. It was falling into disrepair. Trump asked Lindsay what he thought. "I think he's a sharp guy who has his own agenda," Lindsay told Trump. Someone who knew Trump better might have seen the wheels begin to turn in his head at that very moment. For Trump, the Empire State Building was the quintessential New York building. It had always been pure magic.

Over the coming weeks, Renoir and Lindsay sketched out a proposal for a Trump development in Tokyo. Not another word was said about the Empire State Building. Trump Tower Tokyo, as they began referring to their plan, would be a 1-million-square-foot sister building to Trump's New York crowd pleaser. It would offer, one written proposal said, "Western-style amenities in an opulent setting, offering the largest floor sizes in the city, the finest shopping arcade in the city, and condominiums of the highest quality in one of Tokyo's premier addresses." When completed, it would be worth $2.5 billion, the proposal projected.

By early May, Trump was expressing keen interest. "As per our discussion, I would love to develop your wonderful site in Tokyo, Japan," Trump wrote to Kiiko on May 7. "As a 50/50 partner in this transaction, I believe that I will add much value to the site both in terms of increased zoning capability and with your lending institutions. It would be my intention to use one of the world's greatest architects, perhaps Phillip

Johnson or I. M. Pei, together with a local Japanese architect. When completed, I believe Trump Tower, Japan will be the finest development in the world and a great source of pride to both you and your family."

But first, Trump had to convince Yokoi to swallow a particularly tough nut. In exchange for "negotiating with current creditors" of Yokoi to settle existing debts and get new development financing, Trump said in a letter to Yokoi, he wanted a 50 percent ownership stake in the venture and a plaque on the front naming him developer. Trump did not offer to invest a single dollar of his own capital. Yokoi was unaccustomed to being over a barrel. He had an altogether different idea. In a handwritten response, Yokoi offered to give Trump a 50 percent stake only if Trump insured repayment of the $1.8 billion of debt. Trump rejected the proposal out of hand. "The feasibility of any developer committing 200,000,000,000 Yen to a transaction as a starting point for launching a project is remote at best," Trump wrote. Years later, Trump would recall that his immediate reaction had been a less diplomatic, "I'm not retarded."

Yokoi's lenders were backing him to the wall. Chiyoda disclosed plans to auction the property come November. Appearing before reporters, Yokoi feigned surprise. "The construction of a 50-story office building was to start in the second half of 1993," he lied. Now, Yokoi had little choice but to acquiesce to Trump's demands. By mid-July, a draft agreement was complete. Trump Tower Tokyo would be no less than 30 stories. Trump would get half the stock, a plaque on the front, and naming rights for the skyscraper. In exchange, Trump agreed to personally negotiate with Chiyoda Mutual Life and Bank of Osaka to try to get Yokoi off the hook for $1.8 billion of debt without losing his prized property.

Trump touched down in Tokyo on a United Airlines flight on a steamy Sunday afternoon in August 1993, accompanied by an entourage that included his second wife Marla Maples, his longtime architect Der Scutt, assorted underlings, and Renoir. Yokoi was waiting at the airport with a limousine. Donald, Marla, Kiiko, and Yokoi rode to Tokyo's Imperial Hotel, where Yokoi had reserved suites for Trump and his people. Kiiko was anxious for everything to go smoothly. If it did, Yokoi and Trump would soon be partners on a project that would save her father from ruin. Kiiko had worried that her father would give Marla an embarrassing gift from his stockpile, so she had a pearl necklace made, which she gave to her father to present to Marla. At a festive dinner that night, pictures were taken and toasts were made. Yokoi and Trump took turns boasting about themselves. Spirits ran high.

For two days, the two camps hashed over the deal. Trump visited Yokoi's lenders. He found the executives at Chiyoda Life noticeably cool to his white knight act. "Those guys were such stiffs," Trump later put it. "I sat with them and told them what I was going to do. It was the strangest meeting. They never said a word. I talked to them about buying the debt back at a discount. They nodded. I didn't know if that meant yes or no. The meeting ended. They didn't say anything. And that was it. It was the strangest meeting. They were really dopes."

Nonetheless, by Tuesday night, it looked as if Kiiko's fondest wishes would be fulfilled. Trump and Yokoi, everyone believed, had agreed to a deal. Champagne was opened. Trump and Yokoi agreed to meet at Trump's suite at nine o'clock the following morning to sign final documents. Then the two tycoons would appear at a press conference set up by Renoir.

Yokoi had never been a realistic man, particularly when he was running out of chips. That evening, he apparently couldn't shake the feeling that he was being snookered. He had never liked outsiders meddling in his business. He hated his lenders.

He had doubts that the value of the Hotel New Japan had fallen as much as the Americans were telling him. He harbored unrealistic hopes that the criminal case against him would ultimately collapse. He resented having to give up control of his crown jewel in Japan.

At nine the following morning, Trump and his entourage were waiting. Yokoi was nowhere to be seen. Renoir ranted about Yokoi. Kiiko rushed off to look for him. When she found him, Yokoi told her he had changed his mind. Kiiko fumed at her father. You have to tell Trump yourself, face-to-face, she told him. Yokoi arrived at Trump's suite an hour late. The deal was off, he told Trump. Trump was angry. Trump, Yokoi, Kiiko, and two translators settled onto two couches to see if they could repair the breach. They got nowhere. Yokoi was in a bad mood. An awkward quiet fell over the room.

"Let's talk about something else," Yokoi said. "Let's talk about the Empire State Building. Maybe Trump can help us."

"Did you get it?" said Trump. His surprise appeared genuine enough.

"Yes, I got it," Yokoi responded, brightening.

Trump said he had been interested in bidding on the property. He'd be happy to help out with it, he said.

The meeting broke up under a cloud of disappointment. Trump went off to the press conference, where he spoke vaguely about looking at opportunities in Tokyo. Renoir was disgusted with Yokoi. It seemed to Renoir as if his father-in-law had just blown his last chance to keep his empire intact. Kiiko, too, was distraught, but she was intrigued by Trump's expression of interest in the Empire State Building. She asked her lawyer, Henry Bubel, to think about how Trump might help. Perhaps there's an opportunity for some kind of joint venture, she told him.

When Renoir returned to New York, he fulminated to his friend Charles Lindsay that Yokoi was likely to lose everything. Trump, however, was ecstatic. That, in any event, is what he would claim years later. "Honestly, I wasn't thrilled about buying a hotel where I had to travel 24 hours in an airplane," he said. "Eighty people were killed, which I also don't like," he continued, inflating the death toll at the Hotel New Japan by nearly 50. "It had bad luck. It never thrills me to take over something that has bad luck. Ninety-nine percent of my effort was in order to be nice to them to get my position in the Empire State Building. If that meant talking enthusiastically about a hotel, perhaps that would be part of it." Possibly sensing his listener's skepticism, he added, "You understand."

To Trump, a native New Yorker, the appeal of owning the Empire State Building was so obvious it hardly bore explaining. It was a New York icon. It had that unique quality that Trump had always sought in his own projects: It captivated people. Yet there was an added bonus to getting involved with its new owners. It offered Trump an opportunity to make life difficult for a woman who, over the prior decade, he had grown to despise. It would allow him to antagonize, once again, his archenemy in the New York real estate industry, Leona Helmsley.

6

Old Guard, New World

To fully understand the collision of titans that was rapidly approaching, one must look back to the 1950s, the era of the man in the gray flannel suit, when the Empire State Building reigned as perhaps the most valuable single building in New York. At that time, Harry B. Helmsley and his investment partner Lawrence Wien were widely viewed as New York's most astute and powerful real estate men. Wien, a real estate lawyer, leased space in the Empire State Building. Walking through its soaring marble lobby each day, studying Manhattan from his office window, Wien had decided it was the greatest building in the world. He coveted it. Badly. When Alvin Silverman came to see Wien to apply for a job in late 1952, the young lawyer told Wien that he worked for the law firm that handled eviction work for the Empire State Building. Wien leaned back in his chair, looked the young man in the eye, and declared with unwavering confidence, "Some day I'm going to buy this building."

By the late 1940s—when the booming postwar economy

lifted the Empire State Building from near bankruptcy to enormous profitability—the sight of New York's tallest building rearing skyward had become irresistible to a great many property men. John Raskob's creation was no longer a symbol of the excesses of the 1920s, but a monument to what could be accomplished by those with ambition and pluck. Whether vanity was driving the real estate magnates who came to covet it or simply raw ambition is impossible to know. But in the years to come, the Empire State Building would be their Holy Grail. The pursuit of it would become a test—much as it had for Raskob and du Pont—of their ability to balance prudence and desire.

If it came from just about anyone other than Larry Wien, a vow to buy the Empire State Building could have been dismissed as bluster fit for a barroom. But Wien, son of a prosperous Russian-born silk manufacturer, and his partner Helmsley, who had worked his way up from the industry's bottom rung, had already devised a way to buy nearly any building they desired. Wien, a square-jawed graduate of Columbia Law School, had worked out a way to buy large buildings with capital pooled from numerous investors while avoiding corporate taxation. He had invented real estate syndication. For several years, before copycats materialized, Wien bought buildings with the ease and abandon of a man printing his own currency.

In Harry Helmsley, four years his junior, Wien had found the ideal partner. A shy man with a receding chin, prominent glasses, and a close-cropped mustache, Helmsley had gotten his start in the 1920s as an office boy for a real estate management firm. During the Depression, he wore out his shoes dunning cash-strapped tenants in Hell's Kitchen, a gritty patch of the Manhattan's West Side filled with tenements, warehouses, whorehouses, rail yards, and factories. Helmsley developed a keen eye for sizing up buildings, and he worked assiduously to cultivate ties with the bankers who were seizing properties right and left. Soon Helmsley was brokering sales and buying buildings. He concluded that the way to make money in real estate was to leave no detail overlooked, no dollar wasted.

The two men complemented one another perfectly. Wien, whose strength was structuring deals and tapping the moneyed crowd, was hungry for deals. Helmsley had a block-by-block, encyclopedic knowledge of Manhattan real estate and an uncanny knack for determining the right price to pay for a building, whether it be a decrepit fixer-upper or a bankrupt trophy. They struck a deal: Helmsley would find buildings for Wien. Wien would award Helmsley the lucrative management contracts and a piece of the investment. They became an incomparable act: Wien, a gregarious man-about-town with aspirations to leave a mark on the social and cultural life of the city, and Helmsley, an introverted workaholic who carried two briefcases home each night and seemed to care about little else but his holdings.

For the next 30 years, Harry found the properties and haggled over purchase prices with the tenacity of a man spending his last penny, and Larry found the money, staggering sums of it. Like an occupying force, the two men swept through Manhattan, skimming the cream of the city's property—the Lexington Hotel, the Lincoln Building, 120 Broadway, then the nation's third largest office building, the Graybar Building, the Hotel Taft, and a raft of lesser properties in New Jersey, Pennsylvania, California, Florida, and Tennessee. Wien's public limited partnerships raised money almost as efficiently as the U.S. Treasury, raising more than $150 million from some 3,000 eager investors between 1950 and 1958 alone. The two of them made, Wien would later say, "an awful lot of money."

To Wien, it seemed that his dear friend Helmsley wanted nothing less than to be the wealthiest man in the real estate world. But Helmsley appeared convinced that it wasn't likely to happen if he threw money down the drain on himself or his buildings. He saw no reason to trade up from his two-bedroom home in the suburbs, where he cut his own grass and clipped his own hedges. When he bought the New York Central Building, the railroad required him to rename it. Rather than hire stoneworkers to fashion a new sign, he had them rechisel only the C and the T, making it the New York General Building. To Harry, it was all about money. None of his holdings were ever for sale, it was explained to one employee, but any of them could be had if you made the right offer. It's not that he was cheap, he told employees. It was that any expense came straight off of the bottom line.

Wien must have flushed with anticipation when he received a call in 1953 from Roger Stevens. Before John Raskob passed away in 1950 at his Pioneer Point Farm in rural Maryland, he had left instructions with the executors of his estate to sell the Empire State Building as soon as someone stepped forward with an offer of $50 million. Stevens, a 42-year-old wheeler-dealer from Detroit, had somehow convinced the estate's broker he was the best man to organize a syndicate of investors to undertake the biggest real estate purchase in U.S. history. The following year, the Stevens group bought the building for $51.5 million and simultaneously sold the land underneath it to Prudential Insurance for $17 million.

When Stevens called Wien with an offer to sell the building, Wien had no way of knowing that Stevens had no intention of following through. Unbeknownst to Wien, Stevens's partner, Chicago building materials tycoon Henry Crown, had already bought out every member of the ownership syndicate except Stevens and Detroit banker Alfred R. Glancy Jr. Stevens was holding out for top dollar, and he knew of no better team at pricing properties than Wien and Helmsley. Wien prepared a bid, but in October 1954, Stevens and Glancy sold Crown all of the stock he didn't already own.

Wien felt he had been bamboozled. Several months later, he packed up his law office and moved out of the Empire State Building for good, taking space in another stately old office building he bought, the Lincoln Building on Forty-second Street. From his pine-paneled corner suite on the forty-eighth floor, Wien would survey his holdings, which dotted the panorama that unfolded to the south. Five floors above him, from his own more spartan office, Helmsley would do the same. Framed perfectly in office windows of the two budding tycoons, like a racier car glittering in the driveway of the next-door neighbor, stood the Empire State Building, evidence that Wien and Malkin were not yet the kings of Manhattan real estate. Wien was not content to let the matter rest.

Ordinarily, Helmsley refused to engage in the kind of haggling that was the hallmark of most real estate deals. Harry's soft voice and taciturn manner belied a sledgehammer negotiating style. He was tough on sellers. After studying a property's books like a holy text, Helmsley would sit down with its owner and make his offer. Often, it was just below the low end of the seller's targeted range. Low, but not insultingly so. Bidders who didn't know better might throw back a counteroffer. "I'm off the deal," Helmsley would abruptly declare and get up to leave. And he meant it. There were enough other buildings to buy. Word got around. When Harry made an offer, you either accepted it, or looked elsewhere.

With Henry Crown, Helmsley had to temper his style. He had to court Crown, play nice. This, too, was in Harry's repertoire. In 1958, Helmsley began. Crown had the upper hand. Crown was making good money on the building. Between 1951 and 1960, occupancy never dropped below 97.7 percent. It was churning out profits. In 1960, Helmsley caught a break. Crown, after merging his company into General Dynamics, came to the sickening conclusion that General Dynamics was on the verge of going broke. And if General Dynamics went under, he told his son Lester, it could bring down the

Crown empire with it. Crown decided he had no choice but to pay off much of his personal debt. He had to sell the Empire State Building.

Helmsley, of course, had no way of knowing that. He flew to Chicago time and again, jousting with Crown over the value of the building. To Wien and Helmsley, it appeared as though Crown kept changing his mind, raising the price. Several times, Wien gave up the deal for dead, lamenting to Helmsley that Crown's people were impossible. Helmsley persisted. The gangly tycoon paid so many visits to Crown's executive at the building that sharp-eyed employees began speculating that a deal was in the works. Crown told his leasing manager it was a blatant lie, the building wasn't for sale, and he should tell the tenants as much. Helmsley flew back and forth to Chicago to haggle with Crown. Finally, on a flight back to New York in the summer of 1961, Harry announced to his colleague Alvin Silverman, "Okay, Alvin. We're buying the Empire State Building."

Most real estate deals present all the complexity of a sixth-grade geometry problem. But the deal that took shape between Wien, Helmsley, Crown, and Prudential Insurance, which owned the land under the building, was numbingly complex. As rich as they were, Wien and Helmsley could not ante up the $65 million Crown wanted for the building, nor could they hope to raise that much quickly from investors. So Wien pressed Prudential to enter into a three-way deal. Wien and Helmsley would buy the building for $65 million, then resell it to Prudential for $29 million. In exchange for the rock-bottom price, Prudential would lease the entire building to Wien and Helmsley, who would pay just enough rent to give Prudential a respectable 7 percent return on its investment, plus the hefty tax write-offs that flow from real estate depreciation. Wien and Helmsley, in turn, would take over the building as though they owned it, taking all the risks of an owner and squeezing whatever profits they could out of the occupants.

But how long should the sweetheart lease run? Wien suggested 30 years, with three 21-year renewal options, for a total of 93 years. To Wien and Helmsley, then 56 and 52, that must have seemed like an eternity. To Wien's ambitious son-in-law Peter Malkin, a 27-year-old beanstalk of a man who had joined his law firm three years earlier, it didn't. "Dad. It's not long enough," said Malkin.

Helmsley started laughing. "Oh, so you think you'll live more than 100 years?"

"Yes," said Malkin.

"Let's ask for another 21 years," replied Helmsley.

In the end, Prudential agreed to a 114-year lease. Wien and Helmsley would rent the entire building for $3.22 million a year until 1991. The rent would then drop to just $1.84 million for each of the next 21 years (it was later adjusted to $1.9 million), before plunging to just $1.61 million a year for the final 63 years. For a building then churning out about $11 million a year in revenues, that seemed to leave Wien and Helmsley ample margin for profit. And even if the profits didn't flow, the two men had become masters of wringing money out of their deals every which way. Wien's law firm would get a $1.1 million fee when the deal closed, $100,000 a year to supervise the partnership that would hold the lease and act as its lawyer, and another $90,000 a year to act as lawyer to the private partnership that would hold the sublease. Helmsley's brokerage and management firm, Helmsley-Spear, would collect a $500,000 commission and $90,000 a year for building management.

Still, Wien and Helmsley figured they needed to come up with $39 million in a hurry to make the deal work. Wien proposed raising $33 million in $10,000 chunks by offering investors a stake in the lease. Wien would guarantee them a

$900 annual profit, a 9 percent return, a tad lower than other real estate partnerships at the time, but better than the average stock. But Wien and Helmsley added a lucrative twist—lucrative to them, that is. The partnership of outside investors that would hold the lease from Prudential would sublease the entire building to a separate partnership made up of Wien, Helmsley, and a couple of cronies, who would pay investors just enough rent to cover the promised 9 percent return. Here was the real sweetheart deal. Each year, after Wien and Helmsley paid outside partners their 9 percent return, the next $1 million in building profits went directly to them. Then they would split with their investors, fifty-fifty, all the additional cash the building churned out. The two deal makers would treat it as their just reward for a brilliant deal well done and for the risk they were assuming, however remote, that the building might suffer a catastrophic reversal of fortune.

On December 23, 1961, some 100 lawyers, accountants, title insurers, and real estate brokers joined Wien, Helmsley, and Crown around an oval conference table the size of a swimming pool at Prudential's headquarters in Newark. It was a solemn-looking army of white men with short hair and dark suits. Peter Malkin brought his father. Silverman brought the lone woman, his secretary. Ashtrays filled to overflowing. Documents were everywhere. As the men worked methodically through a 100-item agenda, a television crew hovered at the periphery. A *Life* magazine photographer snapped away.

The scores of documents signed by Wien and Helmsley cemented an elegant web of interests. Prudential owned the building, but had no voice in its operation, no claim on its profits, and could derive little benefit if it soared in value. The thousands of investors who financed the deal had a tidy guaranteed return, but virtually no clout. For all practical purposes, Wien and Helmsley owned the landmark. They could set the rents, write the leases, and collect the rent checks. But they didn't hold title to it. To the scores of accountants and lawyers who filed out of the conference room that day, it was a marvel of financial engineering. No one could possibly have imagined that what Wien and Helmsley had engineered that afternoon was a time bomb that would detonate three decades later into one of the most unseemly battles ever to erupt in New York's cantankerous real estate community.

With the skyscraper safely tucked into his portfolio, Wien had a picture window cut into the south wall of his office, giving him a sweeping view of lower Manhattan, punctuated in spectacular fashion by the ultimate trophy property. Five floors above him, Harry Helmsley added his own picture window. He loved to walk to the window with visitors, sweep his arm across the vista, and say, "There's my inventory." He felt like he was playing the world's largest game of Monopoly, and winning.

Wien ordered a thorough wash-down of the Empire State Building. Thirty men used 3,000 gallons of limestone cleaner to rid the building of unsightly carbon stains. The window frames were repainted, the metal spandrels polished. Wien ordered the removal of the garish revolving spotlights (added by Crown) and the installation of banks of spotlights to bath the building's crown in clear white light. As Wien walked down Fifth Avenue from his suite at the Plaza Hotel to his office, the change seemed exhilarating.

By 1961, the Empire State Building had been eclipsed as a beacon of the new, a distinction that now fell to the cool glass boxes that were rising on Park Avenue. But it still towered over New York City like no other building, holding a vaunted status among the general populace that few buildings ever achieved. What other building had been celebrated in so many millions of postcards, paperweights, and indoor thermometers? In 1964, -

Andy Warhol released *Empire,* surely one of the most confounding movies ever made. Warhol's cinematographer set up his camera on a tripod high in the Time-Life Building, pointed it at the Empire State Building, and began filming. Eight hours later, long after dark, he stopped filming. Attentive viewers who chose to sit through all 480 minutes—it has been called the longest opening shot in the history of cinema—reported that Warhol passed in front of the camera five times and that a light in the background blinked on every 20 minutes. Warhol left it up to his viewers to decode his meaning. The safest conclusion, perhaps, is that the Empire State Building was a quintessential American icon.

If there is any certainty in Manhattan real estate, however, it is that nothing will stay the same. Not its prevailing architectural styles, not its reigning kingpins, not the skyline itself. On January 18, 1964, came the startling announcement that the Port Authority of New York and New Jersey, a quasi-governmental agency that ran the region's ports, bridges, and tunnels, would raze a low-rise swath of lower Manhattan and erect two 1,350-foot towers. Each tower would be 100 feet taller than the Empire State Building.

Wien, the consummate real estate businessman, would later insist that the distinction of controlling the world's tallest building played no role whatsoever in his response to the proposed record-breaking new project. The actions of Wien and Helmsley made it a difficult claim to swallow. They rounded up a group of prominent Manhattan real estate men, their fears fanned by the competitive threat of 10 million square feet of new office space being dumped onto an already glutted market, and formed the Committee for a Reasonable World Trade Center. Wien and Helmsley quietly paid the bills. The group challenged the legality of the agency's condemnation proceedings, intent on hamstringing the new development in the courtroom. In April 1964, a frustrated Austin Tobin, the head of the Port Authority, rose before a luncheon of the Sales Executive Club at the Roosevelt Hotel and excoriated Wien for opposing the project. Wien's motives were obvious, fumed Tobin. Where had Wien been when the trade center plan had called for just 76 stories? Tobin asked.

The legal challenges Wien's group lobbed at the Port Authority dragged on for years, but ultimately came to nothing. In 1972, the dual shafts of the World Trade Center bumped the 41-year-old skyscraper from its perch as the world's tallest. Tinkering with their marketing pitch, the managers of the Empire State Building, with pragmatic resignation, began referring to their skyscraper as the world's most famous.

In the offices of Shreve, Lamb & Harmon, the architectural firm that designed it, a more desperate move was afoot. Robert W. Jones, a 35-year-old graduate of Cornell eager to thrust the firm back into the limelight, unearthed the original drawings of the Empire State Building and set out on a personal mission to restore the building to its former glory. "I thought, here's a building that's been the tallest building for 40 years and now it's no longer the tallest," Jones would later explain to a *New York Times* reporter. "Almost with tongue in cheek, I thought maybe we could add a few floors. I called one engineering firm and they said no. Then I called another and they said yes, it's possible. So I wrote to Helmsley and Wien and said, Ha Ha. Isn't this a funny idea?" It is unclear whether Jones ever did contact Wien and Helmsley. (Peter Malkin has no recollection of such a communication.) More telling, Jones had no support from his partners when he shared his fantasy with the world on October 11, 1972: "11 Floors to be added to the Empire State Building," trumpeted the front page of the *New York Times*.

Jones described his plan for dismantling the building's iconic 16-story crown, reinforcing the six stories beneath it, then constructing a new 33-story cap. By Jones's calculations, that would bring the building to 113 stories, or 1,494 feet, 144 feet higher than the World Trade Center and 44 feet taller than plans for the Sears Tower, which was then marching upward toward a new record in Chicago. Jones's drawings struck fans of the Empire State Building as downright appalling. In place of the building's signature needlelike spire, Jones had placed a large rectangular block, capped with a needle. Squint your eyes, and it looked like the World Trade Center. Jones's alternate design was a steeply pitched pyramid, as ominous-looking as tombstone. Jones offered no apologies for tampering with the iconic silhouette. "I think it would be pretentious as hell to do it in the style of the building," he told the *Times,* sidestepping the more obvious question of whether the entire initiative was anything more than an exercise in pretension.

Jones's stunt took Wien and Helmsley completely by surprise. They had never even met the man. Privately, Malkin and his father-in-law convinced themselves that the jolt of publicity would do no harm and would perhaps even boost attendance at the observatory. In a moment of candor, Wien cracked that the only way to pull off the plan would be to jack up the building and add 11 stories to the bottom.

As for Jones, his end run around his partners proved a towering blunder. His scheme was ridiculed by staunch New Yorkers, not to mention his own partners. Shortly thereafter, he was asked to leave the firm. "He had some strange ideas," partner Donald Grossmann would later reflect. Another partner, Harold Bernhard, would write that he thought Jones had been a little too fond of alcohol. Jones's partner, Petroff, shot himself to death. Ironically, his life insurance temporarily bailed out the once illustrious firm that had given the Empire State Building its signature shape, but it was shuttered for good in 1995.

The rise of the World Trade Center, it would later seem, marked the end of Lawrence Wien's golden run through Manhattan real estate. Wien had made up his mind, he said,

The Empire State Building was completed in just 16 months, thanks to an army of more than 3,000 workers eager for employment during the Great Depression. *(Empire State Building Co.)*

Financier John Raskob, right-hand man to Pierre du Pont and a top executive at General Motors, dreamed up the Empire State Building as his first real estate project. *(Avery Architectural and Fine Arts Library, Columbia University in the City of New York)*

On May 1, 1931, former New York governor and Empire State Building president Alfred Smith helped his two grandchildren cut the ribbon, and hundreds of invited guests flocked to the eighty-sixth floor observation deck for the first time. *(Avery Architectural and Fine Arts Library, Columbia University in the City of New York)*

After years of trying, New York real estate mogul Lawrence Wien acquired the skyscraper with Harry Helmsley in 1961. *(Empire State Building Co.)*

Peter Malkin, Wien's son-in-law, played a central role in defending the Empire State Building from an attack by Donald Trump. *(Steve Friedman, © 2001)*

The complex sale and leasing arrangements signed in this Prudential Insurance Company boardroom in 1961 cemented an elegant web
of interests, but were a time bomb that would detonate three decades
later. *(Empire State Building Co.)*

Leona and Harry Helmsley with Ivana and Donald Trump in 1986, in friendlier times. Later, Donald and Leona would exchange insults and lawsuits. *(Steve Friedman, © 2001)*

Controversial Japanese billionaire Hideki Yokoi (seated) turned to his son-in-law Jean-Paul Renoir to untangle a welter of problems with his trophy acquisitions in the United States and Europe. *(Renoir Private Collection)*

Yokoi's illegitimate daughter, Kiiko Nakahara, was his link to the world outside of Japan. Their relationship would sour, though, over ownership of the Empire State Building. *(Renoir Private Collection)*

Kiiko Nakahara and her husband gave Donald Trump a stake in the Empire State Building in exchange for his promise to wage a battle to break the lease held by Helmsley and Malkin. *(Renoir Private Collection)*

The last dance for the Helmsleys: Leona began serving a prison sentence for tax evasion in 1992, as Harry's body and mind gradually faded. *(Steve Friedman, © 2001)*

The Empire State Building's 86th-floor observatory, for 70 years an international drawing card to tens of millions of visitors, from royalty to the suicide-prone. *(Empire State Building Co.)*

not to pursue "the balance of my life in the accumulation of money." He devoted more and more of his time to giving it away, and he dogged others to do the same. Wien took a special interest in the construction of Manhattan's Lincoln Center for the Performing Arts, and when a financial bind arose, Wien pledged $1.25 million of his own to close the gap. To raise the money, he reached into the trophy cabinet for his stake in the lucrative partnership that held the sublease on the Empire State Building. At the time, Wien and Helmsley each held 44 percent of the partnership. To raise money for his Lincoln Center donation, Wien sold Helmsley 20 percent, trimming his stake to 23.75 percent and inflating Harry's to 63.75 percent. At the time, it hardly seemed to matter to the stability of their partnership. On real estate matters, Wien and Helmsley were practically joined at the hip, and protection against potential treachery from one another had never been a concern.

Years later, after he was hip deep in the consequences of Wien's action, Peter Malkin came to view the move as one of his father-in-law's few grave errors. Wien's decision was to put Malkin on a collision course with the new woman who had come into Harry Helmsley's life, a woman who would shake her husband's old guard real estate operation to its core.

In 1972, Helmsley, then 63, stunned his friends and colleagues by divorcing his wife of 33 years, moving from suburban Westchester to a New York penthouse apartment in a hotel he had just finished building, and marrying a twice-divorced luxury-apartment broker 11 years his junior who worked for one of his affiliates. To this day, Harry's closest friends are hard-pressed to understand what drew Helmsley to Leona Mindy Roberts, a brassy, foul-mouthed, enormously ambitious broker who had willed herself to rise above her dreary Brooklyn upbringing. Their personalities could hardly have been more different. Harry, a perpetual twinkle in his eye, always had a warm handshake and a smile for his brokers and building managers. He seldom spoke up or down to anyone, whether the mayor or a doorman. When he wanted to send a message, he usually chose the gentle approach, as when he would pick up the order form at a lunch club and say to the employees who accompanied him: "I'm not drinking anything today, does anyone else want to?" But his new wife had an unmistakable edge. She could treat hired help with a withering contempt, although that was hardly unique among certain New Yorkers.

Empire State Building director of operations Charles Guigno would later recall his first encounter with Leona with the kind of clarity that might accompany an especially embarrassing moment, say, from adolescence. Guigno and his wife had been invited to attend a cocktail party on the eighty-sixth-floor observatory honoring Harry. A colleague introduced Guigno to Leona, and she asked Guigno what he did. Guigno explained that he was in charge of the building's mechanical operations.

"Do you take care of the bathrooms?" Leona asked him.

Guigno replied that he supposed that was one of his responsibilities.

Leona snapped back that she had a friend on the 60-something floor who had told her the bathrooms were dirty and the toilet seats old. "You better take care of it," she told him.

"Yes, Mrs. Helmsley," Guigno replied. He turned on his heel and squired his wife away.

More troubling to Harry's friends was the perception that Leona resented Harry's relationship with his longtime partners. Leona expressed an open contempt for Wien and Malkin, albeit behind their backs, associates recall. Leona seemed to be convinced, said a close associate of Harry's, that everyone derived his or her success from Harry and that everyone was out to suck him dry.

But as Harry's puzzled colleagues scrutinized the couple, they found little reason to be overly cynical about Leona's motives. Although it was tempting to joke that in marrying Harry, Leona had made the greatest real estate deal of all time, Leona fussed over Harry so incessantly and so enthusiastically it was hard to dismiss it as just an act. On formal occasions like the annual Real Estate Board of New York gala, she would fly from halfway across the ballroom, arms open wide, grab Harry's face with both hands, and plant a long kiss on his lips. Harry's more straight-laced colleagues would cringe. But Harry adored it. Like a introverted schoolboy cutting loose at his first fraternity party, Harry took to the town with Leona as if making up for the decades he spent at home with his first wife, a devout Quaker. With his bejeweled new wife on his arm, Harry became a regular on the charity ball circuit, often slipping the orchestra extra cash to play on after regular hours. For years, the couple would brag that they had never spent a night apart, even when Harry was laid up for a few nights in the hospital.

Leona took to the lifestyle of the rich in a way that Harry never had. She invited television crews to their penthouse apartment, eager to show the world her indoor swimming pool and enormous closets packed with designer gowns and bushels of shoes. She threw increasingly lavish birthday parties for her husband, pushing for ever more theatrical productions of her "I'm Just Wild About Harry" theme, which seemed to celebrate Leona as much as Harry. Longtime employees were bumped off the guest list in favor of power brokers and celebrities like Frank Sinatra. After the Empire State Building was illuminated red, white, and blue for the nation's bicentennial, Leona took to telling people that Harry had done it to celebrate her own birthday, which also fell on July 4. Harry, still fundamentally shy, floated through these glamorous, hectic years like a placid man drifting on a cloud. One associate arrived at his penthouse to discuss a business deal to find Harry surveying a flooded apartment, his expen-

sive rugs and couches dripping with pool water. Harry, betraying not a bit of distress, explained sheepishly that he had
neglected to turn off a pool valve following his daily swim.

Unlike Wien, Harry in no way tired of the real estate
game. He began investing on his own, even developing properties, which Wien had always shunned as too risky. Increasingly, Harry pursued business with his wife, not Wien. He
gave up buying office buildings and began building hotels,
eventually amassing a chain of 30 Helmsley hotels, anchored
by New York's lavish Helmsley Palace. Harry installed his wife
as president, and together they launched a ubiquitous advertising campaign featuring a beaming Leona in a low-cut
evening gown. Its slogan, which would later prove a rich target for satirists: "It's the only Palace in the World Where the
Queen Stands Guard." Leona took charge of the design and
decorating of the hotels with a fiscal abandon that seemed
the antithesis of Harry's time-tested nickel-and-dime management style. Indeed, when Harry and Leona were finished
turning the Helmsley Palace into a showcase of luxury, they
had spent $37 million more than was budgeted, sparking an
embarrassing and successful lawsuit by investors who were
called upon to saddle the overruns.

It is rare for any building to escape the despoiling effects of
time. Harry was pouring money into his new hotels but not
into the aging buildings that accounted for the bulk of his
holdings. By the dawn of the 1980s, the Empire State Building had begun to take on the whiff of an antique. To director
of operations Charles Guigno, the building's operations and
leasing office "looked like something out of the 1940s," filled
as it was with old steel desks, metal partitions, even a plug-in
telephone switchboard.

On April 23, 1981, with the building's fiftieth anniversary
a week away, construction workers bored into the wall of a

drugstore on the first floor. Underneath the cornerstone laid by Al Smith, the workers located the time capsule, a flashback to the days when the building seemed new and glorious and immortal. But the copper box had been ravaged by time. Its seams had split open. Water had seeped in. The pictures of Smith and Raskob and Lamb, the copies of the construction plans, the rag edition of the September 9, 1930, *New York Times,* the 50-year-old paper money, were all rotted beyond recognition. All that remained intact was a pitiful handful of coins.

On April 30, a small band assembled in the lobby and began pumping out worn standards like "New York, New York." Al Smith's two grandchildren took bows. A former steel-worker and a onetime water boy were introduced. Wien made a speech. Then everyone rode up the aging elevators to the observation deck for champagne, cake, and lox on pumper-nickel. That night, with great fanfare, two rotating laser beams that had been mounted atop the building, one red, the other blue, were switched on. Calls filtered in to the building, the police, and the newspapers. Frustrated sky gazers, anticipating *Star Wars*–like special effects, could see nothing. Those who made out anything at all saw only two laserlike lines of light, thin as paper cuts. It was a sad drama befitting an aging queen. As an effort to call attention to the building, the manager conceded, it was a bust.

By then, a new wave of development had begun washing across Manhattan, the work of a younger generation of builders who sought to make their mark on the skyline. Donald Trump's father Fred had amassed a fortune of upward of $75 million building apartments and homes for the middle class in New York's outer boroughs. But Donald, who was raised in a pillared Georgian mansion on a hill in Queens, had quickly wearied of the low-rise anonymity of his father's office on Avenue Z in Brooklyn and of the affordable housing empire that was Fred's domain. It was a world where tenants would fling garbage out of their windows rather than walk it to the incinerator and would flee their apartments in the dead of night to skip out on unpaid back rent. Donald found it repulsive.

Donald, who forswore booze, cigarettes, even coffee, decided that his destiny lay not in the blue-collar world of affordable homes and apartments that had made his father a millionaire many times over, but in Manhattan, the land of luxury high-rises and doormen. Not yet 26, Donald rented a tiny studio apartment on Manhattan's Upper East Side and began playing a part that already seemed fully formed in his imagination. He favored suits or blazers, even on weekends, and had his initials stitched onto his shirts and engraved into his gold cuff links. By 1975, although he did not have a single development under his belt and New York City was teetering on the brink of financial ruin, Trump cemented an audacious deal to redevelop the Commodore Hotel, a hulking brick eyesore next to Grand Central Station. He sheathed the building in a curtain of reflective glass, built a 170-foot glass-enclosed restaurant that hung over the Forty-second Street corridor of aging brick-and-limestone classics, and reopened it as the Grand Hyatt. Even critics who loathed its design had to admit it was a financial success.

By the mid-1980s, with the completion of Trump Tower on Fifth Avenue, Trump had vaulted into the ranks of Manhattan's property barons. His insatiable thirst for attention stood in stark contrast to the privacy craved by older-line Manhattan kingpins. His name was splashed across the facade of Trump Tower in three-foot-high letters. The project introduced the world to Trumpian development in full flower: a golden entrance, a soaring atrium clad in rose- and peach-colored marble, an 80-foot waterfall cascading down the middle. Tourists flocked to the building to gawk at its expensive boutiques and the tuxedo-clad pianist hunched over the lobby's Steinway grand. It was as if Trump Tower was the tallest building on the skyline.

Trump reveled in the attention brought by his ballooning wealth, never shrinking from an opportunity to flaunt his patented version of the good life. He opened the doors of his Trump Tower triplex home to lifestyle magazines, boasting unselfconsciously of its 80-foot-long living room, its 12-foot waterfall spilling down the walls of translucent onyx. Donald shrugged off the pounding he took from the cultural elite, who decried the garish opulence of his buildings, and reveled in the financial benefits of the worldwide publicity. Buyers flocked to the condominiums he was erecting on Manhattan's East Side. Asian buyers in particular, enchanted by the Trump look, were leading the way.

Upstart builders like Trump, aided by banks and insurance companies hot to lend them money, changed Manhattan's skyline forever. A new class of glass-sheathed skyscrapers and condominium towers rose, setting a new standard in lavishness. Thanks to engineering advances, they offered the cavernous open floors favored by financial services firms. The brawny brick and limestone prewar buildings that filled the portfolio of Wien and Helmsley—buildings like the Lincoln Building and the Graybar Building—slipped into the dustbin of the rental market's second tier, dulled by age and deferred maintenance. Up-and-comers like Trump, George Klein, and new generations of old-line New York real estate families like the Rudins, Fishers, and Dursts didn't covet these relics of an earlier boom. To Trump, the old guard seemed ripe for overthrow. During a stroll through Central Park in the heat of a frenzy of deal making, Trump pointed to the buildings on Fifth Avenue and Central Park South and predicted: "I'll be bigger than all of them. I'll be bigger than Helmsley in five years."

The Empire State Building, however, remained in a class unto itself. Although occupancy had slipped to 89.5 percent during the 1970s recession, it had bounced back to 98.5

percent by 1981. But the building's occupants—850 small businesses—were hardly the sort coveted by glamour buildings. There were 302 menswear firms, 74 in the shoe business. There were second-tier lawyers, accountants, and travel agents. Most New Yorkers seldom even set foot in the place.

Yet each year, nearly 2 million people visited the observatory. Some came to get married. Others scattered the ashes of loved ones. Most came simply to take in Manhattan from its best-known building. The souvenir shop sold some 80,000 miniatures a year—two-inch paperweights, six-inch piggy banks, nine-inch thermometers, four-foot statues, key chains, spoons, and pencil sharpeners. The Empire State Building was a pop-culture icon, a one-of-a-kind industry.

Helmsley and Wien had worked hard to keep the building in the public eye. But increasingly, their efforts struck some New Yorkers as off-key, even vulgar. They bathed the top frequently in colored light: blue for a New York Yankees World Series victory, yellow and orange for Thanksgiving, red and green for Christmas. In 1983, to commemorate the fiftieth anniversary of the release *King Kong,* Helmsley's publicity agent contacted Robert Vicino, a San Diego maker of advertising balloons, about making a 10-foot inflatable King Kong for the lobby. Vicino instead proposed an 84-foot replica of the giant gorilla, to be winched up the mooring mast.

The 3,000-pound balloon arrived deflated and folded into a crate. But the measurements had been bungled, and the crate wouldn't fit into the elevator. Kong was unpacked, manhandled into the elevator, lifted to the eighty-sixth floor, rolled onto the terrace, and hoisted up the mooring mast. As excitement mounted, the inflation began. The balloon, alas, was hopelessly tangled. From the sidewalk, it looked like an oversized garbage bag blown up off the street. Workers lowered it to the deck, untangled it, and raised it again. When Vicino began pumping, Kong sprang a leak on the shoulder. Vicino and his wife pleaded with scores of reporters from around the world to go away. Kong's second assault on the building was playing out more like a farce. But the press, no doubt invigorated by the unfolding disaster, stayed put.

Helmsley was scheduled to appear on network television the following morning, a fully inflated Kong framed in his window. With fear knotting his stomach, Robert Tinker, the building manager, visited Helmsley to brief him on the fiasco. To Tinker's astonishment, Helmsley merely laughed. Let the air out, Helmsley said. "We'll get more attention out of it this way." The newspapers played the story as comedy. Kong's shoulder was patched, and as darkness descended the following day, inflation began anew. The wind rose to gale force. Worried about his workers, Vicino ordered them to lash down the flaccid ape. Kong stuck to the building like a wad of chewing gum. The next morning, when the wind subsided, Kong was hastily inflated. But by that time, the newspapers had already tired of the weeklong drama. That night, as the wind mounted to near 100 miles per hour, Kong tore once again. Vicino and his wife declared victory and hustled the balloon down. The inflatable Kong lived out its days touring the country, until one humid and stormy afternoon in New Orleans a bolt of lightning popped it like a party balloon.

Commercial real estate in America was still very much a father-son industry. Successful entrepreneurs groomed their sons to succeed them, aspiring to earn a place among the circle of family dynasties that dominated New York real estate. As a business model, however, it was fraught with peril. Fathers hoped against hope that the riches they amassed did not make their sons slothful. Their sons struggled with the temptations of entitlement. Some stumbled. The two sons of Alexander DiLorenzo, who accumulated a trove of Manhattan buildings in the 1960s and 1970s, frittered away a portfolio once worth some $600 million through reckless investment, erratic behavior, and inattention to detail. An adage arose about such post-war real estate fortunes: The first generation creates it, the second enjoys it, and the third destroys it.

It has been said that Peter Malkin, like Leona Helmsley, married well. Neither Malkin's wife nor his wife's sister chose to follow their father, Larry Wien, into the real estate business. As Wien devoted more and more time to philanthropy, Malkin eagerly looked after the family's lucrative real estate holdings. By the mid-1980s, the knotty question of succession in the Helmsley empire must have begun weighing on Malkin. Harry Helmsley—whose holdings were then gushing personal income at a rate of $25 million a month, according to longtime associate Peter Ricker—had no children. Leona's only child, Jay Panzirer, had died suddenly in 1982 of heart disease.

Like many driven men who work well into old age, Harry Helmsley was being interrupted more and more by his own frailty. He stopped coming to quarterly meetings for buildings he controlled with Wien, including the Empire State Building. There were operations on his eyes. Rumors circulated about a mild stroke. Employees began noticing that Harry's steel-trap mind took a bit longer to digest the particulars of a deal. The strings of trenchant questions that Harry typically fired at them during their presentations were a bit slower in coming. Peter Ricker decided that if Harry wasn't lucid during any given conversation, it was best to just stop talking business until later. Word began leaking out that Harry had lost a step. Increasingly, employees were reluctant to bother Harry with the countless small matters that crop up when running millions of square feet of commercial real estate. Decisions were postponed. The properties began to slip.

Leona became fiercely protective, erecting a shield around Harry. In years past, associates of Harry who were not involved with his hotels had little difficulty steering clear of his wife. No longer. Leona's differing approach to business hit them like a kick in the groin. She issued curt memos announcing wholesale changes in policy. Over the phone, she sent secretaries hammering on the doors of men's rooms in search of their bosses.

Carol Mann, a veteran Helmsley employee who specialized in co-op conversions, had been hearing stories of Leona's abusive behavior and vulgar tongue for years, but had dismissed them as the exaggerations of insecure men not accustomed to headstrong women. Mann simply couldn't believe that the Harry she knew, a consummate gentleman, would put up with such antics. Then Leona called Mann for the first time.

"Hello, Mrs. Helmsley," Mann offered cheerily.

"Who the fuck are you and what the fuck do you do here?" Leona demanded.

Mann stammered out the name of her boss.

"Let me tell you something, you little bitch," Leona growled. "You work for Harry Helmsley. Don't you ever forget that."

One day, when Empire State Building director of operations Charles Guigno was out in the building, a command crackled over his walkie-talkie to return to his office immediately. Mrs. Helmsley was on the phone. When Guigno arrived, his heart pounding, he found the partnership's comptroller with the phone to his ear, weathering the storm. When the comptroller hung up, he informed Guigno that Leona had discovered that Guigno had been bringing Brooklyn bagels to the building's weekly staff meeting, and reimbursing himself out of petty cash, as he had been told to do. "She wants to know why we can't have breakfast at home," the comptroller told Guigno. "Why does she have to pay?" At first, Leona demanded repayment, but cooler heads prevailed, and the matter was dropped. Guigno stopped bringing bagels.

Those summoned to Leona's office on the fifth floor of the Helmsley Palace hotel came to accept with a grim resignation that nothing good was likely to come from such an encounter. As Helmsley-Spear property manager Stephen Heyman steeled his nerves outside Leona's office one day, he reminded himself to control his temper and not to take anything personally. Inside, he could hear Leona cursing like a longshoreman. It gradually dawned on Heyman that Harry was being fitted for a pair of trousers, and Leona was less than pleased with the tailor. Eventually, the hapless tailor scurried out, head down, followed by a smiling Harry, who offered Heyman a warm handshake. Heyman walked into Leona's pastel-colored office and sat down. Leona accused Heyman of stealing $2.5 million. "What in the world are you talking about?" Heyman replied. With some difficulty, Heyman clarified for Leona a controversy involving tenant improvements in one of the buildings. On his way out, Heyman saw Harry once again, and received an identical cheery smile and greeting. Heyman detected no sign in Harry that they had already chatted minutes earlier.

Several months later, Heyman was back in the hot seat outside Leona's office. The building engineer who accompanied him, a man made huge and tough by power-lifting and karate, was terrified, despite having gulped down a couple of drinks for his nerves. They listened as Leona tore into a room-service waiter who had brought her poached salmon. Finally, Heyman and his associate were summoned into a conference room. Heyman could see the engineer's jaw muscles flexing with anxiety. Leona accused the two men of accepting kickbacks on a garage deal. She screamed at the engineer to stop clenching his jaw. Heyman convinced Leona that she had her buildings mixed up. Leona's chief financial officer confirmed the mix-up. Without so much as an apology, Leona moved onto the next subject.

Empire State Building manager Robert Tinker picked up the phone one day to find a woman bellowing at him. He recognized Leona's voice immediately. "How dare you write a memo like that without making me a copy," she roared. "Don't you think we talk?" Tinker, momentarily confused, recalled that he had just written a routine memo to Harry about a new bidding procedure he had instituted at the building. He absorbed the tongue-lashing and hung up.

The next time he met with Harry, Tinker brought up Leona's tirade in the most delicate way he could muster.

"I just can't seem to satisfy Mrs. Helmsley," Tinker said.

"Well, she jumps in and muddies the water at times," Harry replied. "But sometimes that's a good thing."

Tinker realized then that the Helmsley organization had changed for good. Thereafter, he grew accustomed to Leona's phone calls, which never ceased to astound him. It wasn't just her salty language, but her unwillingness to brook any sort of reasoned response. Tinker learned to sit and take it, because saying anything seemed to enrage her all the more. Leona fired employees with astounding frequency. Sometimes, in an effort to alleviate the chaos that was creeping into his organization, Harry would quietly hire them back. Tension between Leona and the Wien family seemed palpable, no more so than when Leona skipped the 1986 funeral of Larry Wien's wife of 57 years. Eventually Harry stopped coming to the office altogether. It was only in retrospect that Malkin would realize that Harry Helmsley was showing the first symptoms of a failing mind.

It is widely believed that disgruntled former employees were behind the newspaper reports that landed Leona and Harry Helmsley in the kind of trouble from which a billion-dollar fortune provides no ready reprieve. In April 1988, Harry and Leona were indicted by state and federal authorities for income tax evasion. Prosecutors said they buried in their business accounts $3 million of expenses connected to the renovation of their sprawling 28-room country estate in Greenwich,

Connecticut. For a man who had forged a reputation as a scrupulously honest negotiator whose word was as good as his signature, it was a cataclysmic blow that spelled the end of his run at the top of the New York property industry. Ironically, the legal battle that followed would only delay the day of reckoning that was looming between Leona and Peter Malkin, the two likely heirs to the Wien-Helmsley fortune.

Larry Wien, who by then had fallen seriously ill with cancer, could scarcely believe that his longtime partner, Harry, had been accused of dishonesty. To Wien, it was a tragedy. "This trouble he's in today, I'm convinced, and most of his friends are, that he never knew anything about it," he told an oral historian from Columbia University. "He's really a fine human being and it's sad. It's sad because he has absolutely nobody in the world besides his wife. He had one brother, Walter, I mentioned, who died. His wife died. They have no children. He had no brothers and sisters other than Walter. He has no father, no mother, no cousins, no nieces, no nephews. He has nobody. And the only person he has, worth well over a billion dollars, is his wife." Wien paused. "And I'm not going to characterize her." After writing farewell letters to many of his friends, Larry Wien died at his home on December 10, 1988. He left his son-in-law, Peter Malkin, in charge of the family's vast real estate holdings, including its partnership stake in the lucrative Empire State Building lease.

Harry's once-keen memory would now come and go. Leona never spelled out to Harry's colleagues just what was ailing him. According to longtime associate John Trainor, who met with his boss each week, Harry had developed a condition in which fluid would build up on his brain. Shunts were implanted to drain it off. When the tubes clogged, said Trainor, Harry would develop strokelike symptoms and would be rushed to the hospital for treatment. A neurologist who examined Harry on August 2, 1988, concluded that he had "a memory loss which is severe for immediate, recent and remote facts," according to a sworn statement Harry's lawyer later provided to the trial court. "This memory loss is attributed to accelerated cerebrovascular disease due to hypertension and age." A neuropsychologist who examined him separately, Harry's lawyer said, had reported that his "memory for recently presented information is particularly impaired and . . . his problems severely compromise his ability to fully integrate conversations and arguments with previously presented material." Harry's lawyer asked the court to postpone his trial indefinitely. In June 1989, a judge declared Harry incompetent to stand trial.

A month later, his 69-year-old wife went on trial in federal court in lower Manhattan. Leona's lawyer, Gerald Feffer, conceded to jurors that his client was not a popular person, but said she was not being prosecuted for "being a tough bitch." The elaborate false-invoice scheme alleged by federal prosecutors, he suggested, was designed by employees to "work around" their boss, of whom they were so afraid.

Thanks to saturation news coverage that summer, Leona Helmsley became the "hotel queen" that New Yorkers loved to hate. The newspapers reveled in the delicious details: false billings for silver-plated trivets, Coalport bone china, striped butler's vests and embroidered maids' aprons for the mansion staff, and a $45,681 silver-gilt clock built in the shape of the Helmsley Building, a birthday present to Harry. Perhaps most galling of all was the statement Leona allegedly made to one former housekeeper: "We don't pay taxes. Only the little people pay taxes." Mayor Edward Koch, front-running the jury, declared Leona guilty of "chintziness," adding that to New Yorkers, she was akin to "the Wicked Witch of the West."

On August 30, the jury convicted her of evading $1.2 million of federal taxes. Long after the courtroom cleared, Leona remained slumped in her seat. She had become a felon. At her sentencing later that year, she sobbed uncontrollably as she pleaded with the judge not to separate her from Harry. "I feel as though I'm in the middle of a night-mare," she declared. "I beg you. Don't let me lose Harry. Please don't. Our whole life has been work and each other. We have nothing else." Judge John Walker, after reminding the billionaire that "no person, no matter how wealthy or prominent, stands above the law," sentenced her to four years in prison and fined her $7.1 million. As she and Harry descended the broad courthouse steps, hecklers taunted them.

Donald Trump joined with apparent eagerness the chorus of Leona detractors. "Nobody knows her as well as me," he told a reporter. "I feel so badly for Harry. He's a great man, a wonderful guy. . . . But she's a sick woman. As bad as he's been portrayed, she's worse. I can feel sorry for my worst enemy, but I can't feel sorry for Leona Helmsley. She deserves whatever she gets."

Manhattan real estate tycoons tend to butt heads over deals with some regularity. By the late 1980s, no feud was more public, more irresistible to the newspapers, than the acidic relationship between "The Donald" and the "Queen of Mean." Trump liked to suggest that Leona simply couldn't countenance a smart, handsome, and successful young man stealing thunder from the Helmsleys. That may or may not have been true. When he was getting his start, Trump would say, Leona enjoyed having him around, inviting him to her parties. At one such party, Trump later wrote in a book, he appeared with a willowy fashion model clinging to his arm.

"How dare you bring that tramp to one of my parties?" Leona snapped, looking the girl in the eyes.

The following day, Leona called Trump at his office, Trump wrote. "You fucking son-of-a-bitch," Leona snarled. "I watched you politicking the room and all of my guests in order to get your convention center passed. Don't do that on my time. And don't bring pretty girls to my parties anymore, especially girls that make the other women in the room look like shit. Fuck you!" Leona hung up.

Over the years, as the two clashed over various deals, the chill deepened. Trump helped torpedo a Helmsley land deal on the East Side of Manhattan. Leona erected roadblocks to a Trump deal in Atlantic City. Twice, Leona gave Trump the finger across crowded New York ballrooms, Trump said. Trump regularly lambasted her for delighted reporters, branding her "a disgrace to humanity," a "vicious, horrible woman," and "a living nightmare." Although Leona was seldom baited into striking back in the newspapers, she delivered the most memorable riposte of the long-running feud, saying of Trump: "I wouldn't believe him if his tongue were notarized."

When Trump realized in 1993 that he had an opportunity to do a deal with the new owners of the Empire State Building, the thought of antagonizing Leona Helmsley must surely have crossed his mind.

7

East Meets West

After returning from Tokyo in the summer of 1993, Donald Trump never again laid eyes on Hideki Yokoi. For years to come, Trump would refer to him simply as the "Japanese billionaire" or, inexplicably, as Nokoi. It is impossible to know whether Trump was simply unable to commit Yokoi's name to memory or trying to distance himself from the controversial man. In any case, when Trump returned to New York, he seemed eager to cast his lot with Yokoi's daughter. He began introducing Kiiko as "the richest Japanese woman in the world."

Kiiko and Renoir, for their part, believed Trump had a great deal to offer them. The Empire State Building, while nifty to own, was a dog of an investment, thanks to that long-term lease to Helmsley and Malkin. Oliver Grace's lawyer had reviewed the lease and concluded that Helmsley and Malkin's interests were well protected. Grace told Renoir it was as good a lease as he had seen and that he didn't want to get mixed up in any bid to break it. All that would be accomplished, he said, is that a bunch of lawyers would get rich. Renoir told Grace he needed someone more prominent, like Donald Trump.

In meetings, Trump treated the couple to his patented brand of hyperbole. The building was a landmark, *the* symbol of New York City, one of the two most visited sites in the city, he told them. And it was in a decrepit state, he insisted. It had become a seedy building. Helmsley was managing it horribly. Something had to be done to revive it, he told them, to bring it back as a prime Manhattan property.

Plenty of crack real estate lawyers had already examined the Empire State Building lease in detail and had been unable to locate a chink in it. The building was 62 years old, after all. It wasn't built like a modern office tower. But Trump asserted to Kiiko and her husband that it was worse than that. The Helmsleys had maintained it so shamefully, Trump said, that Kiiko and Renoir had a case to evict them. Who better than Donald Trump to take on Leona Helmsley and restore the building to its former glory? he asked them. What could be more spectacular, and lucrative, than high-end condominiums on the upper floors?

Not everyone Renoir consulted believed Trump had much to contribute. Charles Lindsay, who was well aware of the ill will between Trump and Helmsley, told Renoir he thought involving Trump was the wrong approach. He likened it to throwing gasoline on a fire. Lindsay urged Renoir to arrange a meeting with Leona in Greenwich, without Trump.

But Renoir was taken with Trump, whom he regarded as the premier developer of upscale Manhattan projects. Trump had told Renoir he could negotiate with Helmsley, that he had done so successfully on a deal in the past. Kiiko felt she would get along well with Leona, that she and Leona might even be able to bond in the face of the alpha male tendencies of Trump and Yokoi. Renoir would later quip that a meeting between Yokoi, Trump, and Leona would have made for "fabulous entertainment."

Kiiko instructed Henry Bubel to try to structure a joint venture along the lines of the busted Trump Tower Tokyo deal. Bubel told Kiiko he didn't think Trump would want a slice of the ownership in return for his services, because Trump would have to pay taxes on his stake right away. Bubel came up with a different proposal. Trump would get half of whatever value he could add to the Empire State Building above $45 million, which is more or less what Yokoi had spent after all the transaction fees were taken into account. If Trump managed to throw out Leona and Malkin, that kind of stake could be worth hundreds of millions. If Trump struck out, well, he'd end up with not much more than a lot of attention, which for a man like Trump was not inconsequential.

In October, Trump signed a letter agreement for just such a deal. Trump wouldn't put up a nickel for his interest in the building, but would only devote his skills to increasing the building's value. On the same day, title to the building shifted from one holding company, NS 1991 American Trust, to a wholly owned subsidiary, NS 1999 American Company. The president of that new company was Jean-Paul Renoir.

Back in Tokyo, Yokoi, true to form, had changed his mind about Trump and the Trump Tower Tokyo proposal. He begged his daughter to bring Trump back to Japan to resume negotiating. Kiiko told her father to write to Trump himself. Yokoi's time, however, was running out. The Tokyo High Court had already rejected his appeal of his three-year prison sentence. In late November 1993, the Supreme Court did the same. The five-judge panel was unanimous. Yokoi had been aware the Hotel New Japan's fire-prevention systems were inadequate, the presiding justice ruled. Correcting the problems would not have been difficult, the court said. But Yokoi had done nothing. His conviction for criminally negligent homicide and his three-year sentence would stand.

Eleven years and nine months after the fire, Yokoi had reached the end of his rope. His once imposing domain was falling apart. His lenders were soliciting bids for the Hotel New Japan. Setsuichi Akiba, the president of creditor Tokyo United Technology, proclaimed to a reporter that the Yokoi family was finished.

The Japanese criminal code allows prosecutors to forgo prison time for convicts who are 70 years old or older. Yokoi, then 80, checked into a Tokyo hospital, complaining of frail health and possible heart problems. Doctors said he was suffering from high blood pressure and had suffered a stroke. He underwent glaucoma surgery. Yokoi asked prosecutors not to send him to prison.

Nevertheless, in May 1994, prosecutors decided he had recovered well enough and that the sorrow of those left bereaved by fire should be taken into account. Yokoi phoned his friend Hisakazu Honjo. In two hours, he told Honjo, the police were coming to get him. He was going to prison. Still, Yokoi grasped for a way to hold together his empire. He asked Honjo to get back in touch with an American firm that years earlier had expressed interest in redeveloping the Hotel New Japan. "It's too late for that," Honjo told him.

Law enforcement officials drove Yokoi to the Tokyo Detention House, where he was subjected to a week-long battery of medical exams so authorities could decide whether his 80-year-old body would withstand the rigors of the standard prison environment. In the end, Yokoi was deposited behind the high concrete walls of Hachioji Medical Prison, on the outskirts of Tokyo, where 260 prisoners were warehoused behind barred windows in six-bed wards. It was a prison for the bedridden, the senile, and the demented. Yokoi was none of those, just old and feeble—and in the eyes of some detractors, clever enough to figure a way to stay out of a harsh general prison population. Because of his fame, Yokoi was given his own room. Its single steam heater was shut off at night.

When summer turned to fall, Yokoi complained of the cold. As the weeks passed, his meticulously died black hair began growing in white.

On June 28, 1994, less than two months after Yokoi went to prison, Kiiko and Renoir entered into a final joint-venture agreement with Trump. Trump Empire State Partners was born, a New York general partnership owned jointly by NS 1999 American Company, the holding company set up by Kiiko and Renoir, and by Trump Empire State Incorporated, a new Trump holding company. Kiiko and Renoir saw to it that title to the Empire State Building was contributed to this new partnership. Trump kicked in about $115,000 in cash, his share of the transaction fees. After the final documents were signed, Renoir presented Trump with a miniature Empire State Building fashioned by Louis Martin Jewelers, along with a commemorative plaque, which Renoir bought for $1,071.

To Trump—who had taken to measuring his deal-making prowess by weighing how much he got against how little he put in—it must have seemed like a splendid deal. Day-to-day management and control of the venture rested exclusively with Trump, along with absolute authority to deal with television, radio, newspapers, and all other media. If he could squeeze more rent out of Helmsley and Malkin, half of it would be his. If he evicted them, his 50 percent upside would be a bonanza. In a sale, the first $45 million would go to his partners' firm, NS 1999 American, then Trump would get half of the rest. For Trump, that added up to powerful incentive to cook up a legal version of a tire iron to the kneecaps of the woman he despised, Leona Helmsley.

For Kiiko, the horizon must also have looked bright. She expected to redevelop New York's most famous skyscraper with New York's highest-profile real estate man. She shuttered her fashion business in Tokyo. She had a notion to go to architectural school in New York and work for Trump. She went on the payroll of Trump Empire State Partners at $10,000 a month. Trump arranged a new $11.7 million mortgage on the Empire State Building. Kiiko and Renoir used part of it to buy an apartment in an expensive condominium building on West Fifty-seventh Street, one of three they would eventually purchase there. They set to work renovating it at once. Kiiko designed a streamlined, open plan calling for Japanese-style screens. It would be their home and office while they worked on the Empire State Building, Renoir later explained.

Renoir saw Trump as the ideal partner to restore pizzazz to the aging skyscraper. Renoir viewed Trump Tower and Trump's condominium projects as proof of that. "With Trump, you don't need to discuss a lot," he explained. "I know the way he thinks. I am completely in harmony with his way of doing things in New York." As Renoir saw it, Trump knew how to attract that important class of rich people Renoir called "the expensive SUV generation." Some were Wall Streeters. Others had invaded New York from Hong Kong and Japan. Renoir talked with Trump about targeting that class of people.

Renoir and Trump agreed on a concept. They would remake the skyscraper from the ground up. Renoir allowed himself to think big. He envisioned upscale retail and commercial space on the lower floors, as in Trump Tower. They would bring in classy tenants, like media companies. In the soaring tower, Renoir saw luxury condominiums, good restaurants, and a hotel. Renting a room in the Empire State Hotel, he felt, would be an unbeatable draw. And up top, of course, gold-class condos. The condos were Trump's idea. Renoir liked it. Renoir envisioned exterior elevators buried discreetly in two corners of the building, which would offer a thrilling ride to tourists. Renoir even began plotting to buy the drab, low-rise buildings that flank the skyscraper on the west, so that he could knock them down and give the Empire State Building a fourth street-level facade. The whole project would cost hundreds of millions, Renoir figured.

Renoir's dream was to empty the building and gut it completely. Only the limestone facade and the marble entrance hall were worth keeping, he believed. All the tiny offices would have to go, along with the hundreds of no-name tenants that Renoir considered beneath the building's stature. So would the colored lighting that was the legacy of Malkin and Helmsley. To Renoir, it was garish. "The kind of things Malkin does gives a bad name to Jews," Renoir would later say with disgust. "And I'm half-Jew. You should be thrown out of the Empire State building for doing these things." The redeveloped building, he dreamed, would have classier management, someone like Hilton Hotels or Donald Trump.

In an important sense, of course, the bold plans Renoir began hatching were no more than a pipe dream. Helmsley and Malkin still had a lease on the building until 2076. Unless Renoir and Trump devised a way to oust them, they would have no more right to begin tearing the building apart than they would to parachute off the observation deck. There was also another curious aspect to this deal with Trump. Kiiko would later acknowledge that the documents outlining the joint venture were never translated into Japanese, and that she had no idea whether they were forwarded to her father before the deal was completed. Kiiko would insist that she never thought she needed her father's approval.

In late June, as a reporter for *The Wall Street Journal,* I picked up on rumors of a change of ownership of the Empire State Building, along with a suggestion that Trump was somehow involved. Like nearly everyone in the New York real estate world, I assumed the building was owned by Oliver Grace, who, like a lot of rich men, simply felt no obligation to talk about what he did or didn't own. City records, however, were now telling a different story. The skyscraper, the records said, was owned by Trump Empire State Partners. The paper trail was confusing. Grace's company, it appeared, had sold the building to one NS 1999 American Company, which had then transferred the deed to the Trump company. The investors behind NS 1999 were a mystery. People who were involved in the deal were cagey. Henry Bubel admitted to me that he represented the mystery investors, but refused to name them. Trump was uncharacteristically restrained. He wouldn't tell me who his partners were, how much money he had invested, or how much of the building he owned.

On July 7, 1994, I reported in *The Wall Street Journal* that the Empire State Building had been purchased for approximately $42 million by a group of Asian and European investors, who had in turn brought in Donald Trump as a partner. Three people involved in the deal, I wrote, said that Trump and the offshore group were equal partners. I raised questions about whether Trump—who still had liens on many of his assets left over from his brush with bankruptcy—had put any money at all into the deal. I noted that the return on the investment looked to be minuscule. "The offshore people don't have much experience with New York real estate," I quoted Henry Bubel as saying. "They thought Mr. Trump would be helpful."

Trump responded to the publicity with characteristic relish, firing out a press release that morning: "TRUMP BUYS EMPIRE STATE BUILDING." Trump's announcement referred to his partners only as "Asian/European investors." It cleared up none of the lingering questions, made no effort to clarify what kind of ownership stake he actually had in the New York landmark. Trump boasted he would be responsible for day-to-day affairs for the partnership. "This is a great deal for me," Trump crowed. "It solidifies my position as New York's Native Son. I get 50% of all the upside and I intend to make my position worth a fortune." Malkin and Helmsley couldn't fail to recognize the opening cannon shot Trump had directed at their bow. "It is my intent to take the actions necessary to restore the Empire State Building to its rightful position as a world class real estate asset," Trump said. Trump concluded with a peculiar comment that read like a jingoistic backhanded slap against his unnamed foreign partners: "I've always said that New York is the greatest city on earth, and I'm giving native New Yorkers the guarantee that it will remain our city." The following day, the front page of the *Daily News* ran the ego-stoking headline: "The New Trump Tower."

After two weeks of digging, I reported in a second newspaper article that Trump's new partners included Jean-Paul Renoir, a French-born investment banker, and his Japanese wife, Kiiko Nakahara. Kiiko, I wrote, was the daughter of Hideki Yokoi, who was currently residing in a Tokyo prison. Yokoi had been a financial backer on the deal, I wrote, although it could not be determined whether his investment had occurred only through his daughter. Kiiko and Renoir's lawyer, Bubel, continued to deflect dicey questions about the particulars. "My clients have asked for anonymity," he said. "In many countries in the world, private citizens try to hide their wealth, because they're susceptible to things like kidnapping." When pressed about Yokoi's involvement, Bubel told me, "If you think some guy in Japan is the owner, you're mistaken." This was all true. But it was also all terribly misleading.

When they read about the deal in a Tokyo newspaper, Yokoi's family members were thunderstruck. Yokoi's brother-in-law, Hishida, would later insist that no one in Tokyo knew anything about the transaction. According to Hishida, Yokoi had told him that his holding company, Nippon Sangyo, owned the skyscraper. Hirohiko, Yokoi's second son, brought the puzzling newspaper report to his father in jail. According to Hirohiko, Yokoi was shocked and furious. This wasn't his plan, Yokoi fumed. He ordered his son to do something about it.

Renoir would later despair that Trump had not been more discreet about the matter. Kiiko had expected her half brothers to be jealous. Now Trump was making it sound as though Kiiko had given him a stake in the building. Kiiko's brothers must have told Yokoi that Kiiko had "pledged to a new lord," Renoir would complain.

Who really owned the Empire State Building? The Yokoi family members running things in Tokyo no longer had any idea. Had Kiiko stolen it from her father? Kiiko invited Hishida to her office in Tokyo one evening to talk about it. Hishida asked Kiiko to explain what happened. He was worried she had transferred the Empire State Building to her own name. Kiiko assured him there would be no reason to put the building under her name, because she would have to pay taxes on it.

Two months after the news broke, Kiiko resigned from the board of Nippon Sangyo. At a board meeting, Hirohiko, Kunihiko, and two of Yokoi's associates agreed unanimously to launch an investigation into what had happened in New York and, if necessary, to file a lawsuit to protect the interest of Yokoi's company.

From prison, Yokoi demanded the best lawyer in New York. His sons were momentarily flummoxed. How does one find a top New York lawyer? Hirohiko and his associates hadn't a clue. They called people they knew in Tokyo. A Japanese patent lawyer named Toshio Honda knew a man named Kakuda. He wasn't a lawyer, but at least Kakuda lived in New York. Honda offered to call him. Kakuda, as it happened, had played golf with a New York lawyer named Steven Rosen. In Japan, it is exorbitantly expensive to play golf. To become an ace golfer in Japan, it helps to be a wealthy businessman. Rosen, a scrappy solo lawyer nearing 50, was an excellent golfer. It was not because he was wealthy. Rosen's father had worked in the golf business. Rosen was not a bad lawyer. He had learned trial law working for a prominent matrimonial lawyer, which made him no stranger to dysfunctional families and bare-knuckled tactics. But as a solo practitioner, he would not have been near the top of anyone's list of the best lawyers in New York. Nonetheless, the Yokoi family hired Rosen. They instructed him to find out whether Yokoi had been cheated out of ownership of the Empire State Building.

Rosen ordered a title search on the skyscraper. Trump Empire State Associates was the name that came back. By itself, the information meant nothing to Rosen. He wasn't about to call Trump for an explanation. That would have tipped his hand. So Rosen hired Kroll Associates, an international detective agency of considerable repute, to investigate the building's ownership. Kroll specializes in discreet corporate sleuthing for Fortune 500 companies. Rosen asked the detectives to turn a sharp eye to the interests of Kiiko and Renoir.

On September 28, Kroll reported back to Rosen. Since 1991, title to the property had been transferred three times. First, Prudential sold it to E. G. Holding in a cash transaction. Then someone transferred ownership to NS 1999 American Company, apparently for no money. Finally, title shifted to Trump Empire State Partners. The transfer tax, Kroll reported, valued that final deal at $50,000. In addition, Kroll reported, Yokoi's $22.5 million white elephant on Long Island, Oheka Castle, had been transferred in 1993 from Nippon Sangyo to something called NS Trust. Again, the lack of transfer tax suggested that no money had changed hands. The Kroll report did little to dispel the confusion over who really owned the Empire State Building. But it left one thing abundantly clear: Yokoi's company, Nippon Sangyo, didn't own the building, and it never had. As for the baffling string of holding companies, Yokoi's people in Japan said they had never heard of them. The report didn't say who really owned or benefited from these companies. Hirohiko grew suspicious of his half sister. "Neither Nakahara nor Renoir were provided with any authorization to enter into a partnership with Donald Trump or entities owned or controlled by him, or to sell or transfer the Empire State Building to any such partnership or other entity," Hirohiko would later maintain in a sworn statement. "Any transfer of the Empire State Building would require a written resolution of [Nippon Sangyo] as well as Hideki Yokoi's approval." And Yokoi had never approved such a move, he said.

Yokoi ordered Takenosuke Sakakura, the ex-husband of his eldest daughter, to fly to New York to confer with Rosen. Sakakura told Rosen that Yokoi was itching to sue Kiiko and Renoir immediately. But Rosen knew that any legal complaint would be torn to shreds if he didn't gather specifics to back it up.

"I need documents," Rosen told Sakakura over and over again.

There are no documents, was the word that came back from Japan.

"That's ridiculous," said Rosen. "There has to be a room full of documents somewhere. And I have to see Yokoi."

Trump remained largely in the dark about the severity of the brewing storm. As far as Trump knew, Yokoi still wanted him back in Tokyo to help clean up the mess with his lenders. Trump had no interest in going back to Japan himself. He was still laboring to get his own financial affairs back on track in New York. He asked Abraham Wallach, one of his real estate executives, to fly to Tokyo. Wallach, a mild-mannered but nervous 53-year-old with wiry, rust-colored hair, had worked on the Empire State Building deal. Wallach knew the players. He liked Kiiko. To Wallach, she seemed sweet, innocent. Renoir was a different matter. It was nothing Wallach could pinpoint. Renoir just seemed a bit too flip, arrogant. Wallach wondered whether Renoir was taking advantage of Kiiko and her family fortune, although Wallach had growing doubts about how much of a fortune remained. Wallach hoped that in Tokyo he would be able to figure out whether Trump had anything to gain by wading into Yokoi's problems in Japan. He also wanted to meet with Kiiko and her brothers and to visit the old man in jail. Wallach wanted to help smooth over this ridiculous family discord and convince Kiiko's half brothers that Trump just wanted to help them. "We knew real estate, and they had real estate, and frankly, they didn't know the first thing about it," he would later explain.

Henry Bubel, who had handled the Empire State Building deal for Kiiko and Renoir, joined Wallach on the long flight to Tokyo. When the two New Yorkers arrived in Tokyo, Bubel parted from Wallach for a meeting with Mitsuo Hishida, Yokoi's brother-in-law and longtime associate. Hishida complained to Bubel that he had asked Kiiko for a copy of the agreement with Trump on the Empire State Building, but had received nothing. Yokoi wanted to see it, Hishida explained. And why had Kiiko taken an $11.7 million mortgage on the building? Hishida asked. Bubel told Hishida the Trump agreement was in New York. He would be happy to send it, he said, if Kiiko allowed him. The next day, Hishida asked Bubel again. He got the same answer.

Bubel, in fact, had relayed Hishida's request to Kiiko. "It's none of his business," Kiiko told Bubel. "I don't trust him and

I don't know what he's up to. Don't give him anything." Bubel didn't.

Trump's man Wallach was surprised by the look of Tokyo. Compared to New York, much of downtown Tokyo seemed poorly built. The buildings looked like lackluster 1950s-era stock, second-tier construction by New York standards. Tokyo reminded him of low-budget *Godzilla* movies. Wallach sat down with Yokoi's eldest son, Kunihiko, in the offices of a law firm. Kunihiko, who had once aspired to become a chef, was reputed to be only dimly interested in following in his father's footsteps. Wallach told Kunihiko that Trump wanted to help the family with its real estate holdings in Japan and help resolve the dispute that was budding over the Empire State Building. The Empire State Building was wasting away while the family dithered, Wallach said. What was needed was a united front. Kunihiko said little. To Wallach, the family members seemed secretive, unresponsive.

Bubel showed Wallach a complex chart he had been laboring over. It was supposed to show who owned the companies affiliated with Yokoi and to decipher the complex ownership of the Hotel New Japan. It listed no fewer than three of Yokoi's holding companies and 20 different individuals. Yokoi, his wife, his mistress, his children, legitimate and otherwise, his brother-in-law, all were said to have a stake in Yokoi's empire. A tangle of lines connected the boxes. Wallach had never seen anything like it. "It was impossible to decipher," Wallach later recalled. "It was crazy. It was typical of Jean-Paul. Everything was convoluted. Everything was complex. Everything was a mystery." Do I really need to know all this? Wallach wondered. He decided to ignore it.

Buildings were one thing Wallach felt comfortable sizing up. Early one morning, he slipped into the passenger seat of Kiiko's red convertible for a tour of what remained of the Yokoi empire. Kiiko turned to Wallach. "Abe, I didn't steal the properties from my father," she said. "My brothers never wanted to be in the business. My father asked me to take care of the business affairs of the family." To Wallach, Kiiko seemed sincere. He was inclined to believe her.

Kiiko popped an opera tape into the cassette player and turned up the volume. Jet lag was killing Wallach. As Kiiko roared toward her father's properties, Wallach dozed. Kiiko showed him office and apartment buildings in downtown Tokyo, an eight-story bowling complex once billed as the world's largest. They visited a slew of *pachinko* parlors, small, smoky, dens where legions of blank-faced men and women plugged metal balls into cacophonous machines, hoping to win prizes. Wallach played and lost. They drove to the abandoned Hotel New Japan, where Kiiko, anguished over her father's fate, began to cry. She maneuvered her convertible through the narrow winding streets of Denenchofu, pointing out her father's valuable homes. She drove all the way to the Pacific Ocean, more than an hour away, to show Wallach a shuttered hotel on the beach. There were buildings and land even farther away, Kiiko told Wallach, near Kyoto and Mount Fuji.

Wallach would later come to view his trip to Tokyo as notable chiefly for how little he was able to discover about the depths of the family's problems. "To me, it was real simple," he would later reflect. "A building in New York was wasting away. We wanted to help. But we got involved with all of these characters. This was well beyond what you're used to in New York. People in New York, they have a goal. The mission is to make money from a property. But this was well beyond the issue of making money. People here were defeating themselves. It was more about vengeance, and getting back at family members, and conspiracies, and all such manner of things. At least in New York, if I sit down with Peter Malkin, I know what he's after and he knows what I'm after. Here you couldn't make a deal. You couldn't even figure out what the issues were."

At the time, Wallach had no way of knowing that the long knives had already been taken out. While Wallach was trying futilely to bond with members of Yokoi's dysfunctional family, some of them had already decided on another course of action that would kick off an epic family feud. "Right then and there, the lawsuits were being prepared," said Wallach. "As Donald says, it was like Pearl Harbor."

PART TWO

Tower of Discord

Who Owns the Empire State Building?

hortly before Hideki Yokoi was taken away to prison, he handed a briefcase to his second son, Hirohiko, for safe-keeping. Inside the case was a key to the old safe that sat next to Yokoi's desk. As far as Hirohiko and his older brother knew, it was the only key in existence to their father's strong-box. Hirohiko placed the briefcase into his own safe, his curiosity firmly in check.

Hirohiko, then 48, had always been a quiet man, so defer-ential to his father that some family insiders assumed the old man intimidated him. Hirohiko would later complain about his father's stinginess, recalling that on his birthday, his bil-lionaire father had given him a measly bunch of flowers. But Hirohiko typically kept such thoughts to himself. Yokoi seemed to have grown to trust his second son, making him vice president of Nippon Sangyo and president of two of his other holding companies.

Hirohiko's brother Kunihiko, three years his elder, had a far rockier relationship with his famous father, other family members have observed. Yokoi gave his firstborn son executive positions in various family firms, but Kunihiko didn't show any trace of his father's raw ambition. It seemed as though Kunihiko was less interested in his father's business than in his own red Ferrari and in having fun. Years earlier, Kunihiko had moved out of his father's residential compound, swapping his house there for the house of his father's sister. Since then, he had had little to do with his father, family members said.

Now, with his father locked away, Kunihiko urged his younger brother to open the safe. Kunihiko had heard rumors about overseas purchases, about photographs of castles floating around the office, about a famous castle in France. Perhaps he and his brother could discover the truth in Yokoi's safe.

Yokoi had been in prison for a couple of months before Hirohiko mustered the nerve to insert the key. He swung open the heavy door, curious about what the old man had deemed worthy of protection. Inside, he found a very old wallet, but no money, no jewelry, no stock certificates, and no will. He also found some papers and a thick bound book, in English. Hirohiko recognized it as the book his father had shown him in Kyoto a year earlier, when Yokoi had boasted about owning the Empire State Building. Although Hirohiko understood little English, he discerned that the document had something to do with the purchase of the Empire State Building. He paged through the book, looking for the name of Nippon Sangyo, which he had understood to be a party to the deal. He didn't find it anywhere.

The two brothers pored over the material from the safe, trying to unravel the mystery of the overseas properties. The contracts and papers revealed that Yokoi had purchased far more foreign property than they had realized. But to Kunihiko, the contracts looked like a mess. He and his brother passed the Empire State Building book, along with other material they didn't understand, to someone at the Bank of Tokyo, asking for an explanation. By then, the extent of their father's holdings was a matter of some importance to both of them. Kunihiko had pledged his house and other land in Denen-chofu to his father's lenders to delay a forced auction of the Hotel New Japan. Hirohiko had mortgaged his home in Atami and given the money to his father for the renovation of *pachinko* parlors. His house in Denenchufu carried four or five separate mortgages.

The brothers agreed that the foreign buildings were the least important holdings of their father's company. They discussed selling them quickly to repay the banks. They agreed this was a good idea. Because they were running things now, Kunihiko told his brother, it was unnecessary to consult their father about what to do. Kunihiko, in fact, was not to pay a single visit to his father in prison. He would later say that he had no idea whether Hirohiko ever discussed with Yokoi their intention to sell the Empire State Building and the other overseas holdings.

But who really owned the Empire State Building? To Kunihiko and Hirohiko, the book in Yokoi's safe provided no answer. The investigators they hired, however, were coming back with disturbing details that seemed to bear out the murky newspaper reports that had enraged their father. Documents in America, the investigators reported, made clear that Nippon Sangyo neither owned nor controlled the Empire State Building. The building's confusing chain of ownership passed through various offshore companies, ending in an Isle of Man trust. The beneficiaries of that trust, the brothers would eventually discover, included Nippon Sangyo and Kiiko Nakahara. But when Hideki Yokoi passed away, Kiiko would become the sole beneficiary.

Did that make Kiiko the owner? Not literally. Henry Bubel, Kiiko's New York lawyer, would later describe Kiiko as "the beneficial owner" of the Empire State Building, explaining that she and her husband controlled it through the trust structure. Bubel said he had gone over the ownership structure in detail with Yokoi. But Kiiko herself had been doing the translating.

Hirohiko, on the other hand, would later assert "with absolute certainty" that Nippon Sangyo "never agreed to make a gift of the Empire State Building to Kiiko Nakahara, or to make a gift to her of the monies used to purchase the building." His half sister, he said, "had no authority to take title to the Empire State Building, in such a way that she was the ultimate and primary beneficiary of it. . . . Furthermore, neither Nakahara nor Renoir were provided with any authorization to enter into a partnership with Donald Trump."

Had Kiiko stolen the Empire State Building from Hideki Yokoi? Had Yokoi promised it to her, changed his mind, then lied about ever having told her he would give it to her? Had Yokoi promised to give Kiiko the skyscraper without any intention of ever following through, only to discover that his daughter had taken it anyway? Given Yokoi's history of reneging on agreements and stiffing his lenders, could his allegation of skullduggery by Kiiko be taken at face value? In the fall of 1994, with Yokoi shut away in the recesses of Hachioji Medical Prison, it was difficult to reconstruct just what Yokoi and his daughter had said to one another about the famed New York skyscraper.

Hirohiko and Kunihiko were prepared to assume the worst about the half sister they barely knew. One month after Kiiko resigned from Nippon Sangyo's board, Hirohiko, Kunihiko, and the two other remaining board members met to discuss their options. The minutes of their meeting indicate an unwillingness to wait for answers. "In connection with the overseas assets that our firm owned, it had been revealed that Kiiko Nakahara, a former director on the board, handled two properties in the US, four properties in the UK and eight properties in France in an irregular manner," the minutes read. "Against such background, it was explained that we were intending to accuse her of embezzlement by presenting all the necessary documents to the Supreme Court of the State of New York in the US. When we referred this matter to the floor, it was approved unanimously."

There has always been a gulf between the public perception of the Empire State Building and the reality of the building as a workaday office building. By the mid-1990s, the disconnect was wide. To the thousands of visitors who each day streamed through its marble lobby and shot up to its awe-inspiring eighty-sixth-floor observation deck, the building remained an urban marvel, an essential part of the fabric of New York. For tens of thousands of New Yorkers who hadn't set foot in the edifice in years, the allure was more ephemeral. If the sky was clear as twilight fell over the city, the Empire State Building seemed to take on a luminescence in the indigo sky, providing a jolt of beauty to weary and jaded commuters.

Yet on dozens of floors filled with small businesses that far fewer people ever found a need to visit, the Empire State Building revealed itself as something with a lot less luster. When Suzy Smith moved to New York from Connecticut in 1992 to take a secretarial job with a textile company on the fifty-sixth floor, she was thrilled at the prospect of working in the landmark tower. To Smith, it was the epitome of urban glamour. When she reported for work, however, she was taken aback by the dreary reality of a building showing every bit of its 61 years. It didn't take long, in fact, for Suzy Smith to grow altogether disgusted with the Empire State Building.

Smith, a newcomer to the big city, certainly could have been accused of naïveté. Anyone who has worked or lived in an old building knows that maintaining it can be a never-ending exercise in triage. The Empire State Building was not—and likely would never be—as pristine as a suburban office building in Connecticut. Most buildings of its vintage were not. Longtime New Yorkers grow inured to the irritations and indignities visited upon them by life in the city, from riding grimy subways to working in worn-out buildings. Smith, on the other hand, allowed herself to be filled with indignation. She was also that rare person possessed of the quintessentially American notion that she should do something to correct what she saw as wrong with the world. It was as if her birthright as an American was to sound off about her new office. If she had had any inkling that she was about to become a pawn in an ugly clash between bellicose New York real estate titans Donald Trump and Leona Helmsley, Smith might have thought longer and harder about what she was about to do.

It started innocently enough for Smith, an attractive, thirty-something woman whom a more taciturn person might describe as a motormouth. As assistant to the president of Copen Associates, a tenant in the Empire State Building for more than 20 years, Smith had the thankless task of calling Helmsley-Spear, the building's manager, to complain about this and that. And complain she did, with a terrier-like intensity. Smith complained about wires hanging from the ceiling. She groused about small holes cut into the corridor and office ceilings for repair work. She complained that the replacement windows being installed throughout the building leaked during heavy rainstorms. A building representative told her that the caulking of the new window frames was not yet finished and gave her sausage-shaped sandbags to place around the window frames during storms. When a particularly nasty downpour soaked a copy machine that stood by a window, Smith demanded that Helmsley-Spear cover the damage. It happened again. Again Smith called to complain, then followed her call with a letter. "I was informed that we were number 66 on the list for complaints about window/ flooding," she wrote. "Our business should not be subject to flash floodings."

Several months later, Smith's boss, Copen Associates president Barry Emanuel, pointed out in a letter to the building's director of operations that part of the ceiling over his desk had collapsed. A maintenance man told him, he wrote, that plumbing problems were to blame. Mold was beginning to grow on the exposed pipes, Emanuel noted. In a second letter, Emanuel complained that "the mold all over my office wall is growing rapidly." It was becoming a health problem, he claimed.

Smith also began carping about mice. Vermin are an embarrassing reality in many New York City office buildings, both old and new. Smith found it revolting. To her, the rodents seemed fearless. They would emerge in broad daylight. Everyone would scream. Smith insisted they were rats, that one that emerged regularly was as big as a gerbil. Adding insult to injury, Helmsley-Spear charged tenants to place traps, then charged them again to retrieve the snared vermin. Smith complained about the charges and threatened to stop paying for the traps. Helmsley-Spear senior vice president John Trainor Jr. would later maintain that "every building" charges tenants for extermination and that "some tenants are pigs."

One day, Smith emerged from Copen's office to find a menacing-looking man urinating in the hallway. She slammed the door and called building security. She was told that a janitor would be sent up. Security in the building, Smith decided, left much to be desired. More than a year had passed since terrorists had detonated a bomb under the World Trade Center. Many New York office buildings had begun limiting access. For four or five months, the Empire State Building had done so too, but lines of visitors waiting for clearance had snaked out onto Fifth Avenue. Management soon reverted to an open-door policy. Early one morning, Smith heard a woman screaming in the corridor outside her office. She called security. Later that day, Smith discovered that an office worker had been mugged for her bracelet.

Smith's persistent complaints about the windows and rodents put her on a collision course with Michael Cassidy, a lawyer who handled cases for the building. Cassidy told Smith and her bosses to file a claim for the damaged copier with Copen's own insurer, Smith would later recall. Smith's boss refused. Smith fired off a memo to Cassidy saying the same, once again blaming the building for the damage. Smith demanded that Helmsley-Spear replace the copier. Copen began deducting money from its rent.

Over the phone one day, as they argued further about who was liable for the damage, Cassidy told Smith she was fighting a lost cause, Smith would later claim. He told her she was up against a team of some of the best lawyers around. "You're a nobody," Smith remembered him saying. "You're just a secretary."

"This is America," Smith said she told Cassidy. "We have rights. You think I'm a nobody. You just watch."

Cassidy would later say he had no recollection of speaking to Smith and that he would never say such a thing to anyone. Whatever was said, Smith hung up the phone in a fury, she later claimed. In Connecticut, Smith had helped organize antiabortion protests as a lobbyist for the state's chapter of the National Right to Life Committee. She was no stranger to public trench warfare. Smith decided it was time to step up her campaign against the building, which thus far had been an exercise in frustration. But who owned the Empire State Building? Smith wondered. She hadn't a clue.

That night, Smith's husband told her that Donald Trump had recently bought the building. Smith was astonished. "I can't believe that a millionaire like Donald Trump owns that building, and it's run so crappy," she said. "People would die if they saw it."

Smith composed a short letter to Trump complaining

about problems at the building. She threatened to begin organizing tenants in the building unless Trump started addressing the problems. She faxed it to his Trump Tower headquarters. Smith wasn't the type to wait patiently for an answer. She phoned the Trump Organization and asked for Trump himself. Instead, she got his longtime assistant, Norma Foerderer. Smith told Foerderer she wanted Trump to come to the building and meet with tenants. "If he doesn't set up a meeting with me ASAP, I'm going to picket this building," Smith blurted out. "I'm going to start a 'Dump Trump' campaign."

Trump phoned back within the hour. Smith poured out her litany of complaints. The building's lawyer, she added, had been "an asshole."

"You've got it all wrong," Trump told her. "You're confused." He told Smith that although he was an owner of the building, the Helmsleys ran it under a 100-year lease. Trump asked Smith if she was absolutely certain about all her complaints. Smith assured him she was.

"Before you do anything, I want you to calm down," Trump told her. "Please come over and talk. Just don't start picketing my building."

Smith could find no other tenants to join her on such short notice. She hadn't been prepared for this sudden audience with Trump. She wasn't even wearing makeup, she worried. She dumped a stack of photographs into a Macy's shopping bag, along with one of the sandbags Helmsley-Spear had distributed to plug the leaky window frames. When she arrived at Trump's office on the twenty-sixth floor of Trump Tower, she was nervous. Trump's lawyers were waiting. Smith and the lawyers were escorted into a spacious corner office. Behind a large, tidy desk beside a wall covered with laminated magazine covers of Donald Trump sat the man himself.

"Oh, you're young," Trump told Smith. "I thought you were this old hag, the way you were talking. I hear you have a lot of problems with my building. What happened?"

"I don't even know where to begin," Smith replied. At times, Smith seemed to find it difficult to edit what came out of her mouth. Moreover, when she was excited, she tended to speak much too quickly. Smith told herself to speak slowly and articulately. She handed Trump a list of complaints. She described the security, told him about the mugging. She complained about inadequate fire safety systems, a lack of smoke detectors and fire extinguishers. She told him there were mice and rats. When she turned to the problem of the leaky windows, she jumped up from her seat, reached into her Macy's shopping bag, and pulled out the sandbag. When she looked back at Trump, he seemed to be rising from his chair in alarm. Smith realized she was freaking him out. He thinks I'm going to hurt him, she thought.

Smith urged Trump to call her boss for a second opinion. Trump asked if he could do so right away. Trump's lawyer advised against it. Saying he always ignored his lawyers, Trump reached for the phone and called Copen Associates. Copen chief executive officer Carin Trundle told Trump that all she wanted was a safe and clean building.

After he hung up, Trump told Smith that this wasn't the way he ran his buildings. In Trump Tower, he said, if there was a hole in the wall, the tenant didn't pay rent until he fixed it. He rambled on and on about his buildings. Once, a guy in the soaring retail atrium of Trump Tower snatched a lady's pocketbook, Trump told her. A Trump Tower security guard grabbed the man, hung him over a high railing, shook him, and ordered him never again to set foot in the property. There was no need to involve the cops, said Trump. "And you know what?" Trump said. "He never came back."

Smith asked Trump if he had walked through the Empire State Building before he bought it. Trump replied that he hadn't. (Trump later pointed out that he had, of course, been in the Empire State Building.) Smith expressed disbelief that he would buy the building without examining it closely.

"Susan, it's the Empire State Building," Trump said. "It's like the diamond of New York."

"Well, your diamond is like a piece of coal," Smith snapped back. "It's disgusting." Smith asked Trump to walk through the building, not just the bottom floor. Just go to 10 floors, she told him, 10 out of 102. Just look at them, she said. Again, Smith had the nagging feeling that Trump thought she was crazy.

Trump reminded Smith that under the long-term lease to Helmsley and Malkin, he had little power over how the building was run. "There's very little I can do to help you," he said. Leona Helmsley, he continued, "is a witch. Harry's a kind man. She destroyed him. She wrecked him. This is a woman who destroyed a good man. She's a bitch." Smith was taken aback by the profanity Trump used when discussing Leona. Trump described a deal in which he felt he had been double-crossed by Leona. "I wanted to take her scrawny neck and strangle her," Trump fumed, Smith would later recall. Smith noticed that Trump's face was red and he was shaking with anger. She felt the sudden need to get out of Trump's office. Trump claimed Leona wasn't putting any money into the Empire State Building, and was only sucking money out.

"I'll look at the building. How's that, Mrs. Smith?" Trump said.

Smith thanked Trump, and hurried out of his office.

Trump phoned Smith several days later and told her he had examined the building. As he described his visit, Smith noticed that the word "shit" kept coming up over and over. Trump said he would help her. He told Smith he would force Helmsley to fix up the Empire State Building.

But as Trump prepared to take action against his longtime adversary, the question that was threatening to tear apart the Yokoi family—who owned the Empire State Building?—

suddenly came to roost on Trump's own desk. On November 2, 1994, on behalf of Yokoi's Nippon Sangyo, New York lawyer Steven Rosen filed a lawsuit in the Supreme Court of the State of New York against Kiiko Nakahara, Jean-Paul Renoir, Trump Empire State Partners, and a half dozen holding companies. The lawsuit accused Kiiko and her husband of keeping Yokoi in the dark about the complex series of transactions involving the skyscraper, of failing to identify the shareholders in the shell companies, and of neglecting to send either stock certificates or documentation to Yokoi.

Rosen didn't accuse Kiiko and her husband of flat-out stealing the building. But he came about as close as one could. When the Empire State Building was purchased, the lawsuit said, Kiiko "represented" to Yokoi that she would take title either under the name of Nippon Sangyo or through entities created for the company's benefit and under its control. Kiiko had no authority from Nippon Sangyo to use the acquisition vehicles she used, the lawsuit complained, unless "legal title" would ultimately rest with Nippon Sangyo or entities it controlled. Kiiko had never told the company that she and her husband, in fact, controlled the building, the suit said. Nor had she told anyone at the company about the deal with Trump, about which Nippon Sangyo still knew nothing. What's more, Kiiko hadn't consulted Nippon Sangyo about the new $11.7 million mortgage, which, the lawsuit charged, she had taken for her own use.

The lawsuit didn't stop with the Empire State Building. It accused Kiiko of improperly transferring Long Island's Oheka Castle and two of the British properties, and of buying Juniper Hill and Thame Park, the two other British castles, through unauthorized vehicles. It complained that companies controlled by Kiiko and Renoir had taken over all the properties and were refusing to give them back.

The lawsuit demanded the return to Nippon Sangyo of the Empire State Building and all of Yokoi's other baubles, and a full accounting by Kiiko and Renoir for all of the money Yokoi had forwarded to his daughter. Nippon Sangyo asked for $250 million in compensatory damages and an equal amount in punitive damages.

As a solo practitioner, Rosen was well aware of the consequences of filing such a blistering lawsuit against well-heeled opponents when the stakes were so high. Top-drawer law firms were likely to step into the fray. Teams of lawyers would attempt to snow him under with paper. They would wage a campaign of attrition. Rosen took that much as a given. He braced for the worst.

Several weeks after Rosen filed the suit, he and Kakuda, the New York businessman who had referred Rosen to the family, boarded a jet for the long flight to Japan. Kiiko and Renoir had already moved to dismiss the case. The clock had begun ticking for Rosen to file a response. It was time for Rosen to meet his client, to get the story directly from Yokoi.

When Rosen touched down in Tokyo, he was exhausted. He looked forward to collapsing into his hotel bed. He had not accounted for the Yokoi family's hospitality. Yokoi's second son, Hirohiko, rounded up a family posse of a dozen for a welcoming dinner. For the next 10 days, Rosen felt as though he was being shadowed by this family pack, which arranged all of his meals and left him scarcely enough time to catch his breath.

When Rosen arrived at the Hachioji Medical Prison, he was escorted into a small visitor's room, where he took a seat facing a Plexiglas screen. Rosen noticed right away that the guards were not carrying guns. The facility looked relatively benign. A short, elderly man walked in and took a seat on the other side of the glass. He wore a light blue uniform, which looked to Rosen like pajamas, over a white T-shirt. Hideki Yokoi looked thin, but not frail. He appeared a bit disheveled. Rosen introduced himself. A prison official hovered over Rosen's shoulder ready to take notes.

Rosen knew he needed to be absolutely certain that his client wanted to wage war on his daughter. Yokoi made it abundantly clear that he did. He flew into a rage, screaming to Rosen about what had happened. Yokoi kept yelling, inexplicably, "three hundred million dollars," apparently his muddled tally of the value of the overseas properties he said had been taken from him. Rosen asked Yokoi whether he wanted to negotiate with Trump. Yokoi fumed that Trump hadn't spoken to him about the deal and had gone behind his back. He forbade Rosen to bargain with Trump.

"Can we negotiate with Kiiko?" Rosen asked.

"No. Everything has to come back to the company," said Yokoi.

Rosen asked Yokoi if he wanted to try to avoid a prolonged fight by settling the case.

Again, Yokoi said no. He told Rosen he had his daughter and her husband on the run and that he felt they would land in jail for what they had done. Yokoi left Rosen with the clear impression that he wanted nothing to do with his daughter, that he had no desire to reconcile.

Rosen returned to Yokoi's Tokyo office to begin laying a foundation for the protracted legal struggle that he saw looming. In a conference room, Rosen spotted a large, perplexing chart mounted on an easel. He asked what it was. Someone explained that an American lawyer named Henry Bubel had visited recently. This baffling tangle of boxes and lines was Bubel's attempt to explain to Trump's representative the numbingly complex ownership structure of the hotel. Rosen stared at the chart. "The more I looked at it," Rosen later recalled, "the more I understood how deeply Trump was involved. He must have known that he couldn't deal with Kiiko without checking with her father. He knew the relationships too well. It was impossible for him to say, 'I didn't know.'" To Rosen, the chart suggested that Trump knew more about this bewildering family empire than he was letting on.

Rosen eventually found the roomful of documents he knew had to exist. He asked for copies of every one of them and settled in for the mind-numbing chore of plowing through them all. He read from eight in the morning until seven at night. When he got back to New York, he was literally shaking with fatigue. He had one week to respond to Kiiko and Renoir's motion to dismiss the lawsuit.

It is impossible to know whether events would have unfolded any differently if Hideki Yokoi had assembled a crack team of high-priced lawyers and advisers at the outset. Rosen proved to be a capable enough lawyer, given his limited resources. But Yokoi had always placed his trust, first and foremost, in family members. So when he resolved to find out what had become of his beloved French châteaux, he once again looked for help within the family. During a prison meeting, Yokoi asked Takenosuke Sakakura, the ex-husband of his eldest daughter, Chizuko, to take stock of his holdings in France. Takenosuke apparently remained on good terms with his ex-wife, for Chizuko, then 51 years old, was soon on her way to France with instructions to meet her ex-husband's cousin, an artist named Peter Bal, who was then residing in Paris.

At the age of 37, Bal, a tall, dark, handsome man with hazel eyes and an athletic gait, had long been at ease in both America and Europe. His father hailed from Belgium, his mother from Japan. Bal himself was born in the upscale New York suburb of Bronxville, but had moved to Belgium at age eight and had made regular visits to Japan. He learned to speak French and Flemish, studied sculpture and painting in Belgium, then returned to New York City on his own in 1983 to make a life as an artist. Like many young men with such aspirations, Bal landed on Manhattan's Lower East Side, where he set up a studio in a small rented room in a Soho building with access to a 3,000-square-foot roof. Bal took a shine to painting on the roof, adapting his techniques to endure foul weather. He also dabbled with the electric guitar and began playing in rock bands. Like most young artists, Bal held a series of undistinguished day jobs. He worked for a week as a messenger on Wall Street, delivered sandwiches, worked in construction and industrial cleaning, and finally, making use of his artistic skills, built architectural models for design firms.

By the summer of 1995, when Takenosuke Sakakura phoned him in Paris, Bal had been working as an artist nearly full-time for seven years. Bal's cousin explained to him that his ex-wife, Chizuko, was in France. Chizuko spoke no French. Takenosuke asked Bal to meet her at the Hotel Le Temouill, then drive her to a few châteaux. He didn't say why. The request struck Bal as odd. But this was family, so he agreed without pressing for an explanation.

Chizuko greeted him warmly and exchanged small talk about the family. She said nothing about the growing suspicions of treachery within it. She asked Bal to pick her up at the hotel the following morning and drive her to various places. Chizuko told him she was unfamiliar with France and felt more comfortable with Bal than with a stranger.

When Bal returned in the morning, Chizuko introduced him to Kakuda, the New York businessman. Bal couldn't figure out why Kakuda was there. A man who supervised the château at Rosny guided the group to three stately properties. Bal learned they were the property of Chuziko's father, Hideki Yokoi. Chizuko explained only that her father had asked her to report on their condition. From what Bal could tell, their state wasn't good. The staff charged with their upkeep had been dismissed. The historic structures seemed to be in horrid condition. The warden of one complained of damage and told them that movable objects had disappeared. Chizuko and Bal also discovered that real estate brokers had been showing the properties to prospective buyers.

To Bal, it seemed that Chizuko was eager to be done with her tour and leave the country. When she left one week later, she told Bal she thought he could help the family with this troubling business in France. Bal politely declined, pointing out that he was an artist and knew nothing of business. Chizuko left carrying a stack of photos for her imprisoned father.

Peter Bal could recall meeting Hideki Yokoi only once in his life, more than a decade earlier. Bal had been visiting his cousin in Tokyo. A doorbell woke Bal from a sound sleep, and he staggered to the door and opened it. Outside, he saw a limousine. A short man in a tuxedo stood on the doorstep.

"Where is Sakakura," the man demanded.

"I don't know," said the groggy Bal.

"Get out of the way," barked the man in the tuxedo, pushing open the door and striding into the house.

In a flash, it dawned on Bal that this was no limousine driver. No Japanese driver would be so rude. Bal looked more closely at the man's face and detected a resemblance to his cousin's wife, Chizuko. This must be her infamous father, Bal realized.

Now, years later, Bal was understandably leery of getting involved with Yokoi. But he wanted to help his cousin. He referred Chizuko to Basile Ader, a French lawyer he knew. A few weeks after Chizuko left, Ader informed Bal that one of the châteaux was being sold. Ader wanted to do a title search to determine who actually owned the properties, but he was having problems, he told Bal, communicating with Japan. He was unsure from whom he was supposed to be taking instructions. He asked Bal to help. Bal arranged for one of Yokoi's executives in Japan to sign a document instructing Ader to protect the French properties from being sold.

Bal was reluctant to be dragged into the mess any further. He spoke to friends who were lawyers.

"Peter, you do not want to get involved in this," Bal later recalled being told. "This is complex international business. You know nothing about it. Go back to your painting."

9

Trump's Broadside

Many ironies would eventually color the story of Yokoi and Kiiko's trophy-hunting spree. The largest was probably this: To turn their prized holding, the Empire State Building, into a desirable investment, Kiiko and her husband would have to portray it as a thoroughly tarnished gem, to figuratively tear down the beloved building by felling the titans most closely associated with it—Leona and Harry Helmsley. Kiiko and Renoir could have found no better henchman than Donald Trump. Their deal with Trump presented him with an unparalleled opportunity to embarrass Leona. If Trump could dislodge her from her most famous asset and fill the tower with Trump condominiums, he would score such a monumental victory at Leona's expense that she would have a hard time not carrying the sting to her grave. Yet Trump faced exceedingly long odds on breaking the lease held by the Helmsley/Malkin partnership. The building's previous owner, Prudential, had never claimed the partnership had violated the lease in any meaningful way, much less run the building into the ground. And it was now clear to anyone who read the newspapers that Trump had a towering incentive to do just that.

The appearance in Trump's office of Suzy Smith, the amped-up Empire State Building office worker, must have seemed serendipitous. After his first meeting with her, Trump phoned Smith to tell her he planned to take action on the building. For Smith, it was all the encouragement she needed. In the bargain bin at Barnes & Noble, she found *Guerrilla P.R.—How You Can Wage an Effective Publicity Campaign Without Going Broke*. She bought it for $1.99. Smith drafted a crude petition, addressed to Leona Helmsley. "We, the Tenants and Workers from the Empire State Building, are dissatisfied with the safety/services provided by your Management." Smith, a gregarious woman by nature, started buttonholing people in the elevator on her way to and from work, gathering signatures and trying to whip up support.

Smith knew from her work with National Right to Life that mounting a demonstration wasn't particularly difficult. She unearthed a few old "Stop Abortion Now" placards she had once carried and covered the word "abortion" with the name "Leona." The most important part, she had learned, was not the number of protesters she could muster, but the number of reporters she could lure. On November 16, 1994, she faxed a press release she had drafted to dozens of news organizations listed in the public relations book she had purchased:

TENANTS OF THE EMPIRE STATE BUILDING WANT CHANGE
STOP LEONA NOW!

Smith's press release described the building as a house of horrors. It complained of muggings, men urinating on hallway walls, homeless people wandering the corridors, faulty windows, floods, rodents roaming the workplace during working hours, bad smells, mold, and bursting water pipes. Two days hence, the press release said, a tenant petition drive would be launched in front of the building. Smith invited reporters to attend, adding that the building was "a must see," and offering to produce other unhappy tenants. "THIS IS A CRY FOR HELP," her release concluded.

Thirty-five minutes before the rally was to begin, John Trainor, the Helmsley-Spear senior vice president responsible for the Empire State Building, walked into Smith's office with two other men. One of the men was director of operations Charles Guigno, the other a private investigator wearing a concealed recording device. Smith, a bundle of nervous energy, told Trainor she didn't have time to talk. Come back later in the afternoon, she told him. Trainor, a beefy man with silver hair, hooded eyes, and a baritone voice, made no move to leave. Smith's boss asked Trainor to make an appointment for later. Trainor began grabbing the petitions and handouts that Smith had prepared for her demonstration. Smith told Trainor to put them back. "No," Trainor told her. "I have a right to this material." He stuffed the papers into his jacket.

Smith could scarcely believe what was happening. She told Trainor the papers were hers, and that she didn't want him to have them. If he didn't put them back, she told him, she would tell the press. The way Trainor saw it, if Smith planned to hand the fliers out to strangers on the street, he was entitled to read them, too. He later recalled being frustrated at Smith's refusal to answer his questions. Nonetheless, Trainor returned the papers to the conference room table. But according to Smith, he didn't leave quietly.

"If you go out there," he warned Smith, pointing at her menacingly, "you're going to be sorry you did." Trainor would later deny issuing any threats, or even raising his voice. "I'm known as the biggest pussycat in the business," he said.

In any case, Smith grabbed her bullhorn, her "Stop Leona Now" signs, a stack of press releases, and the press packages she had assembled, then headed for the sidewalk with a few people from her office. Reporters and television cameramen were waiting. Smith was nervous. She had participated in antiabortion protests in Connecticut, but this was New York City. Only a few tenants stood with her. She switched on the bullhorn and began speaking.

"John Trainor just told me, if I came out here, I'd be a sorry young person," Smith began. "Please. If you care about the Empire State Building, if you care about our national landmarks, please sign the petition." Smith went through her litany of complaints about the security, the vermin, and the condition of the building. It was a story tailor-made for the tabloids and local newscasts. To Helmsley-Spear's horror, reporters began combing the building for dissatisfied tenants and broadcasting stories about Smith's complaints. Helmsley-Spear scrambled to keep the cameramen out.

Not long after the rally, Helmsley-Spear assistant vice president Thomas P. Sullivan came to talk with Smith's boss, Barry Emanuel. Within earshot of Smith, Sullivan told Emanuel that he had an unstable person working for him. Smith pressed the record button on her own tape recorder. According to Smith, who would later claim to have lost track of the tape, Sullivan asked Emanuel whether he agreed that Smith was crazy to be doing what she was doing and suggested that Emanuel get rid of Smith. (Sullivan would later recall alluding to Smith's stability, but not suggesting her dismissal.) The office was falling apart, Emanuel shot back. Sullivan suggested that Smith was exaggerating the problems. Copen had already withheld several thousand dollars in rent in the dispute over the copy machine damaged by rainwater. Emanuel was eager to see what kind of terms Helmsley-Spear would offer on a new lease. When Sullivan finally left, Emanuel asked Smith to stop the rabble-rousing, at least temporarily.

To Smith, it seemed that matters were turning sinister. The atmosphere was charged. She noticed two men had begun shadowing her when she left the office at night. They were tall men in suits—not gray or blue, she noticed, but colorful ones. She alerted Trump, who told her to ignore them. Instead, she began snapping pictures of the men. Within days, they were gone.

Trump was intrigued by Smith's description of her confrontation with Trainor. He sent a couple of men to install a hidden camera over Smith's desk, apparently eager to catch the Helmsley-Spear men doing something improper. But none of them came back to Smith's office in the coming days, so the camera was just as quickly removed.

Smith was too stubborn to buckle under to the pressure. Her father, a lawyer, instructed her to stop running her campaign from her workplace immediately. She met with Trump to brief him on the disturbing turn of events. Smith told him she planned to carry on her effort from her apartment. She told him she needed a fax machine and a printer. Trump unplugged a fax machine and gave it to her, right then and there. Later, he shipped her a printer the size of a stove. It was too large for Smith's apartment, so she arranged for Trump to donate it to charity.

Smith wasn't about to allow Trainor's visit to her go unanswered. She complained to the police that Trainor and Guigno had threatened her. The next thing Trainor knew there were two police officers in his office asking questions. Eventually, everyone was hauled in front of an arbitrator. Both Trainor and Guigno denied threatening anyone. Trainor told his lawyer that the secret audio recording of the visit would prove it. As the hearing stretched on, Trainor later recalled, he snapped at his lawyer, "Play the fucking tape so I can get out of here." The tape was never played. Shortly after the hearing, Trainor had a heart attack and spent 18 days in the hospital. He later blamed it on the stress brought on by Smith's accusations. The dispute over Trainor's visit eventually fizzled out without any finding of wrongdoing by anyone.

By now, Peter Malkin was well aware that Trump was preparing to attack the long-term lease. Trump himself had practically said as much months earlier, when he had announced to Malkin over the phone that he was buying the Empire State Building. Malkin had an obvious line of defense. Several years earlier, he had launched a $60 million program to modernize the Empire State Building. Workers were already replacing all 6,400 windows, refurbishing the skyscraper's 60 elevators, installing a new air-conditioning plant, repairing the limestone facade, and renovating the observation deck.

To Malkin, it was inconceivable that a woman like Suzy Smith would attack the building for no other reason than to bring about improvements. Malkin told reporters Smith's employer was behind on rent and angling for a cheaper lease, an allegation that Copen denied. Malkin insisted that Trump's press agents were behind Smith's press releases and public comments.

One bitterly cold morning shortly after her first rally, a television reporter interviewed Smith on a sidewalk near the Empire State Building. The reporter told Smith the building's managers had described her as a mouthpiece for Donald Trump, then asked if Trump was paying her.

"Absolutely not," insisted Smith. She was here to represent the tenants of the building, she explained. Smith complained about the security and the condition of the building. "If you care about our national landmarks," Smith told the television audience, "call the mayor. Ask him to review the situation and clean up this filthy building." Smith held up a sign with the phone number of the mayor's office.

Later that morning, Trump called. He told Smith that when he saw her urging people to call the mayor, he had spit his coffee on his newspaper. The mayor's office had called, Trump said. Trump told Smith he had denied having anything to do with Smith's plea. Smith had the impression

Trump was beginning to regard her as something of a loose cannon.

On December 20, 1994, Peter Malkin's partner, Alvin Silverman, received a letter by certified mail addressed to Empire State Building Associates. It was from Trump Empire State Partners, Trump's partnership with Kiiko and Renoir. "Gentlemen," the letter began. "Please take notice, that we are the landlord and owner of the Empire State Building and do hereby notify you of the following defaults of your obligations under the lease." The letter laid out the findings of the team of lawyers and engineers Trump had ordered to scrutinize the lease and the building. It rambled on for 71 pages. Trump found fault with the building's fire safety systems and insurance. He complained of a "severe rodent infestation problem." He faulted Malkin for not seeking approval from the owner for much of the work being done on the building, for not doing the exterior work properly, for inferior security that "exposed the building's tenants to an increased risk of muggings."

Above all, Trump complained about quality, accusing Malkin and Helmsley of failing to maintain the Empire State Building as a "high class" building, as required by the lease. "The plastic laminate interior cabs installed by you in the elevators are of a class of interior elevator cab not found in a high class building," the letter said. The elevator cables "are causing a poor ride quality." The replacement windows "are inexpensive, low quality windows," inferior to windows available for use in "high class buildings," the letter said. The tenant base, Trump complained, was "made up primarily of small high-turnover tenancies rather than large, prestigious tenancies," such as major law, accounting, advertising, or engineering firms.

"Please take notice," the letter concluded, "that pursuant

to Article 19 of Lease you are required to cure said breaches on or before March 31, 1995, that being more than sixty days after the service of this notice upon you, and that upon your failure to cure the Landlord will elect to terminate your tenancy in accordance with paragraph 19.01 of the Lease and in accordance with applicable provisions of the law." The letter was signed by a Trump executive.

Trump was only too happy to simplify his complaints for reporters. The Empire State Building was "a mess," he told them, "a laughing stock." The condition, he said, was "absolutely deplorable." There was, Trump said, "a lack of quality throughout."

It is doubtful that Harry Helmsley was capable of grasping the fact that Donald Trump had set out to take away the building he had once coveted more than any other in the world. Although Leona never spoke of it in public, Harry's friends took it as a given that he was slipping rapidly into the twilight world of senility. Ever since Harry had stopped coming into the office, John Trainor had been meeting with him nearly every week to run through various business matters. By the early 1990s, Harry was having difficulty following Trainor. "John, stop," Harry would tell him. "I can't follow this any more." Harry was still capable of signing things, recalls Trainor, but Trainor began making more and more decisions himself based on what he thought Harry would have done.

In 1992, just before Leona left to serve her prison term for tax evasion, Peter Malkin met the couple in their Manhattan penthouse apartment. While Malkin and Leona talked business, Harry sat on a couch and stared straight ahead. Out of the blue, Harry said, "Larry [Wien] and I had great times together," Malkin later recalled. Then Harry lapsed back into silence.

Thanks to the deal made years earlier by Malkin's father-in-law, Larry Wien, Harry Helmsley held a far bigger stake than Wien's heirs did in the lucrative partnership that controlled the Empire State Building lease. And now Leona held a power of attorney to act on his behalf. But the legal troubles that descended on Leona in the late 1980s left Peter Malkin as the de facto caretaker of the landmark. Malkin grew accustomed to calling the shots and to treating the abrasive, temperamental, seventy-something Leona with kid gloves.

While a slugfest between Trump and Leona would have quickened the pulses of many a New York tabloid editor, Trump in fact faced a more formidable foe in Peter Malkin. To casual acquaintances, Malkin presented a picture of courtly charm. Following the lead of his illustrious father-in-law, Malkin was an active philanthropist and was committed to various civic groups. But some in the real estate industry regarded Malkin as a first-class pest, a control freak with a spine of steel. Malkin was a lawyer who expected people to hew to the letter of the law, and he was likely to unleash a blizzard of correspondence on those who did not. A guest at one dinner party at Malkin's red brick Georgian recalls that Malkin leaped from his dinner table when he detected the drone of an airplane, threw open the doors, and shouted that the plane was flying lower than allowed. He exhorted his guests to join his crusade against the Westchester County Airport, supplying them with the phone number of the Federal Aviation Administration. When the house next to his own came up for sale, Malkin bought it, then put it back on the market with restrictive covenants regarding noise and lighting. When no buyers materialized, he tore it down. The way Malkin saw it, he was just trying to improve the quality of life in his community. "When anyone makes an effort to have things done correctly," he later explained, "there will be people who won't be happy that things they have done incorrectly will be found lacking."

Malkin regarded Trump's complaints about the Empire

State Building as nitpicking of the highest order. Malkin wasn't one to be cowed into cutting a deal. On February 14, 1995, less than two months after Trump declared the Helmsley/Malkin partnership in default on its lease, Malkin challenged Trump's move in New York State court. He asked the court to extend the deadline for fixing the alleged defaults until a court could decide whether Trump's complaints were valid. Trump's claims, he insisted, were "baseless." Malkin pointed out that the partnership was in the middle of a $60 million renovation program, which was more than Kiiko and Renoir had even paid for the building. The default notice, Malkin argued, "is not from a landlord genuinely fearful of its economic investment in the property but from a hired gun without any economic investment in the property whose compensation depends on breaking or burdening a long-standing and previously unblemished contractual relationship."

On March 21, Judge Edward Lehner of the New York State Supreme Court granted Malkin's request, pointing out that no city authority responsible for public safety had issued to the Empire State Building any violation notice that supported Trump's claim that the skyscraper was a danger to the public. Judge Lehner blocked Trump's effort to toss Helmsley and Malkin from the building until Trump's claims could be examined in greater detail.

If Suzy Smith had hoped to ferment a groundswell of outrage among other tenants in the building, she was coming up short. But she did find sympathetic ears within a number of other offices in the building. Before long, she had gathered dozens of signatures on her petition to Leona. Attorney Jacques Catafago, who was irate about being billed for rodent extermination, began working with Smith and threatened to file suit over the extermination bills.

When Jack Brod phoned Smith in December 1994, she recognized immediately that Brod could bring significant attention to her cause. Brod, then 85 years old, was a living link to the Empire State Building's storied past. Merely visiting his office was like a trip back in time. Brod had moved into the Empire State Building in 1931, and his company, Empire Diamond Corporation, had been peddling gold, silver, and diamonds from a warren of small, drab rooms in the building's upper reaches ever since. Slow moving, ruddy-faced, with the unblinking gaze of a very old man, Brod looked as timeworn as the building itself.

More than a decade earlier, when Brod was opening his office safe, he had felt the barrel of a gun pressed to his head. A voice said, "Don't turn." Brod didn't. Five armed bandits wearing wigs and fake mustaches handcuffed and hog-tied Brod and his employees. The thieves loaded about $250,000 worth of gold, silver, and valuable coins into bags and fled. For the next couple of years, Brod kept shotguns hidden behind his drapes. Brod told Smith he thought the building's security was deficient and that he still carried a gun to protect himself. He suggested forming a security arm of the tenants association. Brod boasted of his ties to the Federal Bureau of Investigation. He volunteered to head the new group, and Smith readily agreed. She issued a press release announcing Brod's involvement, which said the group was preparing "survival tips" for tenants, including the formation of "neighborhood watches" and the carrying of mace.

The timing of Suzy Smith's actions left Peter Malkin convinced that it was Trump who was calling the shots. On February 15, 1995, Trump Empire State Partners sued Helmsley, Malkin, and their partnerships in New York State court, repeating the allegations Trump had made in the default notice and branding the building "a second rate rodent infested commercial building." Trump demanded $100 million in damages. The very next day—timing that struck

Malkin as suspicious—Smith issued a press release announcing a "Stop Leona Now" campaign and a rally at noon the following day. Smith bought a bag of 300 large plastic whistles from Toys "R" Us. She announced that she intended to distribute them on the sidewalk to Empire State Building tenants for use in the hallways, spurred, she said, "by a morning mugging and several robberies." The Empire State Building Tenant/Workers Association, explained Smith, aimed to "stop Leona Helmsley from operating the Empire State Building like a low income housing project."

On the morning of the rally, as reporters arrived at the building, Smith handed them lists of tenants with complaints who were available to interview. Helmsley-Spear employees, however, barred reporters and cameramen from wandering through the building. Smith, who was beside herself with anger, telephoned Trump. Trump wrote a letter authorizing reporters to enter the building and faxed it to Smith. Smith presented it to Helmsley-Spear and distributed it to the reporters. Helmsley-Spear insisted that Trump had no authority to do such a thing. Security personnel kept the reporters at bay. "That Trump had no right to enter the Building in this fashion—that his act was in fact a violation of the Leases—did not daunt Trump," Malkin's lawyers later complained in court papers. "The result was a chaotic and disruptive scene at the Building that produced no evidence of Trump's baseless claims but nevertheless furthered the impression of a building in trouble."

Shortly before noon, as Smith prepared for her sidewalk protest, Jack Brod, her new ally, telephoned.

"I think we're going about this the wrong way," Brod told her. "We're going after the wrong person. If Trump breaks the lease, he's going to double the rent. We can't do anything to help him."

"We're not doing it to help anyone," Smith responded. "We're doing it to help the building."

"Let's think about it," Brod persisted. "Let's not go out there today. Let's stop this right now. We have to figure out a different tactic."

Smith told Brod she was going ahead anyway.

Out on the sidewalk, Smith sounded her now-familiar themes to the gathered reporters. She was surprised to see Jack Brod shuffling over to the group.

"This is the safest building around," Brod declared to the reporters. "I wouldn't think of having my diamonds anywhere else."

A look of astonishment crossed Smith's face. Later, when she saw Brod in the elevator, she called him Judas. Brod, for his part, offered no apologies for his sneak attack. "I have a love of the building," he later explained. "It's been part of my life for 69 years. . . . I felt she was being used by Trump, and doing damage to the building. That's when I stepped in and tried to nullify the thing. I got nothing out of it."

After the fiasco on the sidewalk, Smith invited a local television crew back to her office for an interview. Charles Guigno, the building's director of operations, arrived to head them off. He brought the building's security chief, an ex-cop, who aimed a video camera at Smith's group and began recording. Guigno told the television crew to leave. Smith's boss protested, and tried to prevent the security man from coming into the office. "I believe she slammed the door in his face," Guigno later remembered. The television crew left.

Thanks to Suzy Smith and Donald Trump, relations between the new owners of the Empire State Building and the building's longtime lessees, Helmsley and Malkin, were now in tatters. Trump called Malkin to suggest that the two of them discuss matters over lunch at the Plaza Hotel. With litigation in full swing, Malkin was wary of talking to his adversary. Instead, the partnership's lawyer, prominent New York litigator Arthur Liman, agreed to meet with Trump.

Over lunch, Trump told Liman he had made a spectacular deal with the Japanese and had nothing to lose. Liman told Trump he had "nothing to gain other than a black eye," Liman recalled to a reporter for the *New York Observer*. Liman told Trump that his association with Hideki Yokoi would cause him nothing but grief, because New Jersey, where Trump's casinos were located, took its gaming licenses very seriously. Trump did not need to be reminded that state licensing officials looked dimly on contact with reputed gangsters.

If nothing else, the lunch demonstrated how wide the breech had become. Trump boasted to the *New York Observer*: "Arthur Liman, in my opinion, had one thing on his mind at the lunch and that was to buy out our position, because they know they are in total violation of the lease and they know how badly the building is run." Yet Malkin later said he was thinking nothing of the kind. Malkin figured Trump was trying to convince Leona and him that the fight over the lease would be long and costly. Malkin assumed Trump was angling to compel him and Leona to either buy the Empire State Building from Trump and Kiiko or to sell them the long-term lease.

Manhattan's other real estate luminaries watched Trump's attack on the Empire State Building unfold with a mixture of amusement and outrage. Over the years, Malkin and Leona had crossed sabers with many of them. But other owners were reluctant to root for Trump in an action many of them considered a frivolous attempt to break a lawful lease. Bernard Mendik, who owned dozens of Manhattan buildings, had had differences with Malkin over control of the Grand Central Partnership, a midtown business improvement association. But he was so outraged by Trump's lawsuit that he told Malkin he'd be willing to testify for him.

Powerhouse Manhattan real estate broker Julien Studley was no fan of Malkin's stewardship of the Empire State Building. Studley owned units in the partnership that held the lease. Four years earlier, he had sued Malkin and his law firm, accusing them of milking the partnership for fees. Malkin had denied Studley's claims. The two men were locked in protracted litigation. Yet Studley, a world-class poker player, didn't think Trump had come to court against Malkin with clean hands, he would later say. Trump's motives for challenging the lease were purely financial, he said. And Studley, an expert on leases, viewed the Empire State Building lease as unbreakable.

Trump invited Studley to lunch at the Plaza Hotel. He asked Studley what the two of them could do together on the Empire State Building. "If you want to break the lease, there's nothing for us to talk about," Studley responded. "If you want to improve the building, then we can talk." With that, the conversation turned to other deals.

Yet however confident Malkin felt about his ability to defeat Trump in court, he was concerned about how Trump's attack was affecting business at the building. John Trainor watched the Empire State Building's occupancy level slide from 91 percent to 82 percent, evidence, he later explained, that Trump and Smith were "substantially affecting the value of the building." Thomas Sullivan, the building's director of leasing, also noticed the fallout. "The building became something of a laughing stock," he said, "and it was affecting my ability to negotiate leases."

With the costly refurbishment program in full swing, suddenly profits to the two partnerships that controlled the lease all but dried up. The more than 2,000 investors in the partnership run by Malkin had always counted on their 50 percent cut of the excess profits to boost their guaranteed 9 percent return. In 1995, for the first time, there were no such profits. The separate partnership that subleased the building, the partnership owned primarily by Harry Helmsley, also felt the squeeze.

Ironically, the financial pinch came during a period of

nearly unrivaled prosperity for New York City. The city was flush with the wealth of a long bull market in stocks, its streets sanitized by the tough policies of its law-and-order mayor, Rudolph Giuliani. Business was booming, office vacancies were melting away, and tourists thronged the midtown streets. More than 2 million visitors a year flocked to the observatory of the Empire State Building, oblivious to the clash of titans that was raging over it.

On May 30, 1995, Malkin struck back against Trump. On behalf of the two partnerships that controlled the building's lease, Malkin sued Trump, Hideki Yokoi, Kiiko Nakahara, and Jean-Paul Renoir in the Supreme Court of the State of New York. The suit accused Trump and his partners of running "an illicit and reckless campaign"—orchestrated by Trump in conspiracy with Yokoi and his daughter—to deprive the Helmsley/Malkin partnerships of their rights under the lease. Trump's aim, the suit alleged, was to "threaten and diminish the value of the leaseholds in order to force plaintiffs to buy peace with Trump." Donald Trump, the suit said, "knew all too well the kind of outrageous claims—of rodent infestation, of homeless people roaming the halls, and of the risk of terrorist attack—that would most easily attract a tabloid headline, prey on the fears of existing tenants, and diminish the value of plaintiff's leasehold interests." Suzy Smith, the suit said, was nothing more than an agent of Trump, the "one person out of the 15,000 who work in the building everyday to launch his scheme." Malkin and Helmsley demanded $100 million in damages.

In spite of her tense run-ins with Helmsley-Spear employees and the mixed reception she had received from her bosses, Suzy Smith refused to abandon her quixotic crusade to force improvements at the building. She was developing a real flair for the tabloid gesture. At one point, she decided to ask all the building's tenants to save their dead rodents to contribute to some kind of lurid display. Trump, emerging as the cooler head, scotched the idea. Smith exasperated Trump on a regular basis. When Smith proposed voicing support for union elevator attendants during their dispute with Helmsley-Spear, Trump again called her off, warning that messing with the union could be dangerous. Smith had the distinct impression that she was driving Trump crazy. One day Trump told her, "It'd be a nightmare if you were in one of my buildings and this kind of stuff was going on."

When Smith heard that Leona Helmsley had declared the Empire State Building fit for a queen, it struck her as ripe for the kind of dramatic gesture she had read about in her guerrilla public relations book. She grabbed her Polaroid camera and snapped pictures of freshly killed rodents and holes in the ceilings. Smith constructed a crown of cardboard, and pasted on the photographs. She dashed off a poem, "Fit for a Queen," and faxed it to Leona's office. She placed the crown in a hatbox and called reporters who had covered her campaign. Smith and her crown landed on the local news.

After the broadcast, Smith's phone rang.

"Is this Susan Smith?" said a woman's voice.

Smith said that it was.

"You are a fuckin' sick bitch," growled the voice.

The caller hung up.

Is that her? wondered Smith. She decided that it must have been.

The French Front

Hideki Yokoi remained separated from the brewing tempest in New York by a language barrier, the Pacific Ocean, and the high walls of Hachioji Medical Prison. As his first winter in captivity began warming into spring, he received a letter, dated March 18, 1995, from the daughter he believed had betrayed him. "My dear father, how have you been?" Kiiko wrote. "I have recently read a book about Japanese prisons. What was described in it was beyond my imagination, and I am very worried for you, father, especially because of your advanced age. And it is my great regret to have to write a letter like this to you, when you are in such an extraordinary environment."

Japanese newspapers and magazines, Kiiko wrote, had twisted the story of what had happened. She had spoken to his brother-in-law, Hishida, and explained her actions, Kiiko continued, but Hishida had misunderstood. The trust company that held the Empire State Building, she insisted, "was set up in line with directions from you, and I don't know how, but he

[Hishida] misunderstood these and created the problem that we are facing now." A "misunderstanding" with Yokoi's Tokyo lawyer, Kiiko wrote, "has caused a bunch of lawyers to attack me in court in foreign countries. And New York tabloids are repeatedly writing scandalous stories about me.

"Rather than talking to lawyers and newspaper reporters, I think it would be best if I could meet you, father. If I did anything wrong, I will correct it immediately. I will wait to hear your opinions. I will listen to anything you say. I hope to see you as soon as possible. I pray for good health of my precious father. To my beloved father, Kiiko Nakahara."

On April 20, the old man composed a meandering and somewhat disjointed letter of response. For a man who had filed such a blistering lawsuit against Kiiko, Yokoi took a curiously gentle tone. He reminisced about the success of his overseas purchases, singling out the Empire State Building—which he erroneously referred to as the "world's biggest building,"—as their proudest accomplishment. "It was thought that I was sent by God to the Japanese business world," he wrote.

Abruptly, his tone changed. "After that, Mr. Trump became involved, as did Mr. Renoir, and things have changed, which Nippon Sangyo has had no knowledge of. . . . Consequently, at this time, I am not taking either Mr. Trump or Mr. Renoir into consideration, so please have them discontinue their efforts as soon as possible. Since there may be opportunities in the future for us to seek cooperation from Mr. Trump as long as we operate our businesses in the U.S., please send him our polite decline." Yokoi complained that Trump "never intended to offer a single yen" for the Tokyo hotel project. "Now I can recall that Mr. Trump said at that time that he had failed previously because he had tried to use his own money and that he would never fail again since he would use other people's money. Nippon Sangyo will negotiate and deal directly with the issues concerning the Empire State Building. So, please do not worry, and if there is any talk from

Mr. Trump, please put it off for now." Finally, like a scolding father, Yokoi rejoined his daughter to get back into line. "Kiiko, you made those purchases under proxy for Nippon Sangyo. . . . Let's get together and solve this whole thing once and for all as soon as possible." Yokoi asked his daughter to visit him in prison right away.

It is impossible to know whether Yokoi actually believed that a handwritten edict from him would eliminate Trump and Renoir from the picture and win back both his daughter and the Empire State Building. That July, Kiiko wrote back to one of her father's representatives. She apologized for having been unable to visit her father right away. She had been in Italy, she explained. She asked the representative to arrange a prison meeting for late August. But by that time, the dispute had snowballed beyond the point where a simple solution was possible.

By midsummer, it had become clear to Yokoi's advisers that Nippon Sangyo was not the owner of record of most of the trophy properties. Shut away from his family in prison, Yokoi worked himself into a fury. He didn't bother to wait for the confusing paper trail to be deciphered. His conciliatory tone vanished. On July 18, he fired off a letter to Sakakura, his ex-son-in-law, referring to Kiiko and her husband as "the evil husband-and-wife swindlers." Yokoi instructed Sakakura to take charge of the properties. "Since the couple has been keeping all of their personal belongings at Juniper Hill [one of the British castles], please seize the entire thing. Please seek attorneys' advice and impose prohibitive injunctions against them, such as prohibiting them to enter, use, dispose [of] the mansions and buildings in Europe and the U.S. and take any personal belongings out of those properties so that they will be completely bogged down. Therefore, please change the locks of the entrances, gates, and doors, and put out 'Keep Out' signs and notice boards which say 'No admittance to unauthorized parties by the court' at the gates.

Please keep a strict watch, having the caretakers use new keys every time they enter." As for Kiiko, he said, "ask the attorneys to cease her right of inheritance after my death."

After seething for another three weeks, Yokoi sent a second letter to Sakakura ordering a more aggressive attack on his daughter and her husband. "I saw photographs of France," Yokoi wrote. "It seems to me that they have sold off most furniture, furnishings, decorative accessories, and tapestries, that no gardening has been done, and that many of them do not even have caretakers." He worried that Kiiko and Renoir might sell all four English castles. "It is a must for you to file a complaint against them to the Scotland Yard and retain excellent solicitors in the U.K. in order to prevent them from: selling or entering into the properties; using, transferring, or selling furniture, furnishings, accessories, tapestries, monuments, and their personal belongings; clearing gardens and living trees; transferring their funds from their bank accounts; and so forth. Please take every possible measure and every thorough action so that they cannot make any move at all. . . . Mr. Sakakura, you must go to the U.K. and file a complaint with solicitors to the police department and the prosecutors office. At the same time of thoroughly taking care of them with a civil suit, also immediately deal with these international thieves, such consummate villains, by charging not only breach of trust under the commercial law but also fraud, embezzlement, and unauthorized sale of registered important cultural properties. They are criminals worse than robbers are. We must carry out actions right now. Please swiftly transfer the names of the title. . . . With regard to the Empire State Building, we must file a complaint and expropriate it from Trump."

Around the time Yokoi was penning his vitriolic letters, Kiiko and Renoir were engaging in a series of transactions in

France that would swiftly come back to haunt them. They formed a new company called Châteaux Holdings and transferred ownership of the châteaux from Yokoi's Nippon Sangyo to the new company. Nippon Sangyo received stock in the new company. But between August 10 and October 25, Nippon Sangyo and another Yokoi holding company were stripped of their shares in Châteaux Holdings, French government investigators would later conclude. Most of those shares wound up under the control of a trust called the Hideki Yokoi Legal Issue Trust, of which Kiiko appeared to be a beneficiary. There would later be considerable dispute about just how Hideki Yokoi and his other children benefited from this trust. Kiiko's lawyers would claim that Yokoi's eight recognized children all benefited from it. But investigators became convinced of one thing: Nippon Sangyo no longer controlled the properties.

Peter Bal, the New York artist who had guided Yokoi's eldest daughter around the châteaux, arranged for Nippon Sangyo to retain a French lawyer to delve into the ownership question. In September, that lawyer told Bal that the title search had turned up the name Châteaux Holdings. Kiiko appeared to have transferred title using a power of attorney purportedly supplied by Kazuo Sato, an aide to Hideki Yokoi, a document that had been filed with the French Consulate in Tokyo in October 1992. Bal wondered whether the document gave Kiiko the right to do what she had done. On September 28, the Nippon Sangyo board of directors, under the control of Yokoi's eldest sons, voided Kiiko's authority to act on behalf of Nippon Sangyo in France.

For Bal, it was becoming more complicated by the day to understand what had happened. Ever mindful of the warnings from his lawyer friends, who had advised him to stick to his painting, Bal had been deflecting entreaties from the Yokoi family to take charge of matters in France. "Why do you want to get involved in this case?" Bal recalled being told by friends. "You don't know anything about it, and you are probably going to go through hell. So if you do, ask for a sum that if they do accept it will be worth your while. Otherwise, stay home."

In October, Bal flew to Tokyo, carrying the French documents. When he arrived, he was introduced to Hirohiko for the first time. Bal handed him the papers. It quickly became clear to Bal that Yokoi's sons were at an utter loss about how to proceed. "They didn't understand anything of foreign business, and I think they lost confidence in the lawyers," Bal later explained. "They wanted somebody to be able to supervise what was going on and give them some sort of report." Hirohiko again asked Bal to help. He introduced Bal to Kazuo Sato, then president of Nippon Sangyo. Sato told Bal that Yokoi had already filed a lawsuit in New York accusing his daughter of taking the Empire State Building. Bal was astonished.

Having seen the condition of the French châteaux firsthand, Bal bluntly advised Hirohiko to cut his losses on the properties. They were costing lots of money and attracting far too much unfavorable attention. The repairs and complaints would be constant, Bal worried. Get rid of them, he advised. If the family wanted to keep one or two, he said, that was understandable.

Bal may have been a fledgling artist with a bohemian streak, but he knew how to drive a hard bargain. He told Hirohiko he wouldn't get involved without the proper paperwork. Hirohiko was reluctant. After speaking to his father, Hirohiko agreed to enter into a formal agreement. Bal made sure it was lucrative. Bal would receive $6,000 a month to coordinate the litigation—in itself more than he could hope to make as an artist. But the deal was potentially far richer. Bal would help with the effort to regain title to the French properties for Nippon Sangyo and to sell them. In exchange, Bal would receive 20 percent of the total value of whatever properties were sold. Bal's life as an artist was over. As career changes go, it was a jarring shift. He was now a mercenary for Hideki Yokoi, a job he quickly discovered to be rich with tension and intrigue.

Before Bal left Japan, he received a power of attorney to act on behalf of Yokoi's company in France. He and Kazuo Sato also paid a visit to the French consulate in Tokyo. Bal wanted to check the validity of the power of attorney he believed Kiiko had used in France. The document contained Kazuo Sato's name, but Sato told Bal he had never signed it. The consulate's records showed that Kiiko herself had come in to have a similar document verified three years earlier. How Sato's name wound up on the document was an open question.

When he returned to France, Bal sent registered letters to all of the parties involved. He instructed them to turn over documents related to the châteaux and to get in touch with him to explain what was happening. Bal received only one response, from a man to whom he hadn't even written. It came from Terrence Jehan, a representative of the Hideki Yokoi Legal Issue Trust, which now owned the châteaux. Bal telephoned Jehan and asked who he was. Bal asked him to explain what was going on. The trust documents were sent to Bal along with a letter explaining that the beneficiaries of the Hideki Yokoi Legal Issue Trust were the eight recognized children of Hideki Yokoi. The protector of the trust was Kiiko Nakahara. Bal didn't even know what a trust was, let alone a protector.

By now, it was clear that the family had much to learn. But one thing was certain: Nippon Sangyo neither owned nor controlled Yokoi's beloved French castles. So on November 7, 1995, Nippon Sangyo filed suit in France against Kiiko and Renoir, accusing them of improperly transferring title to the châteaux. Nippon Sangyo petitioned the court to remove the properties from the control of Kiiko and her husband and to appoint a temporary administrator for them. On November 28 the court did just that.

But the French lawsuit, it turned out, would be the least of the couple's problems. In December, an investigating magistrate in Versailles, Sylvie Petit-LeClair, began looking into the allegations against Kiiko and Renoir, questioning people who had been involved in the transfer of the châteaux. Kiiko and her husband were now the subjects of a criminal inquiry.

Almost immediately, troubling questions arose about the power of attorney that Kiiko had allegedly used in France, the document that her father's associate Sato claimed never to have signed. As it happened, Chou Sothy, an employee of the French consulate in Tokyo, recalled an October 20, 1992, visit by Kiiko to verify the document, which granted Kiiko the power to sell Nippon Sangyo's properties in France. "I remember Nakahara quite well," Sothy said when questioned by a French investigator. "She is a beautiful woman with a very strong temper." According to Sothy, Kiiko had wanted the consulate to witness her own signature as well as the signature of a man who she said was seriously ill in the hospital. Sothy told Kiiko it wasn't possible to verify the signature of anyone who wasn't present, Sothy recalled, and Kiiko told her she would ask the man to sign the document at the hospital. Again, Sothy told Kiiko that wouldn't suffice. Kiiko left. Later, she phoned back and repeated her request. Sothy passed her on to the consul, who then instructed Sothy to witness the signature of Kiiko alone. Kiiko returned, and Sothy did just that. Sothy told investigators that the French consul told her he had warned Kiiko that the power of attorney would not be suitable in France because Kiiko, essentially, had given it to herself. Much later, Kiiko would offer a far more benign take on the power of attorney.

The suspicious behavior, French investigators claimed,

didn't end there. In November 1994, the same month Nippon Sangyo had sued Kiiko and her husband in New York state court to block any further transfers of property, the couple had appeared at the office of Alain Tant, a solicitor-notary in a small town in the south of France. Renoir told Tant, who functioned as something between an American notary public and lawyer, that he and his wife wanted to sell a number of châteaux owned by a Japanese company, Tant later told French investigators. Renoir told Tant he and his wife were in a hurry, Tant recalled. Renoir handed Tant a power of attorney authorizing Kiiko to sell the châteaux. It was identical to the document verified by the French consulate in Tokyo two years earlier, except for one suspicious change. Kazuo Sato's name had been added. It appeared to have been written with a different typewriter. The following year, Tant said, he helped the Renoirs to form Châteaux Holdings, shift ownership of the châteaux to the new company, then transfer ownership again to the Hideki Yokoi Legal Issue Trust.

Had Sato's signature on the power of attorney been forged? Sato told investigators he hadn't signed it. Nippon Sangyo's lawyer told investigators that Yokoi had never intended to give Kiiko the authority to sell or transfer the châteaux. Kiiko would later produce other powers of attorney pertaining to the châteaux and claim that she had used them. Did any of them give her authority to transfer the châteaux? It was far from clear.

Jean Louis Bordenave, Renoir's lawyer in France, told investigators that by the fall of 1995, confusion reigned with respect to various powers of attorneys. Peter Bal had pointed out to Bordenave that he now held a power of attorney for Nippon Sangyo in France, and he showed Bordenave the minutes of the Nippon Sangyo board meeting at which Kiiko had been stripped of her authority to act in France. Bordenave then asked Renoir about the conflicting powers of attorney.

"My wife has always received her power of attorney from

her father himself, without knowing who signed them," Bordenave, when questioned by investigators, recalled Renoir telling him. "It was the same thing for the power of attorney she brought back from the consulate with her signature. She later gave it to her father and Mr. Sato sent it back with his signature." Renoir told Bordenave that before Yokoi went to prison he had granted his daughter "numerous powers of attorney, such as blank powers and extended powers, which enabled her to act the way she wanted."

French investigators discovered that in late October, Alain Tant, the solicitor Renoir hired in the south of France, had received a fax from Sato revoking any powers of attorney that Sato had purportedly given to Kiiko. In early November, a Nippon Sangyo lawyer called Tant and accused Renoir and Kiiko of using a forged document. They were crooks, the lawyer told him. Tant then received an anonymous fax, which he had forwarded to Renoir. Renoir told Tant the fax came from his brother-in-law. "He asked me not to care for it," Tant later told investigators, "for it was family problems."

As the confusion mounted, Yokoi's daughter Chizuko and her ex-husband Takenosuke Sakakura appeared to emerge as the family members Yokoi trusted most. As 1995 drew to a close, Yokoi again wrote to the couple from prison. He complained that his sons were "late to pay a visit to me." He no longer trusted them, he wrote. "It is no one else but I that should be totally responsible for having raised my next generation in a free and easy environment, putting them in the Keio Kindergarten through the Keio University, without letting them make their own effort nor letting them work for others," he wrote. "Therefore, I would like to ask you, the husband-and-wife team, to help the 'stupid' second generation of mine. Chizuko, I have faith in you because you resemble me most among all my children, and you are a businesswoman. Please track down the Renoirs and consult your best friends and the local authorities in France as soon as possible to charge them for criminal matters promptly, so that the trickery will be uncovered immediately."

Yokoi brimmed with a hope that bordered on irrational that he would recover the Empire State Building and his other overseas assets in short order and that his trophy properties would save him from financial ruin. "With a little more push, we will be able to solve everything," Yokoi wrote.

It is unclear whether Hideki Yokoi, as he wrote, was aware that events had already taken an ominous turn in France. On December 22, 1995, French authorities in Versailles indicated that there was sufficient evidence to presume that Kiiko Naka-hara was involved in the use of forged documents and a breach of trust. Kiiko became the subject of a *mise en examen*—literally "put in examination"—a French procedure under which a magistrate wields broad investigative powers against a person suspected of wrongdoing. Kiiko was ordered to appear before the magistrate in Versailles for questioning.

On January 19, 1996, Kiiko boarded an early train from Paris, intent on convincing the investigating magistrate that the allegations against her were nothing more than a grievous family misunderstanding. Through several hours of questioning, Kiiko offered innocent explanations for the questionable paperwork and property transfers in France. She said she had never even seen a translation of the suspicious power of attorney she had sought to authenticate years earlier at the French consulate in Japan, so she had no idea what it said. Her father, she said, had asked her to protect his properties from creditors. She had only been following his instructions, she said. "I did no wrong."

Her explanations apparently proved less than convincing. After the session, two men handcuffed her and hustled her into an elevator. Kiiko would later insist the action so shocked her that she thought she was being kidnapped. The two men drove her to a small complex of buildings in Versailles, the former stables of Marie Antoinette. Only when Kiiko found herself in a room with barred windows did she realize she was no longer a free woman. She burst into tears. Kiiko was locked inside at the women's prison of Versailles.

The French criminal justice system is harsh on those presumed to have committed a crime. French magistrates have the authority to place suspects in provisional detention so they won't try to flee or influence other witnesses. Magistrates can leave them there for as long as a year before ever deciding to turn over the case to a prosecutor for trial. Kiiko was ordered to cease all communication with her husband, who was also under investigation. The nightmarish turn of events threw Kiiko for a loop. She wept constantly. Prison officials refused to give her a single room for fear she might kill herself. Almost no one spoke English. Kiiko couldn't stomach the canned food she was served. Her weight dropped precipitously. Renoir later complained bitterly that French authorities had kept her behind bars "in order to try to destabilize my wife and have her crack up."

Several weeks after his wife was detained, Renoir himself was summoned for questioning. Renoir, a suspicious man by nature, was already skeptical about the intentions of French officials. In 1992, French authorities had accused him of violating laws protecting historical properties because he had moved a couple of outdoor statues at one château without first requesting permission from the French Ministry of Culture. Renoir had said he was just trying to protect them from the winter weather and blamed the action on the politically connected shooting club that leased Yokoi's Château Millemont, L'Association de la Croix Blanche, or the Order of the White Cross. Renoir had unsuccessfully attempted to bar the club from hunting on the property. Ever since, Renoir had believed that the shooting club, together with the village's mayor, who held a long-term lease to live in part of the château, was out to get him. Renoir was convinced that Yokoi's hired gun, Peter Bal, had caught the ear of this powerful local clique.

"I knew the French," Renoir would later fume. "My father had been hounded by the French as a Jew, and they usually did that, sent you to Auschwitz in order to seize your assets. So I was leery of anything that has to do with the French. . . . After what they pulled on me in October of 1992, opening a penal case for a nonsense relating to the movement of statues, I decided that I would not go, because I smelled a trap."

In February 20 letter responding to the summons, Renoir's French lawyer protested that his client "has always been a scapegoat" in the case. "Now again, I notice that people keep believing allegations from people whose quality to act seems quite questionable, since the device is to hit Mrs. Nakahara in order to hit her husband even better." Renoir's lawyer said Renoir would be willing to answer questions in a country "where his freedom wouldn't be threatened." Renoir had no intention of coming to France, the letter said.

In February 1996, the French magistrate issued a warrant for Renoir's arrest, to be distributed around the world. Renoir was wanted for questioning about certain suspected crimes. When Renoir left his castle in England, he headed in the opposite direction, to Canada, where he met with John Markham, an American criminal defense lawyer. In June, Renoir moved into the New York apartment he and his wife had purchased. Jacques Hernot, a French lawyer who had worked with Renoir, phoned a warning to Henry Bubel, the New York lawyer who had helped Kiiko and Renoir set up the web of offshore companies. Hernot told Bubel that the political climate surrounding the matter in France was poisonous, that the local politicians were up in arms, and that the newspapers had stirred resentment about the destruction of the châteaux. Anyone with connections to the Renoirs was now in danger of being arrested, Hernot warned. France now regarded Renoir as a fugitive. In New York, Renoir sank into a deep gloom.

By early 1996, Hirohiko Yokoi had begun asking for Peter Bal to help the family with the Empire State Building case as well. Bal phoned Steven Rosen, the lawyer handling the American lawsuit, and explained that the family had appointed him to be its liaison with the lawyers. Bal said he wanted to come to New York to be briefed on the lawsuit. When Bal arrived, Rosen handed him a copy of the complaint. He told Bal to read it. Bal struggled through the document. He asked Rosen for the supporting documents, then returned to France to study them.

Bal had no illusions about his own capacity to follow the complex paper trail. "I must confess that I didn't understand the whole complaint nor the workings of the trust," Bal would later say. "I was rather clueless about what it was all about." The lawsuit itself proved puzzling to Bal. "I think I must have read it about ten times," he later said, "and still didn't understand most of it until Mr. Rosen had explained to me fully what it was all about."

Bal was desperate for an audience with Yokoi. Already, Kiiko's lawyers were raising questions about Bal's authority to act on behalf of her imprisoned father, accusing him of being a pawn of Kiiko's half brothers. Bal decided that before he committed to involving himself in the fight for the Empire State Building, he would need to discuss the matter with the old man, face-to-face.

But halfway around the world, fate had delivered a devastating blow to any hope that the swiftly intensifying family feud could be resolved through rational negotiation. When Mitsui Hishida, Yokoi's brother-in-law, arrived for his fortnightly prison visit in early February 1996, he was horrified to discover that Yokoi was unable to speak a word. Sometime in

January, the old man had suffered a stroke. Yokoi, like Harry Helmsley, was the glue that had held together an array of dangerously unstable forces. Now, like Harry, he was being robbed by old age of his ability to keep them in check.

On February 22, 1996, as chaos swirled in the Yokoi family, Bal touched down in Tokyo with a bundle of confusing documents. He showed Hirohiko Yokoi the papers he had gathered about the Hideki Yokoi Legal Issue Trust, which effectively owned all of the châteaux, along with a letter asserting that the trust's beneficiaries were the eight children of Hideki Yokoi. The men might as well have been examining documents in Sanskrit. "Nobody really knew what a trust was," Bal would later recall. "And I must admit that at that time, I didn't know anything of these workings myself."

Bal didn't know what to expect from Hideki Yokoi. Hishida accompanied Bal to the Hachioji Medical Prison. The effects of Yokoi's stroke were obvious to Bal. With effort, Yokoi was able to force out words. He gesticulated madly. But conversation was difficult. Nonetheless, Yokoi managed to indicate that he was not happy with how the case was going.

Hishida pointed out to Yokoi that his daughter was now residing in a French prison.

"Thank you very much. Thank you very much. Thank you very much," the old man told Bal in English, his fighting spirit evidently very much intact.

Peter Bal left Tokyo carrying a power of attorney to represent Nippon Sangyo in connection with all of the foreign properties, the Empire State Building included. But Yokoi's shaky mental state had added an unexpected layer of confusion to an already muddled situation.

French investigators did not appear to be prepared to take Bal's word at face value. Kiiko and her husband had raised too many questions about Bal's authority. In July 1996, Petit-

LeClair, the French magistrate in charge of the investigation, flew to Japan to see for herself what Yokoi had to say. Petit-LeClair met with Yokoi at Tokyo police headquarters, in the presence of the French police and two detectives from Interpol. Petit-LeClair submitted her questions to the Japanese police, who in turn put them to Yokoi. Speaking was still a struggle for the old man. But Yokoi insisted that he had never authorized Kiiko or Renoir to sell the châteaux. As for the particulars of what had happened in France, Yokoi seemed to have no idea. To many of Petit-LeClair's questions, Yokoi responded simply that he didn't know.

The magistrate must have wondered about the reliability of the ailing witness, for she requested a thorough medical evaluation from the Tokyo Police Hospital. A police doctor reported back that the 83-year-old man was suffering from hypertension, liver problems, cataracts, and hepatitis. More significantly, Yokoi had suffered a cerebral infarction, otherwise known as a stroke, which made it difficult for him to communicate. "He loses his words and presents a slight case of dementia," the report said. It's hard to imagine that such a report could have given the investigating magistrate rock-solid confidence in Yokoi's version of the truth or in his ability to be a convincing witness if the case were to go to trial.

By now, it appeared, Donald Trump had an inkling that the intensifying war within the Yokoi family posed a threat to his hold on the Empire State Building. Trump had no desire to be marooned on one side of an ugly family dispute, particularly the side of a couple who stood accused of criminal activities. Trump had every incentive to bring this family feud to an end—provided, of course, there was still a place for him at the Empire State Building. In a letter to Yokoi confidant Mitsui Hishida, Trump aide Abe Wallach reminded Hishida of Wallach's previous visit to Japan. "Since that meeting much has happened, and regrettably not for the good," Wallach wrote. Wallach offered to visit Tokyo again, "in order to try and resolve all outstanding issues and litigation. I feel that an honest and frank discussion, principal to principal, is a lot more beneficial than legal actions and courtroom sessions." It was vitally important, Wallach realized, not to be seen as a mercenary in the service of Kiiko and Renoir. "The Trump Organization does not in any way want to harm the Yokoi family nor benefit at their expense," Wallach wrote. "We believe that we are thoroughly conversant in real estate matters and are prepared to create added value at the Empire State Building and the properties in Japan." Wallach received no response to his plea.

In his years as a trial lawyer, Steven Rosen, Yokoi's lawyer in New York, had seen enough nasty family disputes to realize that the Yokoi row was shaping up as a marathon. Yokoi had shown no interest in settling the case, even though the jailing of his daughter seemed to present him with leverage. Rosen realized that as a solo practitioner, he was ill equipped to direct a lengthy legal campaign against large New York law firms capable of churning out copious amounts of paper— particularly given that his own client hadn't been especially prompt in paying its bills.

"Peter, I can't do this any more. It's going to ruin my practice," Rosen told Bal. "This is a full-time war if we go to court. I won't be able to fight it."

Fall of the House of Harry

11

For commercial empires as rife with internal tension as those of Harry Helmsley and Hideki Yokoi, it doesn't take much of a spark to start a conflagration. The decline of a patriarch certainly can do it. So can the rising power of an heir. In January 1994, months before Trump launched his attack on the Empire State Building, Leona Helmsley once again became a free woman. She had served 18 months in federal prison, one month in a Manhattan halfway house, and two months under a 9:00 P.M. curfew at her Central Park South penthouse. "I'm happy to be free and spend more time with my ailing husband," she said. Days later, there was a luncheon bash for her at the Helmsley Park Lane Hotel. At the head table, Harry sat next to his male nurses, motionless, staring straight ahead, Peter Malkin later recalled. Many people went over to him and spoke to him, but he didn't respond in any way. Harry didn't move or blink an eye.

Malkin had good reason to feel trepidation over Leona's return, as did the other longtime partners of Harry Helmsley.

Leona's prison stay had removed her completely from the day-to-day affairs of running the vast Helmsley portfolio. For several years, Malkin had happily called the shots at the Empire State Building. Now Leona, who had always taken a keen interest in the skyscraper, was back. Worse still, Harry seemed to have lost all capacity to rein her in. Irving Schneider, who had worked for Harry since 1946, visited Harry at his Arizona home three times in 1995. Schneider would later attest that Harry "is completely incapable of coherent conversation, does not recognize me, and appears to have no understanding of his immediate circumstances or surroundings."

For years, Harry had been the cement that bonded the sprawling array of partnerships that owned scores of aging New York apartment, office, and industrial buildings. Harry's strong-willed partners, themselves millionaires many times over, respected him too much to take issue with the decisions of his volatile wife. But as Harry slipped away, so did the relative calm that had characterized his partnerships for a half century. Harry, then 87, had no children to keep a steady hand on the tiller. Neither did Leona, then 74. Harry's partners, Irving Schneider, 75, and Alvin Schwartz, 83, seemed to have no succession plan in place other than to exercise an option to buy Helmsley-Spear, the brokerage firm that managed more than 100 buildings, at a bargain price when Harry passed away.

In May 1996, apparently convinced that Harry had lost all capacity to control his empire, Schneider and Schwartz shattered the tenuous peace in vitriolic fashion. They sued Leona and Harry in New York state court, accusing Leona of eviscerating Helmsley-Spear by arbitrarily firing employees, closing branch offices, and siphoning off $40 million of company money over the preceding five years. Leona had withheld $5.7 million in promised compensation from each of them, the lawsuit claimed, while paying herself and her husband more than $13 million. That March, Schneider and Schwartz said, she had attempted to shift management of 17 buildings from Helmsley-Spear to another brokerage company she controlled. Leona's actions, they claimed, amounted to "an egregious campaign to loot H/S and render H/S insolvent." Leona, they complained, was a "pretender devoid of authority." Leona, through her lawyer, vehemently denied the accusations.

Leona certainly didn't act like a woman devoid of authority. At the Empire State Building, her appearances were anticipated with considerable dread. One rainy morning around this time, director of operations Charles Guigno drew the assignment of greeting Leona in the lobby when she arrived for a meeting. The building's director of security offered to accompany him, Guigno recalls, to offer "moral support." When Leona arrived, she complained angrily that her driver had been unable to park her limousine in front of the Fifth Avenue entrance because a police car had taken her spot, recalled Guigno. The security director, an ex-cop, scurried out to ask the policeman to move. Leona glanced with disgust at the rain that had been tracked in on the lobby floor.

"Who's responsible for this?" she demanded of Guigno.

"What do you mean?" he said.

"This floor."

"That would be me," said Guigno.

"It's all wet," Leona told him. "I ought to box your ears as you stand in front of me right now."

"We have a lot of rain," Guigno stammered. "I'm doing the best I can."

"When I come down here, it better not be like this," she said, and walked away.

Peter Malkin, for his part, started bickering with Leona over a comparatively inconsequential matter. Leona had grown convinced that Malkin and Paul, Weiss, Rifkind, Wharton & Garrison, the topflight law firm in charge of rebuffing Donald Trump's grab for the Empire State Building lease, were keeping her in the dark about the litigation. So Leona stopped paying the law firm's bills. By November 1996, 10 months' worth of unpaid bills had piled up. As a crucial hearing approached, Paul, Weiss, which was owed hundreds of thousands of dollars, threatened to pull out of the case. Malkin, together with a Helmsley-Spear lawyer, scrambled to negotiate a payment plan. On the day the first payment was due, Malkin learned that Helmsley-Spear did not intend to pay. That afternoon, Malkin wrote a check from another account belonging to the Empire State Building partnership, an account controlled by his law firm.

Leona was irate. She demanded to be made a required cosigner of the account, which Malkin's law firm ordinarily used to pay rent and various other expenses of the Empire State Building. It was a power Harry Helmsley had never held. Through his lawyer, Edward Brodsky, Malkin refused. Such a change in policy required the approval of 80 percent of the partnership, Brodsky wrote in a brusque December 11 letter to Leona's lawyer. Harry Helmsley controlled 63.75 percent. That wasn't enough. "In light of the above there is no need to discuss the issues raised by having a non-lawyer as a signatory on the account," Brodsky concluded.

Leona "went absolutely ballistic," her lawyer, Charles Moerdler, later recalled. The following day, Moerdler shot off a threatening letter to Brodsky. "It would be a major stride in restoring amicable relations between Mr. Malkin and the Helmsleys if Mr. Malkin would relent on a matter that should not precipitate the confrontation that is beginning to loom large," Moerdler wrote. "While, as a litigator, I am, of course, prepared to ply my craft, I must repeat that it seems to me an unnecessary burden while other, more serious matters, threaten the partnership. That, however, is your client's call. The ball is in your court."

With that, communication between the two tycoons, whose families had been in partnership together for nearly 50 years, ground to a halt. Leona decided to stop speaking to Peter Malkin altogether.

On the morning of January 4, 1997, shortly after her show-down with Malkin, Leona Helmsley called a friend from Harry's bedside in an Arizona hospital. As her husband's health deteriorated, Leona had been at his side constantly. Harry could no longer walk and could hardly manage to smile. This morning, Leona was in tears. She told her friend that Harry's death from pneumonia was imminent. Several employees and bodyguards kept Leona company. Later that day, Harry Helmsley passed away at the age of 87. "My fairy tale is over," Leona said in a prepared statement. "I lived a magical life with Harry." Three days later, Harry was interred in the Helmsley family mausoleum in Woodlawn Cemetery in the Bronx. Leona ordered the lights on the Empire State Building dimmed for a week.

Harry Helmsley left behind a fortune then estimated at $1.7 billion. In a 1974 will, Helmsley had spread his fortune among Leona, her son, her grandchildren, siblings, nieces and nephews, and the New York University Medical Center. It is unclear how many times since then Harry had amended his will. The final will Harry left behind, which he signed on January 25, 1994, instructed that $25,000 be left to his longtime secretary. Everything else, the will stated, was to go to his second wife, Leona.

Peter Malkin's new partner at the Empire State Building, it appeared, was to be Leona Helmsley. She had inherited Harry's 63.75 percent interest in Empire State Building Company, which held the lucrative long-term lease on the property. Malkin, who controlled 23.75 percent of that partnership, phoned Leona at her Greenwich mansion after her husband's death. Leona's secretary answered the phone. Malkin asked to speak to Leona. In the background, he heard Leona say, "You tell him I'm not here."

In a pointed snub, Malkin was left off the long list of real estate luminaries invited to Harry's memorial service.

On the afternoon of February 22, 1997, seven weeks after Harry's death, Ali Abu Kamal, a sad-eyed 69-year-old Palestinian with a neatly trimmed mustache, decided to visit the Empire State Building. A respected English teacher in Gaza, Abu Kamal seemed somewhat confused about what to make of his life. He had arrived in New York on Christmas Eve, bounced between cheap hotels and the couches of acquaintances, retreated to Florida for a spell, then returned to New York. He had spent hours wandering about the city, spending as much as $40 a day on lottery tickets in a fruitless effort to strike it rich. When he returned that day from the Empire State Building, his host asked him how he had liked it. "What a wonderful world," proclaimed Abu Kamal. He smelled of booze and cigarettes.

The following afternoon, a Sunday, as the winter sun dipped toward the horizon, Abu Kamal again rode the elevator to the eighty-sixth floor and joined 90 or 100 happy sightseers on the outdoor deck. He asked one group to point out the Statue of Liberty to him, and they chatted briefly.

"I love Americans and I love America," he said.

"Where are you from?" someone asked.

"I'm from Egypt," he responded.

Abu Kamal walked to the southeast corner of the outdoor deck, drew out the .380-caliber black Beretta, a light but powerful Italian semiautomatic he had purchased in Florida, and began firing as he walked along the deck. He shot Christoffer Burmeister, a 27-year-old Danish guitarist from the local rock band Bushpilots, in the back of the head. He shot Matthew Gross, also 27, Burmeister's New Jersey bandmate, in the head. He shot Argentine businessman Mario Carmona in the back of the head, Swiss tourist Jakoe Schaad in the throat, and Hector Menendez of the Bronx in the right thigh. He shot

French tourists Virginie and Patrick Demange, both of them in the buttocks. Then Abu Kamal pressed the pistol to his temple and pulled the trigger. He slumped to the deck, face up, a pool of blood forming around his gray striped suit and black wool overcoat. His dentures moved in and out as he wheezed, unconscious.

It all happened so fast that many tourists at first confused the shots with popping firecrackers. But the bloodied bodies set off a panicked stampede for safety. On the deck, the building's security guards found the three men shot in the head bleeding profusely. Guards and bystanders grabbed T-shirts from the souvenir stand and attempted to treat the wounded. Within five minutes, police officers were pouring onto the eighty-sixth floor. A witness pointed out the gunman to police officer Jeffrey Stella. Stella noticed that Abu Kamal was still breathing. He rolled Abu Kamal over, looking for a weapon. There was nothing underneath him. Looking around, Stella noticed the Beretta sitting atop a yellow bag. He didn't touch it.

The Danish guitarist was dead. His bandmate was rushed to the hospital in a coma. Abu Kamal was brought to Bellevue Hospital in the company of a police officer. The doctor who treated him discovered a kitchen knife concealed in his clothing, along with several rounds of live ammunition. The doctor also found a two-page handwritten letter stuffed into a pouch that hung around Abu Kamal's neck. Seven hours after he opened fire, Abu Kamal died.

Police quickly concluded that Abu Kamal was not a trained terrorist but a confused man who was angry at the world and looking for a way to settle his grievances in a final blaze of gunfire. Abu Kamal's suicide tract, which he titled "Charter of Honour," raged against four groups of "bitter enemies" who "must be annihilated and exterminated"—a group of students who attacked him in 1993 for refusing to help them cheat in a final exam; another group of students who beat and robbed his son; an Egyptian police officer who beat him; and finally, the nations that oppressed the Palestinians. The Empire State Building, in Abu Kamal's hazy logic, loomed as a symbol of American Zionism. "The Zionists are the paw that carried out their savage aggression," he wrote. "My restless aspiration is to murder as many of them as possible, and I have decided to strike at their own den in New York, and at the very Empire State Building in particular." Police found no evidence to support Abu Kamal's earlier complaints to his family that he had been cheated out of as much as $300,000 of savings by men whom he never identified.

Abu Kamal's murderous rampage seemed to further roil the combatants feuding over management of the Empire State Building. To tenant agitator Suzy Smith, the shooting proved what she had been sounding off about for more than two years—that security was deficient. Jacques Catafago, her tenant association's lawyer, issued a press release bemoaning the security and lack of screening of visitors to the building. He requested an emergency meeting with Donald Trump about Helmsley-Spear's shortcomings.

Trump was also swift to blame the building's managers. Trump's lawyer reminded reporters that Trump had been warning of security lapses for years. A Helmsley-Spear executive snapped back: "Such an inappropriate comment like this we did not expect even from Donald Trump during this tragic time." Helmsley-Spear executive John Trainor would later add: "Who's to prevent some wacko with a concealed automatic weapon from walking into Grand Central Station at the busiest time of day and killing hundreds of people." Two days after the shooting, Trump filed a motion to vacate the state court judge's temporary halt to his lease-breaking effort.

Malkin scrambled to line up security experts to attest under oath that security at the Empire State Building was not lax. Within 24 hours of the shooting, metal detectors had been installed in the second-floor staging area for visits to the observation deck. Armed security guards were posted at the metal detectors and on the eighty-sixth floor. Security personnel began inspecting all bags and packages.

Peter Malkin would later claim that Helmsley-Spear ignored his repeated requests for information on the disaster and Helmsley-Spear's response to it, a charge that the company denied. In any case, the catastrophe proved but a momentary distraction in the intensifying clash of demands and counter-demands that were now zinging back and forth between Leona and Malkin. After Malkin refused to give Leona control over the Empire State Building partnership's bank account, Leona ordered Helmsley-Spear to stop sending money to the account, Malkin said. A lawyer for Leona demanded that Malkin divulge a list of other investors who were part of the 23.75 percent of the partnership that Malkin controlled. Three days after the shooting, Leona's lawyer faxed a letter to Malkin's law firm announcing her intention to replace Wien & Malkin with her own lawyer's firm on a pending challenge to the Empire State Building's tax assessment.

Malkin had ample incentive to protect his law firm's involvement in running the building. Between 1985 and early 1997, his firm's compensation from the two Empire State Building partnerships had exceeded $14 million. Malkin refused to consent to the change of law firms. In a letter to Leona's lawyer, Malkin's lawyer Brodsky noted that the original partnership agreement had clearly stipulated that upon the death of both Helmsley and Wien, all partnership decisions required the approval of at least 80 percent of the partnership interests. Harry's estate did not have 80 percent. "Your firm may not be substituted as counsel of record," Brodsky wrote. Malkin refused to turn over the files on the tax case.

To Leona's mind, Malkin still was not coming clean about the 23.75 percent of the Empire State Building partnership he claimed to control. So on March 13, 1997, she sued Malkin in New York State Supreme Court, demanding proof of Malkin's interest in the Empire State Building partnership and in more than a dozen other partnerships. She questioned the nature of his authority to act as an agent for other investors. Malkin had always been careful never to say that he or his family "owned" 23.75 percent of the partnership, and for good reason. Years earlier, his father-in-law Lawrence Wien had sold much of that stake to other investors under complex agreements that left Wien with voting control of the positions as well as a share of the profits. Wien's heirs had inherited his diminished stake. Leona's suit compelled Malkin to acknowledge that he and his family were "beneficial" owners of—meaning that they received all economic benefits from—only about 5 percent of the Empire State Building partnership.

The 63.75 percent stake owned outright by Harry's estate dwarfed Malkin's holdings. Yet Malkin held voting rights over just enough of the partnership to block Leona from doing almost anything without his approval. The two partners needed each other, and they weren't even speaking. Malkin, in fact, had begun doing his level best to thwart Leona from even taking charge of the stake Harry had bequeathed her. In an April 24 sworn statement, Malkin, exhibiting his powers for hairsplitting, declared that Leona was not even his partner in the Empire State Building partnership. According to the records of the surrogate court, Malkin noted, Harry's estate was his partner.

Leona could not have been pleased. In an open letter dated May 1, she exercised her power as executrix of her husband's estate to officially assign to herself Harry's majority stake. She presented Malkin with an amended business certificate for the partnership, which set forth her name as partner. Malkin flatly refused to recognize the new certificate.

It was going on five months since the warring tycoons had last spoken to one another. That month, they found themselves seated at the same table at a meeting about another building with which they both were involved. Leona averted her eyes from Malkin. When the meeting broke, Malkin approached his prickly partner.

"Lee, this doesn't make sense," he said. "If we can't get along, we should get an amicable divorce and get this over with."

"How dare you speak to me!" Leona snapped back.

Several weeks later, Leona electrified the New York real estate community by announcing her intention to sell most or perhaps all of the holdings she had inherited from Harry. Leona owned or had an interest in some three dozen office, warehouse, and showroom buildings and two dozen apartment buildings in New York, others in Newark and Chicago, and hotels scattered from New York to Florida. Unlike the property empires assembled by the Dursts, Rudins, Fishers, Roses, Tishmans, and a handful of other New York real estate families who had clawed their way to the top, the Helmsley family empire, it now appeared, was to dissipate after a single generation. Leona's timing was opportune. By 1997, the Manhattan commercial property market was booming again, the bust of early 1990s now but an unpleasant and increasingly distant memory. Leona's advisers valued the vast portfolio at close to $5 billion. Neither she nor her advisers made any mention of her intentions with respect to the Empire State Building, still the most famous part of her late husband's legacy.

Peter Malkin, however, did not treat the announcement as an opening for détente in the intensifying war of wills. To Leona's advisers, it appeared that the contrary was true, that Malkin viewed the sales effort as an opportunity to gain further leverage in his fight. Two days after Leona's announcement, Malkin sued Leona and Helmsley-Spear in New York state court. He accused Leona and Helmsley-Spear of "numerous and repeated breaches of fiduciary duty," mismanagement and waste, and breaches of contract in connection with the operation and management of the Empire State Building and a dozen other buildings with a market value of over $1 billion. His lawsuit accused Leona of "actively and arbitrarily" meddling in the management of the Empire State Building and other partnerships, of acting without proper approval from her partners, and of running down the company charged with managing the buildings. Leona had fired the director of the Empire State Building observatory without even telling Malkin, the lawsuit complained, and had withheld money intended for the bank account managed by Malkin's law firm. Leona's "history of fraud and abuse in dealing with properties over which she has exercised control," the lawsuit alleged, put the partnership funds at risk. Malkin also heaped criticism on Irving Schneider, accusing him of mismanaging a number of aging garment center buildings. "Helmsley-Spear's growing level of incompetence and disarray and its threat to the investment entities and the properties that they control result in large part from the arbitrary, irrational, and illegal acts of Leona M. Helmsley," the lawsuit said. "Leona Helmsley and Helmsley-Spear are spinning out of control and virtually all communication from Helmsley-Spear to Wien & Malkin in its capacity as Supervisor has ceased."

Through his lawsuit, Malkin sought to clip Leona's wings in the severest manner imaginable. He asked the court to terminate Helmsley-Spear as managing and leasing agent for the Empire State Building and the other properties and to bar Leona from participating in the management of, or even voting her ownership stakes in, any of the buildings.

In a sworn statement accompanying the suit, Malkin poured fuel on the fire, lambasting his partner for her check-

ered past. "If nothing else, Leona Helmsley's history of corruption, fraud and abuse indicates that she cannot be trusted
to handle other people's money," Malkin said. "Over the past
two decades, Leona Helmsley has demonstrated that she does
not hesitate to perpetrate fraud when it suits her selfish purpose and that she has no right to be a fiduciary for others."

Perhaps most galling to Leona, however, were the aspersions Malkin cast, in a sworn statement that July, on her very
right to inherit her husband's estate. Harry had signed his
last will in 1994, five years after he had been declared incompetent to stand trial in the tax evasion case that sent his wife
to prison. "[T]he legitimacy of the very will under which
Leona Helmsley purports to have inherited the partnership
interests involved here is of doubtful validity," Malkin asserted.
The 1994 document, he said, was signed by Harry "long after
he was universally acknowledged by those who knew him to
have no reasoning ability." The ramifications of Malkin's point
were obvious. "If the will was not validly executed," Malkin
later explained, "it would mean that the designation of Leona
as a successor [to Harry's interests] was not valid. It would be
consistent with a course of conduct that justifies my concern
that Mrs. Helmsley should not be a voting partner."

Leona had long ago given up publicly responding to
attacks and criticism. She felt the press had never treated her
fairly, explained her lawyer, Gerald Fields. On Leona's behalf,
Fields blustered that Malkin had trumped up charges in
order to get "what he can't get through the partnership
agreements. Now that Mrs. Helmsley has taken over Mr.
Helmsley's interests and wants to assert some leadership,
Malkin doesn't like it. He wants to continue running it. She
ain't going to let him." Fields was contemptuous of Malkin's
attempt to raise doubts about Harry's will. "He's not the surrogate of New York County," Fields fumed. "He has no standing. It's nothing but a bunch of balderdash and smoke, and
she found it really offensive."

Charles Moerdler, who was also representing Leona, characterized Malkin's suit in a sworn statement as retaliation for Leona's "refusal to bow to Mr. Malkin's improper attempts to usurp control and to manipulate for his own benefit the partnerships and the 11 properties." It appeared, said Moerdler, that Malkin was out to prevent Leona from obtaining "full value" for the properties she wished to sell. (A property mired in litigation is usually less attractive to buyers.) Malkin's refusal to sign the amended business certificate that would make Leona his new partner at the Empire State Building "is nothing more than a display of petulance and spite," Moerdler said.

Moerdler professed to be unconvinced by Malkin's stated desire to award to a third party the contracts to manage the disputed buildings. Moerdler asserted that Malkin's suit was "a naked attempt, motivated by greed," to wrest the contracts from Helmsley-Spear and award them to WM Management, a real estate company controlled by Malkin and his son. Irving Schneider, who was preparing to buy Helmsley-Spear from Leona, said the same in his own sworn statement and dismissed Malkin's criticism of him and his company as "replete with half truths, false innuendoes, and conclusory unsupportable charges."

The supreme irony of Malkin's attack on Helmsley-Spear, of course, was that he was skating dangerously close to the argument advanced by Donald Trump: that the Empire State Building was being run in a disgraceful manner. Indeed, Leona's lawyer was quick to point out that not so long ago, in the face of Trump's attack, Malkin had mounted a spirited defense of Helmsley-Spear's management of the building.

On September 2, 1997, New York state court judge Ira Gammerman granted Leona Helmsley's request to send the case to an arbitration panel, ruling that it was required by the partnership agreements. "What is happening in this case is like a chess game, and everybody is trying to obtain a slight advantage," the judge observed from the bench. "My suggestion is that everybody just sit tight and go through arbitration, and unless you resolve your differences yourselves, all these disputes will be resolved within the framework of the arbitration."

Malkin had been hoping for a quick courtroom victory. But there was a certain advantage to fighting it out in the privacy of a secret arbitration proceeding. Malkin could heap criticism on Helmsley without handing ammunition to Donald Trump for his crusade to wrest control of the building from Leona and him.

Three weeks later, Leona settled her dispute with Irving Schneider, who had attacked her so viciously 16 months earlier. She sold Helmsley-Spear, the management company that ran the Empire State Building and once dominated the city, to Schneider and Alvin Schwartz, and the two men dropped their suit against her. That freed Leona's lawyers to concentrate on thwarting Peter Malkin, whose attack on her had cast a cloud over her efforts to turn her late husband's empire into hundreds of millions of dollars in cash.

12

Sibling Rivalry

s it ever possible to reconstruct the unvarnished truth? In his spellbinding 1950 film, *Rashomon,* Japanese director Akira Kurosawa told a single story four times, through the eyes of his four main characters. Each version left out events that cast aspersions on the teller. People fighting for their honor sometimes spin self-serving versions of reality. Not surprisingly, in the months after Kiiko Nakahara was detained in France, she and her husband offered an altogether different take on the Empire State Building dispute. Their explanation for the property transfers in New York and France—and for the anger they'd sparked in Japan—was poles apart from Yokoi's version.

"Before going to jail, in his last few weeks at the hospital, [Yokoi] told Kiiko to protect the European properties," Renoir said in a sworn statement. "He made it very clear that he wanted it in a separate structure because he was afraid that the creditors would seize it." Kiiko also claimed that she was merely following orders from her father. She suggested that

Yokoi himself had added the name of Sato to the power of attorney that French authorities suspected of being a forgery, as he often did to company documents. She said her father had instructed her to transfer ownership of Oheka Castle, the rundown mansion outside New York, to protect it from his lenders.

With respect to the Empire State Building—the one piece of the sprawling overseas portfolio that was undeniably of great value—Kiiko offered an explanation that would test the limits of what Americans were prepared to believe about free-spending Japanese during the bubble era. Kiiko said her father had intended to give her the skyscraper as a gift. "My husband and I have always managed the assets of the NS Trust [the holding company for the Empire State Building], sub-ject to my commitment to my father to make the annual income available to him, on demand, as I have done in previ-ous years, prior to his incarceration," Kiiko said in a sworn statement in 1995. "My father told me in 1991 that, following his death, the assets of the trust would be mine to do with as I wished, and that before he died, he expected only the right to the income."

But why, French investigators wondered, had Kiiko trans-ferred properties in France after Yokoi's company filed suit against her in New York State? Kiiko had an answer, although she had precious little hard evidence to support it. Kiiko saw the lawsuit as the work of her half brothers, who during jail-house visits with her father, had turned Yokoi against her. "I didn't think [Yokoi] did it," said Kiiko of the lawsuit. How could anyone have manipulated her famously bullheaded father? "Because he was in prison," Kiiko offered. "Your imag-ination can go to hell."

"This is not about some corporate employee who has been caught with his hand in the till," Kiiko maintained in her sworn statement. "Rather, it is one part of a multi-faceted fam-ily feud being carried on in extraordinary circumstances by a highly dysfunctional family solely because of a drastic change in the financial condition of my father's empire and his loss of the iron grip with which he once dominated everyone in fear. . . . As a result of reverses in the Tokyo real estate market and the Japanese stock market, several of my half-siblings, who had previously been made quite comfortable by my father, now find themselves unable to meet their financial obligations. They look to me, and to the assets I have acquired in the United Kingdom and the United States during the past twelve years, as their only salvation."

Kiiko's story was certainly plausible. Yet Kiiko and her husband faced a daunting problem: Yokoi had denied much of it, both indirectly, through his company's lawsuit, and directly, to his lawyers and to a reporter for *The Wall Street Journal*. And there were no documents to support Kiiko's claim that Yokoi intended the Empire State Building as a gift to her. That, of course, did not prove Yokoi hadn't made the gift. During Yokoi's controversial career, he had demonstrated himself capable of treachery. Was it possible that Yokoi was lying? The answer seemed to rest in long-ago conversations between Yokoi and his daughter, conversations to which there were no other witnesses. It would be up to the French investigators and American lawyers to determine who was telling the truth.

The significance of Yokoi's stroke, impaired speech, and possibly addled mind would make the search for truth an even more dubious exercise. Pascal Narboni, one of the Yokoi's French lawyers, termed Yokoi's stroke "providential" to his daughter, for it rendered Yokoi unable to tell his story cogently. Kiiko, for her part, had every incentive to make it appear that her father had lost his mind altogether. In her 1995 statement, Kiiko claimed that as early as 1994 she had observed "very significant declines in both his physical and mental abilities. Correspondence from him since that time confirms my view that he has lost his ability to think rationally and for himself."

Renoir offered an even more convoluted theory about the motive for the lawsuit. A "clan" within the Yokoi family headed by his elderly bookkeeper, Ohashi, was out to get Kiiko, Renoir claimed. "We did not perceive that that paper company, Nippon Sangyo K.K., action in the United States had anything to do with what Hideki Yokoi really wanted to do," Renoir said when questioned under oath. "But it had to do with some half siblings and some adopted siblings and a very conniving former girlfriend and bookkeeper, Ohashi, essentially trying to take over what was left of Hideki Yokoi's wealth. So this is the reason we didn't pay attention to the '94 document filed by Nippon Sangyo. . . . antagonism towards Kiiko was also very strong, based on jealousy that Kiiko was able to bring people like the Trump organization and investment bankers to Japan and his two sons, basically, were only good at going out drinking and driving expensive cars. . . . Hideki Yokoi knew exactly what Kiiko Nakahara had done in relation to the Empire State Building, that it had been ascertained by him that the offspring and the other ones should never know about that. He had kept these undertakings completely secret from them for years after they had taken place."

American lawyers and French investigators faced no small challenge in sorting through the complex property transactions and competing claims about whether Yokoi had authorized Kiiko and Renoir to do what they had done. According to a transcript of questioning by French police in 1996, Bordenave, one of the French lawyers hired by Renoir remarked: "Up to this day, I am unable to say whether Mr. Renoir is lying or saying the truth."

On January 3, 1997, nearly a year after she was locked up in the women's prison at Versailles, Kiiko was released on bail. French authorities kept her passport and forbade her to even speak to her husband or father. Kiiko's 76-year-old mother,

Yokoi's former mistress, was waiting for her in a Paris hotel. They moved to a small home on a quiet island in the Seine River outside Paris. Their yard, dotted with willow and cherry trees, extended to the river's edge, where her German Shepherd could romp while Kiiko watched boats glide by. It seemed a good place to try to recover from her frightening ordeal. She had lost more than 20 pounds. She vowed to stay away from the châteaux and to avoid controversy.

Yet controversy continued to dog her. When châteaux are not maintained, they go downhill fast. They get moldy and mildewy inside. Untended gardens can become a nightmare in a single season. "These things are regarded, rightly or wrongly, as part of the national patrimony," explained broker Patricia Hawkes, who became one of Kiiko's staunchest defenders against press attacks. "If you aren't taking care of them, you are going to be criticized. It was daft to let them deteriorate. She was Japanese, so it made a better story." The newspapers, said Hawkes, "built her up into an absolute demon."

One month after Kiiko's release, a fire ripped through the château de Sully at Rosny. One radio station reported that Kiiko had been involved in a "decidedly murky/dismal affair," that furniture, paintings, and tapestry "were literally pillaged and resold," and that revenge was a motive for the fire. Another station referred to Kiiko on air as "the young Japanese woman who is at the source of the attempted pillage," and later spoke of "Japanese swindlers whose leader was incarcerated at Versailles." Although Renoir had already counted hundreds of negative articles in the French press about himself and his wife, he and Kiiko decided that the radio reports had gone too far. They sued the two radio stations for libel. (Both stations were eventually ordered to pay damages.)

Kiiko and Renoir also went on the offensive against their perceived tormentors within the family. On March 21, 1997, they brought suit in federal district court in Manhattan against Peter Bal, the artist-cum-litigation czar whom they blamed for bringing on their troubles in France. In their lawsuit, they accused Bal of attempting to defraud them of their property rights to the Empire State Building and numerous other properties and of repeatedly accusing them, falsely, of theft and fraud. "As a result of defendant Bal's acts of racketeering, plaintiff Nakahara was improperly held in jail, [and] plaintiff Renoir has been falsely branded as a fugitive, a drug dealer, and a money launderer," the suit said, making reference to a magazine article that said Renoir was rumored to be an intermediary between the *yakuza* and the Cali drug cartel. Kiiko and Renoir demanded $150 million in damages from Bal.

The warnings Bal had received from his lawyer friends had been on target. Bal was now deeply enmeshed in a potentially costly battle. One night that spring, Bal attended an art-world party in the home of New York lawyer Raymond Hannigan. The two men began chatting. When Hannigan mentioned that he was a real estate lawyer, Bal let on that he was in the market for one. Hannigan asked why. Bal checked to see if anyone else was listening. "The Empire State Building," he said.

Hannigan listened raptly to Bal's tale about the Yokoi family dispute. Late that night, Hannigan logged onto the Internet and pulled up newspaper articles about the turmoil in New York and France. He was astonished.

Bal hired Hannigan's firm, Herrick, Feinstein, and Hannigan succeeded in getting the suit brought by Renoir and Kiiko dismissed. Bal also asked the firm to take over the Empire State Building lawsuit from Steven Rosen, the overwhelmed solo practitioner. By mid-1997, Hannigan and his partner, Stephen Rathkopf, were preparing for a showdown.

Ever since Hideki Yokoi suffered his stroke, his brother-in-law Mitsuo Hishida had been lobbying Japanese authorities to release Yokoi from prison for health reasons. In the middle of 1997, at the age of 83, Yokoi hobbled out of Hachioji Medical

Prison two and a half years after entering it, a free man. He promptly dyed his white hair black again. His old friend Tsuneji Sato arranged to see him.

"How are you?" Sato inquired upon seeing his friend.

"Well, I'm so-so," replied Yokoi. "I had a tough time there."

To Sato, himself an old man, Yokoi did not seem the least bit senile. Yokoi boasted to Sato that a fellow prisoner had convinced him to try to get out early by feigning dementia, Sato later recalled. Sato had no way of knowing whether Yokoi was telling the truth. But Sato left his reunion believing that Yokoi had tricked prison officials into letting him out early.

Whatever the truth, it was clear that Yokoi was not the man he once was. The stroke appeared to have permanently afflicted his speech. He began using an aide to interpret his broken sentences and emphatic gestures. To Hannigan, Yokoi's new lawyer in New York, it was now clear that Kiiko and Renoir were intent on using Yokoi's faltering health to bolster their claim that the old man was being manipulated by his sons. The time was fast approaching when lawyers for Renoir and Kiiko would confront Yokoi, would pepper the old man with questions, in a deposition under oath. How would Yokoi stand up under the grilling of crafty American lawyers? Hannigan hadn't a clue.

Hannigan resisted bringing Yokoi to New York for the confrontation, arguing that his client was too frail. Hannigan lost that fight. In August 1997, Yokoi, his two sons, his daughter Chizuko, his brother-in-law Hishida, and assorted employees and aides touched down at New York's John F. Kennedy airport. It was Yokoi's first-ever trip to the United States and, by most accounts, his first journey outside of Japan since he marched through China with the Imperial Army. One of the daughters Yokoi had never officially recognized, Yuriko, had moved to New York years earlier. She met her father at the airport. To Yuriko, her father's mind seemed sharp.

"Kiiko is stupid," Yokoi said to Yuriko about the family troubles.

"You are very angry at her," Yuriko told her father. "But you don't want to give up on her."

From the stretch limousine ferrying Yokoi into the city, Yokoi had his first clear view of Manhattan's famed skyline. His Japanese driver pointed out the Empire State Building. Yokoi gazed at the skyscraper, which seemed to rise like a rocket out of the urban panorama. Eager to pass on some local lore to his strange foreign charge, Henry Olsen, the gun-toting bodyguard hired to protect Yokoi, instructed the driver to explain that the building was lit at night with different colors, depending on the occasion. "I think he knows," the driver told Olsen. "He owns the building."

When Hannigan arrived that evening at the Kitano Hotel on Park Avenue to meet his client for the first time, he found Yokoi dressed dapperly in a suit and bow tie, seated on a couch, surrounded by newspaper and magazine articles about the case. Yokoi rose, a huge smile on his face, and bowed. He playfully punched his fist in the air. Hannigan got the impression that Yokoi was greeting his warrior. Everyone in Yokoi's entourage, Hannigan noticed, addressed Yokoi as "owner." Hannigan tried to prepare his client for his deposition. Yokoi seemed confident about the looming confrontation.

Yokoi's unusual entourage drew double takes when it paraded into the law firm of Patterson, Belknap, Webb & Tyler and settled into an empty conference room. Yokoi had insisted on bringing along his two bodyguards. He said he was worried about Renoir. Out the window Yokoi could see the Empire State Building soaring into the sky. A smile spread over his face. He pointed to the skyscraper, said hesitantly, "Empire," then in Japanese, "owner." He posed at the window with his lawyer for a snapshot. The time had come for the hobbled old man to fight for his prize.

Waiting across the hall for Yokoi were five cocksure lawyers representing Kiiko, Renoir, and Trump, a pair of translators, one for each side, and Renoir himself. It could be said that Yokoi was about to get his first true taste of America. Without question, a gaggle of high-priced New York trial lawyers was about to be confronted with a uniquely vexing adversary.

No sooner had his daughter's lawyers begun questioning Yokoi than it became obvious that something was very wrong. Yokoi gave his name and birthplace without much trouble. Then he began to stumble.

"Are you taking any medicine presently?" asked John Markham, the criminal lawyer hired by Renoir and Kiiko.

"I'm taking two, six," Yokoi replied through his translator.

"What are you taking?" continued Markham.

"Yes, three times a day. Morning, noon, and evening," said Yokoi.

"What kind of medicine?" pressed the lawyer, as Yokoi's own lawyers began to shift uncomfortably in their seats, glaring at Markham.

"For the heart, eyes, and to prevent numbness."

"Do you know the names of any of the medicines you are taking?" continued Markham, bearing down on the old man.

"I don't know well," replied Yokoi hesitantly, his brow furrowing. "The doctor. The doctor. The doctor."

Finally, Hannigan cut in, challenging Markham's line of questioning. Yokoi was clearly confused, and his garbled answers sparked heated disagreements among the rival translators. Kiiko's lawyers, Hannigan figured, were out to trip up the old man, to prove that he quite literally couldn't think straight.

"Do you know why you are here?" asked Markham, in the patronizing tone one might reserve for a senile great aunt.

"Yes," said Yokoi.

"Why are you here?"

"I came to America once in 1984," replied Yokoi wistfully, and apparently erroneously.

"How do you feel physically?" Markham continued.

"My ears are fine," said the old man.

And so it went, the criminal lawyer playing amateur neurologist, peppering the old man with seemingly innocuous questions, probing him for mental incapacity. Yokoi's two lawyers were growing more nervous by the minute.

Markham placed in front of Yokoi a photograph of Donald Trump, Trump's second wife, Marla Maples, and another man, taken during Trump's trip to Tokyo four years earlier.

"Do you recognize the three people in the photograph?" Markham inquired.

"Yes, I know. Okay," said Yokoi.

"Who are they?"

"The name, the name. I forgot the name," Yokoi struggled.

"Do you see a white box in the hand of the female in the photograph?"

"I can see it."

"Do you remember what is inside that box?"

To Hannigan, it seemed as though Markham was trying to prove that Yokoi's memory was shot full of holes. Was it reasonable to expect Yokoi to remember that he had given Marla a string of pearls? Was it even relevant to the case?

Hannigan butted in. "I think the record should reflect Mr. Yokoi just gestured around his neck with his hand," Hannigan offered.

"Chizuko," said Yokoi.

"Chizuko or Kiiko?" asked Markham. "Why doesn't he write down the name he's trying to say on Exhibit 3."

"Nekureso," said Yokoi.

"Again, I'd like the record to reflect Mr. Yokoi's gesturing around his neck," offered Hannigan.

"Kiiko is—wants to give it as a present on her own," recalled Yokoi.

Finally, Hannigan's partner, Stephen Rathkopf, could take it no longer. He rose to his feet.

"Mr. Markham, we're going to object and have a standing objection to every question that isn't in the form of a question that can be answered yes or no. Mr. Yokoi is unable to speak," said Rathkopf, his voice rising in calculated outrage. "I view it as an abusive process to continue to ask questions of a person that is unable to verbalize. You don't need two of us to sit here and watch you go through a series of questions that charitably could be described as abusive. And accordingly, there is no need for me to sit here. As Joseph Wall said to Senator McCarthy, 'Have you no shame?'

"If you choose to continue this way, around day six maybe you will wake up to the fact that this isn't gamesmanship. It's supposed to be a search for truth." With that, Rathkopf walked out.

But Markham wasn't about to change tack, and the confusion got worse. Yokoi appeared baffled, frustrated by his inability to explain himself. He struggled to compensate with frenetic gestures, stabbing his fingers toward Renoir, clapping his hands together, crossing his wrists, and shouting the same raspy phrases over and over. Some questions prompted long silences and blank looks, others sparked responses that, when translated, were non sequiturs. The lawyers and translators bickered constantly. As a search for the truth, the session was a farce.

The following day, Kiiko's lawyers continued trying to prove Yokoi the fool and to establish that his daughter and her husband had done nothing that Yokoi hadn't given them permission to do. This time Yokoi erupted in anger, proving, if nothing else, that his infirmities had not robbed him of the menace for which he was well known in Tokyo.

Yokoi pointed his bony finger across the table at his son-in-law, and hissed, "That guy."

"Are you pointing at Mr. Renoir?" asked Markham.

"Together. They're together," continued Yokoi. "Devils."

"He is a devil?" repeated Markham, in mock horror, pointing to Renoir.

"It's a terrible thing," replied Yokoi. "Until today."

Minutes later, a young Japanese man entered the room, accompanied by an older American man. Hannigan asked Markham who they were. Markham identified the young man as Kiiko's son, Sotn, and the older man as the New Jersey investment adviser who employed him. Hannigan asked them to leave the room.

Markham turned to Yokoi. "Mr. Yokoi, do you recognize—"

Hannigan jumped in to protest.

"No," Markham shot back. "I want to know if he recognizes his grandson."

"What is this?" demanded Hannigan. "You've got to be kidding me." He instructed Yokoi not to answer.

"There's a real question about whether this man can appreciate what's going on, and recognition of people," said Markham.

"I'd prefer to have less histrionics and theatrics, and that's clearly what this is," said Hannigan. "Unless you want to mark his grandson as an exhibit."

"I don't think we need to do that," said Markham.

Kiiko's son left the room, and Markham reluctantly turned to quizzing Yokoi about the French properties, handing the old man a list of them.

"He sold them all," Yokoi snapped. "He sold them all. He did." Yokoi stabbed his finger once again toward Renoir.

"Who owns the French châteaux today?" continued Markham.

"All of them, everyone is a devil," rasped Yokoi. "Of his own will. On his own." Again, he pointed to Renoir.

Yokoi was asserting a strange sort of command over the proceedings. He warded off pointed questions with unresponsive ravings, yet left little doubt that he was angry at what he believed his daughter and her husband had done.

That afternoon, as Markham quizzed Yokoi about his stroke, the old man erupted once again.

"I can tell right away who's bad," he blurted. "Can tell right away bad guys. Can tell right away."

Hannigan, in fact, was not displeased by his client's outbursts. While they may not have been especially cogent, they certainly demonstrated that Yokoi felt as though Kiiko and Renoir had taken his prized properties from him. Renoir, sitting a few feet away from Yokoi, weathered his father-in-law's attacks in silence. Renoir, ever suspicious, was convinced that the aide to Yokoi who was interpreting his mumbles and gestures had been briefed to answer for Yokoi, and that Hannigan was signaling his client whether to answer yes or no, a charge that Hannigan later denied, calling it a figment of Renoir's imagination. "It was part of the scam," Renoir maintained. "Everything he was doing was prompted. Everything was staged."

Through the tumultuous first two days of Yokoi's deposition, Hannigan noticed Donald Trump's lawyers conferring constantly with Renoir's lawyers. Until then, it had seemed to Hannigan that Trump had displayed a sort of indifferent neutrality in the feud, claiming to want nothing more than to be told whom his real partner was. Now, to Hannigan, it looked as though Trump, Kiiko, and Renoir had decided to gang up on Yokoi.

On the third and final day of Yokoi's deposition, Donald Trump's lawyer took a crack at Yokoi, to similar effect.

"Do you love your daughter?" the lawyer asked the now exhausted tycoon.

"I hate her. She did bad things."

"When did you start hating her?"

"Everything," replied Yokoi. "Everything. She tricked me of everything."

"When did you find that out?"

"Bought. What I bought. Purchase. Tricked everything purchased."

A bit later, Yokoi's free association flowered again. "My daughter is lost. Grandson. Daughter. Because she's my daughter. To my grandson, now, these idiots. This idiotic way of doing things. Destroy the company." He squeezed his eyes shut. "Everything. America."

Later that evening, Yokoi and his lawyers celebrated his spirited performance over dinner, with Yokoi himself pouring the sake. "We toasted him as a fighter," Hannigan later recalled. "He loved it. He felt he had really kicked some butt."

Yokoi's withering denunciations could not have been pleasant for Kiiko, who viewed a videotape of her father's deposition in France. It is traumatic enough being attacked by one's father. But Yokoi's statements, it must have seemed, promised to make it more difficult for Kiiko to contend she was merely following her father's instructions.

Two months later, Yokoi's New York lawyer flew to Paris to question Kiiko, who was still barred by French authorities from leaving the country. Kiiko stuck to her story. She had spent a year in prison, she said, "because of the lies made by the person who is sitting there, Peter Bal, these lies made to my father and the French judge."

"Is your father pleased that you were put in jail?" Hannigan asked her.

"Of course he's not pleased," Kiiko responded. "He's very sad."

"Did you watch Mr. Yokoi's deposition on videotape?" Hannigan asked.

"Yes."

"Was he upset that you were put in jail, on that videotape?"

"That portion was not part of that video," she said, "but I could feel that he was very sad that I was imprisoned."

"Did he say that he was sad that you were imprisoned, on that videotape?"

"As you know, he has trouble speaking," Kiiko replied. "So he did not say that. But I could see through the video that he was sad."

Moments later, Hannigan asked her if she had noticed on the videotape that her father claimed she had betrayed him.

"Well, I don't know," said Kiiko.

"Did you see Mr. Yokoi say that he hates you?" pressed Hannigan.

"I am sorry. That was a mistake made by the translator," Kiiko maintained. "He didn't say he hates me."

"What did he say?"

"He said, quote, I am perplexed, unquote. That was because he has a grandchild which is my child. I felt pity for him because he was lied to by some people, by surrounding people."

"Would you say that he is very unhappy with what you did?"

"Of course, it is a happy thing to say truth instead of to lie," she said.

Hannigan asked Kiiko bluntly whether she would return the châteaux to her father if he asked her. Kiiko replied that the French properties already belonged to him. The castles in England, she said, were a gift from her father. He had never put it in writing, she said, for tax reasons.

And the Empire State Building? Kiiko said her father was entitled to receive money from the Empire State Building lease payments. All he had to do was ask. "This was done according to his wishes, and this money is made available to him until he dies," Kiiko explained.

"Has Mr. Yokoi received any of the lease money from the Empire State Building since he has been out of prison?" Hannigan asked.

"I will tell you one more time," she said. "Because people surrounding him lied to him about that being under protection—there hasn't been any request from him because he's been lied to."

Behind Bars

O f all the men and women who were now grappling over the Empire State Building, Jean-Paul Renoir might have been the most out of place. For most of his life, Renoir had been an outsider in one sense or another. He had burned with desire to succeed and had worked hard to do so in the Darwinian world of investment banking. Yet Renoir had vaulted into the realm of the very rich by a chance meeting with an attractive Japanese woman—a potential heir to a billion-dollar fortune. For a brief, shining period of several months, Renoir's boyhood dream of building an empire had seemed within reach. He had moved into an English castle— a fabulous property that smelled of the aristocracy—and was a partner with Donald Trump on perhaps the most famous building in America. By all appearances, Renoir had arrived. But then, just as quickly, it had all turned sour.

Powerful people—jealous people, Renoir decided—were casting him as a villain, a cheat. Renoir was hell-bent on not getting caught up in the web that he believed Yokoi's advisers had spun in France. He could not get over how severely the French authorities had treated his wife. The way Renoir saw it, the whole mess was just a feud within a damaged family. He was livid at the French for treating his wife and him like some kind of common criminals. Renoir vowed not to set foot in France until he and his lawyers had cleared up the matter. He settled into his Manhattan apartment and focused nearly full-time on defending himself. His mood was black.

On October 22, 1997, France secretly requested that the U.S. government extradite Renoir to France for questioning. According to a complaint attached to France's request, Renoir—who had also used his birth name, Perez—had fraudulently transferred châteaux worth about $25 million from Nippon Sangyo and Dai Nippon Fudoson, another Yokoi company, to "entities controlled or represented by the defendant and his wife. The scheme relied on the employment of false documents, including the use of a fraudulent power of attorney."

Extradition requests by France to the United States are governed by a 1909 treaty that was amended in 1970. It allows for the extradition of anyone charged with a crime covered by the treaty and against the law in both countries. The treaty requires France to demonstrate probable cause—that is, to show that it is more likely than not that the accused person committed the crime. On November 19, 1997, federal prosecutors in Manhattan, responding to the French government request, filed an extradition complaint in federal district court in Manhattan. A federal magistrate issued a warrant for Renoir's arrest.

That night at about 8 P.M., Renoir heard a knock on the door of his apartment. He had just returned from the office of his lawyers and had not even taken off his tie. Several weeks had passed since Yokoi's lawyers had grilled him under oath. He believed he had stood up well to their accusations. When Renoir opened the door, he found himself face-to-face with three federal marshals. One of them told Renoir they had a warrant for his arrest. They handcuffed him, walked him out onto Fifty-seventh Street, and put him into the backseat of an unmarked sedan. They began driving north, and soon left the city behind. It was dark. Renoir had no idea where they were taking him. The car exited the highway in Valhalla, New York, some 25 miles north of midtown Manhattan, and pulled into a parking lot at a sprawling complex of low-rise buildings. Renoir had arrived at Westchester County's Norwood E. Jackson Correctional Center.

Renoir spent part of the night in a bullpen with a bunch of street criminals. He figured he'd be out the next morning, as soon as he could raise bail. When morning arrived, Renoir received his first unpleasant surprise. In extradition matters, there is no such thing as bail. Renoir would go nowhere until he either boarded a plane for France or beat the extradition in federal court. Guards escorted Renoir to his new home, a seven- by nine-foot cell. His bed was a steel plate covered with a thin cotton mattress. He had a stool and three shelves on the wall. Renoir traded his suit and tie for two orange cotton jumpsuits, five pairs of socks, five sets of underwear, and a pair of slip-on sneakers.

Through the bars of his cell, Renoir looked out onto a U-shaped cellblock two tiers high. In the common area were two televisions. The din was astonishing, with televisions blaring and prisoners shouting constantly. Renoir and his fellow prisoners were locked in their cells from 10 P.M. to 7:30 A.M., then again from 8:00 to 9:00 A.M. and from 2:30 to 4:00 P.M. When the doors swung open, Renoir was free to mingle with his new neighbors. The men in his block, he discovered, were, like him, in the custody of the federal government, which was leasing the space from Westchester County. There were drug dealers, a few white-collar criminals, and a few killers. They were a rough lot, Renoir realized. He kept up his guard. Given the complications of the extradition laws, Renoir was forced to adjust his expectations. A month, he figured, tops.

One day, two months after he arrived, a new group of men moved into Renoir's block. They knew one another. Their leader, Renoir soon learned, was a young man named John A. Gotti, otherwise known as John Junior, the 33-year-old son of notorious Gambino mob boss John J. Gotti. By then, Renoir had deduced a few simple rules for surviving in jail. Number one: Don't be an asshole. That is, respect people, control your temper, and never talk about other people. Number two: Don't be afraid. Number three, Renoir would later explain, was the most important. As Renoir watched the weak inmates fall under the thumbs of the strong, he recalled what he had learned from the man who had trained guard dogs at his wife's castle in England. With guard dogs, the alpha males must be left alone. You must neither confront them nor cower before them. In jail, Renoir decided, it was the same. The guys who got abused were the guys who bowed to the alpha males. Renoir did not want to be one of the men who carried food trays for the bullies. Rule number three, he decided, was that he must never show insecurity or display a need to belong to any group. When inmates tested Renoir, asking him for his coffee or his soap, Renoir responded with a simple no. When someone offered him something, he said, "No, thank you."

Mike, a 65-year-old member of the Gotti group, began mouthing off to Renoir. More than once, he tried to take Renoir's milk. One night at dinner, Renoir snapped back, "You talk too much. Because of your foolishness, your son's in jail."

Mike approached him, quivering with rage. He punched Renoir twice in the face, two light jabs.

"What the fuck are you doing," barked Renoir, who stifled the urge to fight back.

Later, Gotti told Mike to leave Renoir alone.

Curiously, Renoir found himself befriended by the Gotti crew. They seemed to respect him, Renoir felt. Renoir subscribed to *The Wall Street Journal, Business Week, Barron's,* and *Aviation Week.* Each day, when he was done with *The Wall Street*

Journal, he would swap it for Gotti's *New York Times.* Renoir even became friendly with the man who had punched him.

At dinnertime, Renoir would often join the Gotti crew. The men would pool food from their care packages and, using a microwave, try to approximate home-cooked Italian meals. The man who had punched Renoir worked wonders with the microwave and tomato sauce. Another man could turn graham crackers and apples into pie. Gotti specialized in white sauce.

Each night, they carried their plates of food to the same seats. Initially, Renoir took a liking to the heavyset 54-year-old who sat beside him. Since going 31-6 for the 1968 Detroit Tigers, former pitcher Denny McLain had been in and out of trouble with the law. McLain, previously convicted of stealing $3 million from the pension fund of a meatpacking firm he had purchased, had been brought in with the Gotti crew for allegedly taking part in a telephone calling card scheme. Renoir discussed his case with McLain. One day, after Renoir complained to McLain about another inmate monopolizing the phone, Renoir discovered that McLain had shared Renoir's criticism with the phone hog, a dangerous betrayal in such a charged environment. Renoir decided McLain was a con man and a liar.

One evening, Renoir and the Gotti men watched a television broadcast of *GoodFellas,* the acclaimed mob movie. The Gotti men, who seemed to Renoir to speak in the same locutions of the men in the movie, offered a running commentary on the acting. When a commercial for a television newsmagazine posed the question, "What's the most dangerous place in a car?" the Gotti men roared with laughter. "You stupid fuck," one man shouted at the television. "The trunk!"

In the isolation of jail, Renoir brooded incessantly about his accusers. When I visited him in early 1998, he plunged into a near monologue about the case that stretched on for hours. Rifling through piles of documents, he railed that French authorities were persecuting him. He compared his plight to the Dreyfus affair that divided France a century ago, in which a Jewish army officer was convicted of treason and later pardoned. Renoir spoke of being victimized by a Machiavellian conspiracy involving clans within the Yokoi family. Yokoi's mind, he insisted, had been scrambled by the stroke, turning him into a pawn of his moneygrubbing sons.

"This is a study in insanity," Renoir hissed, his eyes darting. "Have you ever seen the movie *El Cid*?" In the movie's climactic scene, Renoir explained, Spanish soldiers prop the corpse of Charlton Heston onto his steed to lead his troops into battle against the Moors. "That's what they did to Yokoi," he said of his wife's siblings.

"When Yokoi went to jail he created a vacuum. The brothers took over," he said. When they discovered that Yokoi had bought the Empire State Building for Kiiko, they were furious, Renoir continued. "Most of these people hate each other," Renoir said. "But they got together to kill my wife." Renoir dismissed Yokoi's venomous letters denouncing him and his wife as the product of misinformation. "They'd had 18 months to poison Yokoi against my wife. It was so easy when they had access to him in prison."

Now, Renoir claimed, his adversaries within the family were using his detention as a thumbscrew to pressure him to settle the case by giving up what rightfully belonged to his wife. Renoir considered himself the kind of man who could stand up to that kind of pressure. He decided to fight the extradition, to argue that French authorities had not demonstrated probable cause that he had committed a crime, and that, in any case, he and his wife had not formally been charged with a crime in France but were merely under investigation.

Renoir's friends were appalled that he was locked up, with

no end of his plight in sight. Lee Miller, an investor and friend who had worked with Renoir in the early 1980s, drove to Valhalla to visit him. "It shook me to the bone to see this guy walking around in a yellow jumpsuit," Miller later recalled of his visit. "He's in there with hard-core criminals. Murderers. Rapists. This is not a criminal guy. He's a standup guy who happened to marry into a screwed-up situation. It's outrageous."

One day, Gary Melius, the Long Island developer who had sold Oheka Castle to Yokoi, got a call from a woman who identified herself as one of Renoir's Manhattan neighbors. She told Melius that Renoir was in jail. Melius asked her why she was calling him. She told Melius that he was the only guy in the United States that Renoir trusted. Would he help? Melius was puzzled about why Renoir would turn to him. Nevertheless, he offered to put up $5 million for bail, he later recalled. He recommended lawyers. He offered to take up the matter with his senator. It did no good. Renoir stayed put.

For Trump, success against Helmsley and Malkin was proving elusive. Although he had seized every opportunity to hammer the Empire State Building with criticism, he seemed to be getting no closer to gaining control of the valuable lease. In late 1995, a fire had broken out in a Con Edison vault located adjacent to the building's subbasement. Smoke had filtered through the building. Trump promptly moved to set aside the state court order that barred him from terminating the lease, arguing that the building was required to have an automatic sprinkler system. On January 16, 1996, New York state court judge Edward H. Lehner denied Trump's motion.

For Trump, trashing the Empire State Building in newspapers and magazines and on television may have been satisfying, but it wasn't enough. He needed something to use in court. The time had come for Trump to pull out the stops, to turn the building inside out to muster evidence that Malkin and Helmsley had rendered it a hazard. Trump turned himself into a first-class nuisance, bombarding Malkin with the kind of letter-of-the-law demands that were Malkin's stock in trade.

On January 23, Trump demanded access to the building within two days for a team of engineers to inspect fire safety systems. Malkin's lawyers, who complained that the fire department hadn't yet finished testing its new alarm system, proposed February 21. Trump responded with a second notice declaring Malkin and Helmsley in default on the lease. Malkin raced to court to obtain another order to stop Trump from tearing up the lease. Following a February 13 inspection, Trump sent yet another notice of default, claiming that the Helmsley/Malkin partnership years earlier had submitted to a city agency "false and fraudulent documentation" related to air-conditioning ductwork on the eighty-sixth floor. Trump set out to create trouble for Malkin and Helmsley with the city. Trump's inspector sent an urgent letter to the New York City Department of Buildings alleging numerous deficiencies in the fire safety system. And in a supreme act of legal hair-splitting, Trump argued that the Helmsley/Malkin partnership was not authorized to act as "owner" of the building when obtaining permits from the city for the building's ongoing, now $65 million, face-lift. Trump Empire State Partners alone, argued Trump, was the owner of the Empire State Building under the New York City building code. The city building department dutifully stopped issuing new work permits to Malkin and Helmsley.

On February 27, Trump notified Malkin's lawyer by letter that he intended to terminate the master lease in 15 days. Again, Malkin raced to court for an order blocking Trump and for a declaration that the leasing partnership was the building's "owner" for the purposes of the city building code. Again, Judge Lehner ordered Trump not to terminate the lease until the allegations could be sorted out in court.

For Charles Guigno, the building's director of operations,

dealing with Trump's assault became nearly a full-time job. Every week, it seemed, a new group of inspectors or engineers needed access to the building. He spent day after day with the building's lawyers, helping to respond to Trump's accusations. It would later seem to Guigno that the battle consumed nearly two years of his life.

On October 24, 1996, Judge Lehner moved to rein in the squabbling tycoons. He threw out Trump's suit seeking $100 million from Helmsley and Malkin and Malkin's countersuit seeking $100 million from Trump for, among other things, trashing the building in the media. He urged the warring magnates to concentrate on the core issue: whether Malkin and Helmsley were in violation of their 114-year lease. One month later, after a hearing on whether any city agency had cited the building for fire safety problems, he dismantled one of Trump's main lines of attack. Judge Lehner ruled that there were no fire safety violations at Empire State Building.

In the summer of 1997, Helmsley and Malkin finally purged the building of one of Trump's most potent if unpredictable allies. Suzy Smith's employer, Copen Associates, had proposed to Helmsley-Spear terms for a new lease. The building's leasing agent sent Copen's proposal to the Helmsley/Malkin partnership. It isn't clear whether Leona herself made the decision or whether Peter Malkin did. Someone, however, rejected the proposed deal. In an August 18 letter, Helmsley-Spear's Stephen Tole formally ousted Copen and its irksome employee from the building. "During the term of its most recent lease, it appears that Copen has been dissatisfied with the building," Tole wrote. "We do not believe that these complaints have any basis in fact. Nevertheless, since you have been unhappy with your tenancy, a renewal extension of your lease is not appropriate."

Suzy Smith's departure spelled the end of her high-decibel campaign of disparagement. Without her almost manic dedication to complaining, the Empire State Building tenants association swiftly fizzled out. It was one headache that Malkin and Leona must have been pleased to be rid of.

Renoir's jailing could not have been good news for Donald Trump. Trump was eager for this perplexing family squabbling to come to an end and for his two partners to be accorded legitimacy. Just the opposite was happening. Both of his partners had now spent time behind bars. The first time Renoir phoned Trump from jail, Trump urged Renoir to resolve the fighting.

"I hope we can settle this thing fast," said Trump.

Renoir was irritated about being pushed, and he sounded it.

"Listen to me," said Trump. "Before you talk to me in that tone of voice, let me tell you, I've been your greatest believer."

"If I'm speaking loudly," Renoir responded, "it's because it's noisy in here."

Renoir resisted Trump's pressure to settle the case, he would later say, firmly and politely. Trump backed off.

Some time later, the two men spoke again by phone. Trump had not yet submitted to questioning under oath about his involvement with Renoir and Kiiko. Renoir thought a deposition from Trump would assist in his defense. Renoir asked Trump if he had a problem giving one. Trump replied that he didn't have time. Only later would Renoir realize that Trump's loyalty to him and his wife was fading.

Trump must have been nagged by a feeling that he had backed the wrong horse. Yokoi had insisted in his half-incoherent deposition that he had never given the Empire State Building to his daughter as a gift. And Yokoi appeared willing to fight her for it until the day he died. Would a court take the skyscraper from Kiiko and Renoir and leave Trump out in the cold? It was certainly possible. To Trump, that was untenable.

Family warfare was certainly not in Trump's interest. Abe

Wallach, the executive Trump had assigned to the matter, figured the only way to resolve the mess was a compromise. To Wallach, there seemed to be more than enough trophy properties to divvy up so that everyone could walk away feeling like a winner. But reality had to set in among the combatants, Wallach felt. So far, no one appeared willing to budge. "Jean-Paul was not about to compromise," Wallach would later recall. "He was a guy who would fight to the death. It was all principle to him. The way he would speak—'They're liars! They're cheats! I will not stand for this!' Donald would often tell him, 'You need to settle this.' "

Wallach wondered about Peter Bal, who was presenting himself as Yokoi's point man in the battle. Where did Bal come off running this empire? Wallach wondered. Where did he come from? Who is he? Wallach decided it didn't really matter. "This was such a strange thing to begin with, if you find someone with authority, you don't ask too many questions, because you want to make progress," Wallach later recalled. "He seemed to have the ear of Mr. Yokoi. I felt, if I've got a live body who has got the ear of Mr. Yokoi and can help make decisions, I want to keep in good stead with him." Wallach decided to try to work something out with Peter Bal.

Peter Bal was shrewd enough to realize that Yokoi had more than one potential ally in his battle for the Empire State Building. One day, Bal paid a visit to Peter Malkin, who was still laboring to fend off Trump's serial attempts to void the lease. Bal presented Malkin with a figurine he had sculpted, cast in bronze. It was Donald—not Trump, but Duck. Bal told Malkin the sculpture was inspired by New York's own Donald, as in Trump, Malkin later recalled. Like Trump, Bal said, the figure was a cartoon character, it was fake antique, and it was hollow. (Bal later said he didn't recall making such a statement.) Malkin found it uproariously funny, and displayed it prominently on a table in his office. Bal and

Malkin—who had nothing in common aside from the Empire State Building—attempted to size up one another. Malkin was after information about this strange Japanese family. Bal wanted to understand where Malkin and Leona stood.

After Bal left, his lawyers approached Malkin's lawyers, hinting at a cooperative venture between Yokoi and Malkin. If Malkin and Helmsley were willing to help pay Yokoi's legal bills, Bal's lawyers suggested, Yokoi would fight more aggressively to take over control of the Empire State Building from Kiiko and Renoir. And a victory against Kiiko and Renoir, they hinted, would pull the rug out from under Trump, which in turn might end the challenge to Malkin's leasehold on the building. Letters flew back and forth between the two camps outlining terms for a deal. Yokoi's lawyers offered a promise from Yokoi not to try to break the lease if he won control of the Empire State Building. All Malkin had to do was help pay Yokoi's bills. In the end, Malkin declined.

Undeterred, and apparently desperate for financing, Bal and his lawyers turned directly to Malkin's antagonist. Ray Hannigan and his partner Stephen Rathkopf arranged to meet with Donald Trump in his Trump Tower office. All along, Trump had been trying to hedge his bets in the family feud. "Just tell me who my partner is," he had said time and again. Hannigan and Rathkopf offered Trump a deal. For $1 million, Yokoi was prepared to give Trump a release. The release would dictate that if Yokoi won the battle, Trump could retain his interest in the Empire State Building with a new partner: Hideki Yokoi.

"Look. Let's stop talking about me paying anything," Trump responded.

Hannigan and Rathkopf held firm. If Trump wanted to stay in the deal, they told him, he would have to buy this $1 million insurance policy. Otherwise, if Yokoi won his battle against Kiiko and Renoir, the Japanese tycoon would give Trump the boot, they told him.

"We're professionals. We can do a deal," Trump told them.

Trump maintained that he was already bringing his name to the venture. Paying $1 million was out of the question, he repeated. "Why should I put up any money?" he asked. "I have no risk." Trump noted that he had obtained title insurance on the building.

Rathkopf replied that if Yokoi won, it would mean that one of Trump's partners had committed fraud. Title insurance does not cover fraud, Rathkopf argued. The meeting had reached an impasse.

"You guys are too tough for me," said Trump, Hannigan later recalled. "I guess you don't want to settle." Hannigan detected sarcasm. (Trump later maintained that such a comment would be out of character for him.)

"Au contraire," replied Rathkopf. "We're prepared to settle. But we're not prepared to let you guys stay in for zero."

14

A Meeting with Daddy

ideki Yokoi was by no means the only deep-pocketed Japanese investor to be undone by an infatuation with overseas trophy buildings. Like scores of American developers who went bust when the American real estate bubble of the 1980s popped, numerous land-rich Tokyo magnates came undone in the mid-1990s. Each new generation of real estate magnates—whether in New York or Tokyo—seemed destined to repeat the same mistake. Building real estate empires on borrowed money, they discovered, was a perilous practice. Under pressure from banks, Harunori Takahashi, who had once used his own Boeing 727 to hop from one of his Pacific resort properties to another, announced plans to sell office buildings in the United States, Britain, Hong Kong, and Australia. Kitaro Watanabe, who collected vintage Rolls-Royces and was once ranked by *Forbes* magazine as the world's sixth-richest man, halted renovation of his lavish Kona Lagoon Hotel in Hawaii, which quickly fell into disrepair, and announced plans to begin selling assets.

In the United States, where commercial real estate values had declined by 30 percent or more nationwide, the acquisitions that had defined the era of Japanese trophy hunting went belly-up with astonishing speed. Developer Minoru Isutani, who in 1990 paid some $840 million for the Pebble Beach golf resort, surrendered the California club in 1992 to his lead lender, Sumitomo Bank, which subsequently sold it for about $500 million. Sazale Group, the Tokyo hotel company that in 1989 paid $110 million for Los Angeles's swank Hotel Bel-Air, gave it back in 1994 to lead lender Long-Term Credit Bank of Japan, which unloaded it the following year to the royal family of Brunei for about $60 million. Perhaps the greatest blow to the notion of the infallibility of Japan Inc. came in 1995. Mitsubishi Estate Company sought bankruptcy protection for the partnerships that owned New York's Rockefeller Center, essentially walking away from an investment of about $1.4 billion.

By 1996, values of Tokyo property had fallen by half. Some buildings slumped in value by as much as 80 percent. Japanese banks were sitting on more than $300 billion of bad loans. Bottom-fishing American real estate investors—who had already picked clean the American market for distressed properties—began checking into expensive Tokyo hotels, angling for meetings with bankers who might sell them defaulted loans. But the bankers, hoping against hope that property values would rebound, didn't bite. In Japan, non-performing loans, quite simply, were seen as shameful. To sell them for pennies on the dollar, especially to foreigners, would be tantamount to surrender. Japan's bankers were in denial mode.

Of all the stories of personal ruin associated with the Japanese real estate crisis, it would be hard to find one as unlikely, or as devastating, as the ordeal of Jean-Paul Renoir. On the afternoon of February 25, 1998, Renoir walked into an over-heated and nearly empty federal courtroom in lower Manhattan to learn his fate. Renoir wore a standard-issue prison jumpsuit. His hair was cropped close. He appeared to be scowling. In spite of the hardships he had endured in captivity, Renoir was still dead set against returning to France and subjecting himself to a criminal investigative process he deeply distrusted. First, he wanted to straighten out what he still described as nothing more than a family feud that had gotten out of hand.

Renoir's criminal lawyer, Charles Ross, faced a formidable task. Ross had to persuade federal magistrate Douglas Eaton that the French government hadn't met its burden of proof to extradite Renoir. Eaton's duty was not to decide on Renoir's guilt or innocence, only to determine whether the French government had established "probable cause." Ross therefore had to do more than cast reasonable doubt about Renoir's guilt. He had to convince Eaton that a reasonable reading of the evidence would lead to the conclusion that Renoir had not done what the French government said he had done.

Through a day and a half of hearings, Ross labored to do just that. But when Renoir returned to the courtroom on the afternoon of February 25, it swiftly became clear that Eaton harbored considerable doubt about Renoir's version of events.

"Well, my job here is simply to determine probable cause," said Eaton. "I am not here to determine guilt or innocence, obviously. I will hear from the attorneys after I have finished stating my preliminary views, but my strong preliminary view is that the French government has established probable cause." Eaton proceeded to recite the chronology of actions taken by Renoir and his wife in France, taking particular note of the lawsuit brought by Yokoi's company against the couple in New York.

"From my point of view, the important date is November

1994, when the lawsuit was brought against Renoir and Nakahara in New York City," Eaton said. "After November 1994, I
think, it is highly unlikely that Mr. Renoir believed that NSKK
[Nippon Sangyo] was authorizing him or his wife to sell any
of the châteaux or to transfer title in any manner."

Renoir sat silently in his chair, frowning, occasionally leaning forward to scribble notes to his lawyer.

"The November 1994 complaint made several things
forcefully clear to Mr. Renoir," Eaton continued. "First, NSKK
and Mr. Yokoi completely mistrusted Nakahara and Renoir.
Second, NSKK and Mr. Yokoi were attempting to strip Nakahara and Renoir of their most valuable asset, the Empire State
Building. Third, after November 1994, NSKK opposed any
attempt, and so also Mr. Yokoi would strenuously oppose any
attempt, by Nakahara or Renoir to change NSKK's ownership
of the French châteaux."

When Eaton finished, Renoir's lawyer rose to respond.
Ross admitted that the questionable power of attorney cited
by French authorities "really looks bad. It's a power from
Kiiko to Kiiko. It's just very stupid." Gesturing to Renoir, he
asked Eaton: "Does it make sense for a man like this, who has
all of this experience, three years later to pick up this power
of attorney, take it to this remote village and try to use that
power of attorney? Isn't this a smarter man than that?" There
were other powers of attorney, Ross said, documents that
could be interpreted as giving Kiiko the right to transfer
properties.

Eaton interrupted. But all of the documents, he noted,
predated the 1994 lawsuit that put Kiiko and her husband on
notice that they were not trusted. Everything had changed
between Kiiko and her father with the filing of that suit.

Ross hastened to explain. The whole tortured affair, Ross
told Eaton, had to be viewed through the strange prism of the
Yokoi family.

"I think if we go back to the motivations here, it wasn't a

dispute between Yokoi and Kiiko Nakahara," said Ross. "Mr. Yokoi gifted his favorite daughter with the ability to go to France and diversify his holdings, to purchase these castles, these exotic places. . . . And then he gifts her with money to go buy the Empire State Building. What a gift! What a wonderful bequeathment to the favorite daughter. As we say in our papers, I don't think it's just pulling things out of thin air to think these half-siblings are really upset. I think we could all think, if we are sitting home and a sibling gets money from dad to go buy the Empire State Building, we might be a little jealous." The complaint brought in France by Yokoi's company, Ross gamely proposed, was nothing more than an attempt to "influence what's going on over here with the Empire State Building."

"I view it the other way around," replied Eaton. "I think Mr. Renoir was very upset to hear about the November lawsuit, and that he was trying to fight back by taking the French properties and getting them out of NSKK. . . . I don't know what they were planning to do, but it seems to me that the most reasonable view of the evidence is that in response to this New York lawsuit, Mr. Renoir felt that he could get at the very least some sort of bargaining chip by doing exactly what the New York City complaint says they feared: that he would try to transfer title [of] some of the other properties . . . into various trusts. I really think that the crime is completed when NSKK is deprived of its title."

Ross continued to offer benign explanations for his client's actions. Eaton was unmoved. "Maybe it can be justified," Eaton finally conceded. "It seems to me that there may be two sides to the story here. But it also seems to me this is a case that will have to be tried."

With that, Eaton dealt a severe blow to Renoir's hope to avoid a reckoning in his native land. To Renoir's thinking, being shipped to a French jail would hamper his ability to defend himself in New York against the claim that he and his wife had stolen the Empire State Building. He would not even be allowed to speak to his American lawyers by phone. Nevertheless, Eaton said he intended to certify Renoir extraditable. On March 13, 1998, Eaton issued a written ruling, which noted that "the evidence establishes probable cause to believe that the defendant committed the charged offenses," the crimes of fraud and the use of forgeries.

Renoir still harbored hope that if he successfully refuted the accusations made against him in New York, French authorities would view the allegations in France as groundless. Renoir instructed his lawyers to continue to fight extradition. Three days later, Renoir appealed Eaton's ruling by filing a writ of habeas corpus, claiming he had not been formally charged with a crime in France and that the evidence didn't support Eaton's finding of probable cause. Renoir was bent on continuing the battle for the Empire State Building from the familiar confines of his New York jail cell.

Renoir and his wife had good reason to hope that a swift resolution of the New York lawsuit was possible. Just days before Eaton's ruling, Hideki Yokoi had shuffled off a jetliner in Paris, where his prodigal daughter Kiiko was now making her home. Yokoi had never before laid eyes on the City of Lights, or on Europe, for that matter. Yokoi had come to give a statement to the French investigating magistrate. The others who came were after something more elusive. Yokoi's American lawyers flew in, as did his son Hirohiko, his ex-son-in-law Sakakura, and his litigation coordinator, Peter Bal. Even Abe Wallach, Trump's point man on the matter, flew over. All of them were eager for Yokoi to speak to his daughter for the first time since 1995.

To Bal and Wallach, a face-to-face meeting between Yokoi and his daughter seemed a necessary first step to breaking the stalemate over the Empire State Building. Once she saw her father again, Wallach figured, Kiiko might be more open to relinquishing her grip on the building, as long as she was offered the right inducement. The father-daughter reunion, he hoped, would set the table for a deal.

But first, Yokoi had to tell his story to the investigating magistrate in Versailles. Speaking was still difficult for him. He nodded yes or no to some questions and wrote answers to others, his French lawyer, Pascal Narboni, later recalled. Yokoi told the magistrate, said Narboni, that he had not authorized his daughter to transfer ownership of the French châteaux. The magistrate summarized Yokoi's testimony in writing. When Kiiko received a copy, she concluded that her father was coherent again, that his mind had regained its focus. So she and her lawyer stayed up late into the night preparing for the following day, when she and her father would appear together before the magistrate for what French lawyers call a "confrontation."

Hopes of a coherent exchange between the accuser and the accused evaporated, however, as soon as Kiiko's lawyer began peppering her father with questions. Yokoi could scarcely make himself understood. He got anxious and angry. "He had trouble expressing himself," Narboni later conceded, while insisting that his client's mind remained sharp. "He is perfectly able to understand, and has a perfect ability to remember, when he is calm." As an exercise in fact-finding, the session, which lasted for several hours, proved as frustratingly opaque as Yokoi's New York deposition.

Secretly, Narboni arranged for a French doctor to examine Yokoi. The doctor, according to one person familiar with the exam, concluded that a stroke had damaged the left hemisphere of Yokoi's brain, impairing his speech. But for a man of his age, the doctor reported, Yokoi had a sound mind. Narboni kept the results confidential, intending to spring them on the opposing lawyers if they tried to make an issue once again out of Yokoi's mental fitness.

Trump's man Wallach was worried about meeting Yokoi. Wallach was unsure of what Yokoi now thought of Trump. Given the viciousness of the legal attacks, Wallach was expecting the worst. When he met Yokoi, Wallach introduced himself using a few Japanese words fed to him by Peter Bal. Yokoi seemed old and frail, but his handshake struck Wallach as surprisingly firm.

Yokoi smiled and said, "Donald Trump." He reached into his briefcase and struggled to pull out a book. Wallach leaned over to help him. It was a book of photographs. Yokoi opened it and pointed to photographs of Trump's 1993 visit to Tokyo.

"Trump. Yokoi," Yokoi said, pointing to a picture of the two men.

"We want to help the family," Wallach told him through a translator.

"Thank you, I appreciate your effort," Yokoi replied.

The two men talked for several minutes.

"We should resolve all matters between us and get on with the main goal of dealing with the building," Wallach said to Yokoi.

Wallach left the meeting convinced that Yokoi was mentally sharper than Renoir had claimed.

Hopes remained high that when Yokoi and his daughter met privately, without lawyers or a magistrate hovering over them, they would find a way to reconcile. At noon on March 12, 1998, Kiiko was ushered into a conference room at Paris's four-star Hotel Le Tremoille. She was startled to see Takenosuke Sakakura—the ex-husband of her half sister and the cousin of Peter Bal—seated beside her father. Sakakura had to go, she demanded. Sakakura refused to leave, explaining that the old man wanted him there.

"I'm leaving," Kiiko announced.

Yokoi pleaded with his daughter to stay. Peter Bal entered

the room. He told Kiiko he had consulted the magistrate. (The magistrate must sanction any contact between key figures in such a case.) The magistrate, Bal said, had told him it was up to Kiiko to decide whether she wanted the meeting to go forward.

"I'm not comfortable," Kiiko said.

Bal hastily proposed lunch. Over sandwiches, Yokoi asked his daughter about life in prison and joked that he wanted to go back to prison in France. He talked about old family friends who had died. He asked his daughter whether she had found a boyfriend in France. He told her he wanted to live in France, because it was beautiful and because the women were beautiful. To Kiiko, her father seemed to be thinking clearly.

After lunch, Bal again told Kiiko she couldn't meet with her father without Sakakura sitting in, on instructions from Yokoi's son, Hirohiko. Once again Kiiko threatened to leave, and again her father begged her to stay. Finally, Yokoi told Sakakura to leave the room. For 20 minutes, Kiiko and her father talked. No one else heard what they said. About the only thing everyone would later agree on was that tears were shed. That much was clear from the tissues that littered the floor.

"The first thing he said was, 'Lawyers bad,' " Kiiko maintained several weeks later. "He said he wants to finish it. Stupid fight." Kiiko told Wallach that it had been an emotional meeting and that she had been determined not to play "the little Japanese doll," but to be firm. Kiiko said she told her father that she had only done what he had instructed her to do. More significantly, Kiiko insisted that during that brief, teary meeting, her father had agreed that the Empire State Building and two British castles were gifts to her.

That account drew derisive laughter from Yokoi's French lawyer. "It's incredible how much imagination she has," Narboni said that April. During the decisive meeting, said Narboni, Kiiko "didn't stop speaking. That's what her father told me." Whatever the truth, over dinner that evening, according to Narboni, Yokoi told his lawyers that there was no agreement.

Kiiko, however, had left the hotel that day believing that everyone had agreed to regroup the next day at her lawyer's office to complete the agreement she said she had struck with her father. She waited all day, but her father never showed. His absence only fueled her suspicions about manipulation of her father. "When Peter Bal and Narboni saw that father agreed with me, they spirited him away," she said.

Yokoi's lawyers dismissed Kiiko's conjecture as fantasy. Hannigan, Yokoi's American lawyer, said his client "was outraged at some of the things she was saying he said. Kiiko's understanding of how things went and ours are much different. No one was ever aware of any Friday meeting. It might have been something that she imagined." Yokoi's position on the Empire State Building, said Hannigan, was unchanged. He wanted it back.

As Kiiko waited in vain for her father the following day, Yokoi went off to tour the battered châteaux. "He loves them," said Hannigan. "He treats them as if they were his own."

The events in Paris only sowed further confusion among those hoping for a father-daughter reconciliation. Wallach left France "not knowing where things were going or where things were," he would later explain.

When Kiiko's version of the Paris meeting—which had her father agreeing that the Empire State Building was hers—filtered back to Renoir in jail, he allowed himself to imagine that an agreement was at hand that would get him out of jail.

After her father left Paris, Kiiko returned to her island home on the Seine and her life of solitude. It was altogether unclear how French authorities would proceed. They still would not allow her to speak to her husband or to travel outside of France. She spent her days caring for her elderly mother, taking cooking lessons, and painting. She continued to draw her $10,000 monthly salary from Trump Empire State Partners.

Living on the island had helped her recover from the ordeal of jail, she told me when I visited a month after her father had departed. "It took me a year," she said. "Now I'm okay." Over a Japanese lunch prepared by her silent 77-year-old mother, Kiiko said she was lonely. She projected an air of guilelessness, heightened by her tendency to burst into disarming giggles when discussing grave matters. "One day, my father, Jean-Paul, and I, we will all meet and have a talk about prison," she told me with a laugh.

Kiiko would never get the chance.

15

Yokoi's Last Stand

O ver the years, the Empire State Building had proven stalwart enough to withstand the Great Depression, the impact of a B-25 bomber, and a wave of glamorous new skyscrapers. But the mayhem that the feuding tycoons brought upon it in the mid-1990s was proving a formidable threat. It must have seemed to Peter Malkin and Leona Helmsley as though some kind of hex had been cast upon it. Donald Trump and Suzy Smith had shown boundless enthusiasm for denigrating the building and a real knack for attracting bad press. And just when media interest began to flag, a deranged, murderous gunman had rekindled it. Trump's curious deal with the Yokoi family had cast a cloud over the once placid landlord-tenant relations. Vacancies in the tower had grown alarmingly, and dividends to investors in the Helmsley partnerships had evaporated. Lasting damage to the skyscraper's economic prospects loomed as a real possibility.

It may be that Malkin and Leona eventually came to the realization that they weren't helping matters by attempting to throttle one another in court. Without question, it was in both their interests to present a united front against Trump. In the end, neither Leona nor Malkin offered any explanation for why they decided to make peace when they did. Their joint press release of December 18, 1997, read simply: "Leona M. Helmsley and Peter L. Malkin today announced that they had resolved all disputes between them and discontinued all pending litigation. Mrs. Helmsley and Mr. Malkin expressed pleasure at the amicable resolution of their disputes and said that they looked forward to future cooperation in the management and ownership of the properties in which they have interests for the benefit of all concerned."

Their agreement called for Malkin to at last accept Leona as his new partner in the Empire State Building as well as in the other disputed buildings. Malkin also agreed to cooperate with Leona's efforts to sell off the vast portfolio bequeathed to her by Harry. Malkin presumably also gave up his campaign to raise questions about the legitimacy of Harry's will, for nothing more about the matter was ever heard. For her part, Leona agreed to stop challenging Malkin's authority to act on behalf of other investors in the Empire State Building and to drop her efforts to fire Malkin's law firm. When Peter Malkin informed partnership investors by letter that he and Leona had ended hostilities, he stressed that Helmsley-Spear, now controlled by Harry's other two partners, was not a party to the peace treaty. The lucrative contract to manage the Empire State Building would stay, at least for the present, with Irving Schneider. Malkin would fight on against Schneider separately.

It was difficult to escape the conclusion that for all the money and venom the two tycoons had spilled in their battle, precious little had been gained by either of them. They had sheathed their boning knives, and Malkin had reiterated his respect for Helmsley—Harry, that is. "Both parties regret negative implications that may have been drawn from legal papers, and Mr. Malkin especially regrets anything that may have reflected negatively on Mr. Helmsley's very distinguished career," their statement said. "Mr. Malkin said that his long and close association with Harry Helmsley was one of the defining business relationships of his life; and that he had unbounded respect and admiration for Harry Helmsley." Leona and Malkin—whom the lawsuit had revealed to be something less than ideal partners—were still joined at the hip over the Empire State Building.

Their peace treaty coincided with a discernible shift in the fortunes of the Empire State Building. By 1998, a resurgent New York City economy had made office space, once again, a scarce commodity. The renovation of the building, begun in 1991, was finally nearing completion, at a cost that had nudged over $70 million. The new windows were all in place and properly caulked. Every square inch of limestone had been cleaned and restored. The scaffolding was down. The building, quite simply, looked markedly better than it had when Trump rolled out his legal howitzers. Even Suzy Smith—now thankfully out of Malkin's hair—had to admit it. Empty offices began filling. The occupancy rate climbed from less than 85 percent in the initial months of Trump's assault to a healthy 95 percent. The tourists who were once again flocking to Manhattan were buying tickets to the observation deck in numbers not seen in years. Investors in the Helmsley/Malkin partnerships were once again seeing profits.

Yet Malkin had still not been able to snuff out his biggest headache of all. Despite repeated courtroom setbacks, Donald Trump would not let up. He stubbornly pressed ahead with his effort to oust Malkin and Helmsley from the building. Given Trump's deal with Kiiko and Renoir, it was hardly surprising. If he failed to break the lease, his vaunted stake in the building might well turn out to be worth exactly zero.

In 1998, Trump inspected the building once again. According to papers filed by his lawyers, Trump found it "in desperate need of repair." His filing complained that Helms-ley and Malkin had failed to install sprinklers throughout the building, to provide adequate security, to replace the brand-new windows, to correct a "severe rodent infestation," or to correct many fire safety problems. The public was in danger, Trump insisted. "This is the only building in New York City, of which we are aware, that has suffered a serious fire, shooting incident, and elevator crash all in the past few years," Trump's lawyer noted gravely and without elaboration. To Malkin, the new complaints read like more malarkey from an increasingly desperate foe.

In the wake of the fruitless Paris meetings, Hideki Yokoi's lawyers figured they held the advantage in their tug-of-war with Kiiko and her husband over the Empire State Building. Although Kiiko was no longer in detention, she was not out of trouble. The French criminal investigation still hung over her head. Authorities held her passport. Her husband, of course, was worse off by far. The Westchester County jail bore no resemblance to a low-security facility for white-collar crooks. Renoir had come to realize—quite correctly—that while it is possible to delay extradition, it is next to impossible to beat it. Unless, that is, he could deliver a potent piece of exculpatory evidence to the American court. Renoir hoped that if the American lawsuit were resolved in a manner that made the dispute seem no more than a giant misunderstanding, an American federal judge would be reluctant to extradite him. That gave Renoir a powerful incentive to negotiate.

Unbeknownst to Renoir and his wife, in Japan, the two men they imagined as their chief accusers, Hirohiko and Kunihiko Yokoi, were losing their stomach for the fight. Their father had always prided himself on being a fighter. The brothers didn't. They were eager to put the unpleasantness behind them.

In 1998, the two sides began negotiating in earnest to end their feud. If there was one building Yokoi wanted from this whole sorry affair, it was the Empire State Building. At first, Renoir was inflexible about it, one confidant would later recall. A deal was a deal, he argued. But by early 1998, after several months in jail, Renoir began showing a new flexibility. He was concerned, Renoir told his lawyers, that Yokoi's lenders would assert a claim on the skyscraper. Renoir was willing to consider divvying up all the assets, the Empire State Building included. In return, Renoir wanted Hideki Yokoi to write a letter to French authorities asserting that the accusations against them, in hindsight, had been a colossal mistake, that Renoir and his wife had only been following Yokoi's instructions, one of Renoir's lawyers would later recall. Yokoi's lawyers took to calling it the "get-out-of-jail" language.

Yokoi had always been a stubborn man, a trait that hadn't softened with age. He refused to deliver such a statement. What his lawyers offered Renoir instead was far more ambiguous. Yokoi offered to tell French authorities that Kiiko and Renoir had "considered themselves" to be acting in Yokoi's best interests. Renoir complained to his lawyers that such language fell short of the exoneration he wanted.

Strangely enough, it proved easier to divide up Yokoi's tarnished real estate treasures than to agree on words about past intentions. Yokoi's lawyer, Hannigan, would later remark that the exercise resembled a real-life game of Risk. Reluctantly, Kiiko and her husband agreed to shift ownership of the Empire State Building to Yokoi's firm, as long as they could retain a share of the potential profits if Trump succeeded in breaking the lease. Yokoi's firm would get the French châteaux—investments that had always disgusted Renoir anyway. Kiiko would get the British castles, the grand mansion in Long Island, and some of the money that had been piling up in the Empire State Building bank account.

When Hannigan and his partner Stephen Rathkopf arrived

in Tokyo in May 1998 to present Yokoi's board of directors with a formal settlement proposal from his daughter, they discovered that their elderly client seemed to have a constitutional need to carry on the battle. Since his release from prison, Yokoi's friends would later reflect, the once-feared tycoon had become a shadow of his former self. No one would do business any more with the disgraced mogul, his friend Sato explained. No one even paid attention to him.

Newspapers and magazines no longer wrote about Yokoi's power, focusing instead on his slide into economic ruin. His most famous property, the Hotel New Japan, had slipped from his grasp as he sat in prison, unable to pay off his loans. In 1995, after a Tokyo district court failed to find anyone willing to meet the discounted 60 billion yen auction minimum, a subsidiary of Chiyoda Life, Yokoi's financially troubled primary lender, took over title to the burned-out hotel. By then, it was worth just one-fifth of its value during the bubble. The hotel stood vacant in downtown Tokyo, boarded and forlorn, like a totem to Yokoi's downfall. Eventually, a wrecking crew moved in and tore it down.

Business at his bowling alleys and *pachinko* parlors had fallen off by 30 to 40 percent. When Yokoi emerged from prison, his eldest son, Kunihiko, asked him not to visit the properties any more. "If he came, he would say things that were wrong or have impossible requests," Kunihiko explained to lawyers in 1997. "And furthermore, the customers would not like it. So I asked him not to come to those places." Kunihiko said it was the only time he had spoken to his father since Yokoi's release from prison. Yokoi demanded his son's resignation.

The debts of Yokoi's holding company, Nippon Sangyo, almost certainly exceeded its assets. Legal claims asserted by victims of the hotel fire clouded Yokoi's efforts to raise capital by selling other assets, according to a bidder on one property. In Yokoi's diminished universe, his precious overseas properties—and the fight he was waging over them—

loomed large. "It was the only thing he had left," one of his advisers later explained. "He didn't want it to go away."

Hannigan distributed translated copies of the settlement proposal to Yokoi's board of directors, who wasted no time approving the deal. Yokoi, sitting quietly in the back of the room, picked up the document and began reading it. Suddenly, Yokoi shouted, "Zen! Zen!" Everyone turned to face the old man.

"What's he saying?" asked Rathkopf.

"Never," explained Bal.

Yokoi slapped his wrists together, Yokoi's sign, Hannigan had learned, that someone ought to be handcuffed. Yokoi flatly refused to withdraw his allegations against Kiiko and Renoir. He wanted to carry on the fight. Once Yokoi said no, Hannigan later recalled, no one dared challenge him.

What caused Hideki Yokoi to eventually change his mind about making peace with his daughter is perhaps a question only he himself could have answered. One of his advisers came to believe that, as a businessman, Yokoi realized that the longer the fight dragged on, the more the decaying châteaux would cost him. Those properties that had once seemed such a bargain were costing him a fortune. If the stalemate persisted, Yokoi risked losing what little he had left. Whatever the reason, in the months after Hannigan's trip to Japan, Yokoi resigned himself to the fact that settling the case by divvying up the assets—trading some of his other trophies for undisputed claim on the Empire State Building—was in his own best interest.

The letter Renoir wanted from Yokoi, however, remained a major bone of contention. Renoir still wanted his father-in-law to assert that he now understood that Kiiko and Renoir had been acting in his interest. Yokoi told his lawyers he would never make such a concession. He would write only that Kiiko and Renoir considered themselves to have been doing so. Negotiations deadlocked over a few words. His back to the wall, Renoir eventually accepted Yokoi's offer. Yokoi agreed to drop the lawsuit he had brought in France, to withdraw as a party to the French criminal complaint, and to provide the written statement to French authorities.

Whether a letter from Yokoi would convince French investigators to soften their stance was anyone's guess. But Renoir and his wife decided to take what they could get: the British castles, the Long Island mansion, and several million dollars in cash. Yokoi would regain control of the French châteaux and the Empire State Building. On October 6, 1998, lawyers for both sides informed New York state court judge Richard Braun in a court conference that Nippon Sangyo and the Renoirs had agreed in principle to settle the case.

What the two sides had failed to take into account, however, was Donald Trump. Yokoi's lawyers, despite their tough talk to Trump months earlier, had decided they would have to honor the deal Trump had struck with Renoir. Trump's 50 percent stake in the building's upside would remain intact. Trump would get a new partner, but nothing else would change. Trump had known for months that settlement talks were under way. But Yokoi's lawyers had included neither Trump nor his representatives in the negotiations. They hadn't briefed Trump on the deal, nor had they sought his approval. Trump did not appreciate being the odd man out.

Trump's lawyer, Richard Fischbein, arrived at the court conference prepared to make considerable trouble. (Weeks later, Fischbein would earn a place in the annals of legal overkill after a dispute about tables at Angelo & Maxie's Steakhouse on Park Avenue spun out of control. Fischbein refused to pay an 18 percent tip the restaurant levied on his party of 18, the restaurant called the police, and Fischbein brought suit against the eatery in New York state court for false imprisonment, battery, fraud, breach of contract, and slander. The case settled when each side agreed to donate $10,000 to the Children's Aid Society.) Hannigan would later describe Fischbein's tone during the court conference as "particularly pugnacious." Fischbein shattered the conciliatory mood by disputing Renoir and Kiiko's right to enter into the settlement with Yokoi. Fischbein refused to consent to an adjournment of the upcoming deadlines and court dates, including the trial, which was scheduled for the following month. Fischbein, in essence, wanted the judge to compel the Yokoi family to fight it out in the courtroom. What Trump hoped to gain by playing the eleventh-hour spoiler, however, was not something Fischbein chose to spell out just yet.

Three days later, it became clear. Trump asked for the moon. In a cross-claim filed against his partners, Renoir and Kiiko, and a counterclaim against Nippon Sangyo, Trump insisted that Kiiko and Renoir had violated their fiduciary duty to him to refrain from acting in their own self-interest at his expense. No one had given him the right to accept or reject the deal, Trump complained. Trump asked the court to block the transfer to Yokoi's firm of Kiiko and Renoir's interest in Trump Empire State Partners and to award him the option to bid on that interest for $1. In addition, Trump asked for $10 million in damages, and legal fees of not less than $500,000. Trump, it seemed, was trying to grab the Empire State Building for himself.

To Yokoi's lawyer, Hannigan, Trump's counterclaim looked like a holdup. At the very least, Hannigan figured, Trump wanted his attorneys fees covered. Neither Hannigan nor the lawyers for Renoir and Kiiko relished the notion of being strong-armed by Trump, whose stake in the Empire State Building, at least at the present moment, looked to be worth very little indeed.

So Hannigan set out to exert some pressure of his own on Trump. For more than a year, to the consternation of many, Trump had avoided giving sworn deposition testimony about his involvement in the Empire State Building. Just days before Trump's lawyer attacked the settlement, in fact, Hannigan and Fischbein had exchanged testy letters about whether Trump would appear for a deposition on October 15. He didn't. With the Yokoi family settlement hanging in the balance, Hannigan brought this to the attention of Judge Braun and motioned for the court to strike Trump's cross-claim and counterclaim for his "willful and contumacious default in failing to abide by discovery demands."

When the lawyers gathered in Judge Braun's court on November 12, 1998, John Winter, who was representing Renoir and Kiiko, announced to the judge that a draft settlement would be completed the following day. Both sides, he indicated, intended to ask the court to dismiss the case in its entirety. Unfortunately, he said, the dispute with Trump had not been resolved.

Trump's lawyer rose to complain that his client needed to know the exact terms of the proposed settlement.

"This document, whatever the parties have agreed to do, they have done secretly, offshore, hidden away somewhere to avoid whatever they don't want people to find out what the real deal is," he complained. Trump needed to study the deal, he said.

Judge Braun instructed the lawyers to return in a week's time for a hearing on the motion to dismiss Trump's action. When they regrouped before the judge—exactly one week before Thanksgiving—Braun unveiled an unpleasant surprise for Trump.

"We are starting the trial on Monday," Braun announced. "Here is how you are going to try this case. . . . the Court is going to vary the order of presentation of the issues. We're going to be starting with the claims raised by the Trump defendants."

With that, Braun lifted a staggering burden from Yokoi's lawyer and dropped it onto the back of Donald Trump. Trump would have exactly three days to prepare to try his case against Yokoi, Renoir, and Kiiko. Moreover, Trump's lawyers would have to argue Trump's claim—that the Yokoi family settlement violated his joint venture agreement—without even knowing the terms of the settlement.

The next day, Braun added to Trump's burden. He ordered Trump to sit down for his long-delayed deposition the day after his lawyer delivered an opening statement in the trial, just two days before Thanksgiving. "Mr. Trump will have to appear for his deposition this Tuesday," the judge declared, "or his answer will be stricken, and he'll be precluded from testifying at trial."

It was hard to escape the conclusion that Judge Braun himself was calling Donald Trump's bluff. But whatever Braun's intent, his decision prompted Trump's lawyers to make a beeline for the negotiating table. Over the next several hours, they labored to hash out a deal. At first, Trump's lawyers demanded for their client a real ownership stake in the Empire State Building, not just a stake in future upside, one participant would later recall. Yokoi's lawyers flatly refused. Trump's lawyers then trimmed the size of the stake they demanded. Yokoi's lawyers held their ground. In the end, Trump threw up his hands and settled for the same deal he had with Renoir and Kiiko—50 percent of whatever additional value he could bring to the Empire State Building—plus $300,000 to pay his lawyers. Trump would later assert that he never wanted any more than he got.

With the clock approaching 5 P.M., the lawyers filed back into Braun's courtroom and handed him two documents. The judge examined them.

"I have been given a one-page stipulation on the court's stipulation form, as well as the six-page agreement on yellow legal pages," Judge Braun said. "Mr. Hannigan, did you sign both of these two documents?"

Hannigan said that he had, on behalf of his client. The judge asked the same of the other lawyers, who assured him they had.

"I'm very glad you were able to reach this agreement," Judge Braun said. "Obviously, it's in the best interest of all parties, and I'm sure you and your clients are happy."

With that, the war within the Yokoi family over the world's most famous skyscraper, it appeared, was over. Yokoi was going to get his trophy.

The lawyers hurried to draw up papers before any of their erratic clients changed their minds. Hannigan planned to hand-carry the documents to his infirm client in Tokyo. He never had the chance.

On November 30, 1998, Hideki Yokoi awoke, rose from bed, washed his face, and brushed his teeth. A month earlier, Yokoi had moved into the home of his brother and sister-in-law. Under pressure from lenders, he had given up his prized residential complex in Denenchofu. Despite the setback, his health had seemed stable. That morning, unaccountably, he returned to bed. When his sister-in-law called to him, Yokoi failed to respond. She found him unconscious. An ambulance rushed the 85-year-old man to a hospital in Tokyo's Shinagawa district. Hideki Yokoi's heart had given out. He was dead.

Yokoi had not yet signed the get-out-of-jail letter Renoir had wanted so desperately. Almost immediately, people began asking Yokoi's New York lawyer, "What does this mean for the settlement?" Hannigan had to admit he had no idea.

Back in Japan, Hideki Yokoi was cremated. Yokoi's brother-in-law, Hishida, retrieved the bullet that the *yakuza* gunman had pumped into Yokoi four decades before. Hishida gave it to Yokoi's eldest daughter, Chizuko.

Heirs

The death of Hideki Yokoi went largely unnoticed in America, except, that is, within the circle of eccentrics fighting over the Empire State Building, where it produced considerable upheaval. Kiiko Nakahara was devastated that her father had died before the two of them had mended their fractured relationship. She told her lawyers she needed to mourn, that she would be unable to carry on with the settlement for a month.

Weighing developments from his jail cell, Renoir was far less sentimental about Yokoi's passing. In Renoir's view, the dynamics of the battle had changed significantly—in his own favor. Ownership of the Empire State Building was structured such that when Yokoi died, Kiiko would become, in essence, its sole owner. Kiiko was now sole beneficiary of the trust that owned 50 percent of Trump Empire State Partners. And she was sole protector of the trust that controlled the French properties. Moreover, opined Renoir to one of his lawyers, with Yokoi gone, who was left to effectively refute Kiiko's tale that her father had given her the Empire State Building? Kiiko's story, argued Renoir, would be supported by Trump, by the lawyers and accountants who had structured the deal, and by Renoir himself.

Renoir ordered his lawyers to forget the settlement. They are all idiots in Japan, he told one of them. Yokoi's heirs will be under increasing pressure from creditors, he said. They won't know what to do. Let's go to trial, Renoir said. Winning the New York case, Renoir reasoned, would lay the ground-work for a victory in France.

Some of Renoir's lawyers, however, were less than ecstatic about the renewal of his fighting spirit. For one thing, they told Renoir, a New York state judge had already called off the trial after being handed a signed draft of the settlement. Fur-thermore, even with Yokoi dead, the New York case was hardly a slam dunk for Renoir.

Hannigan, the Yokoi family lawyer, was not eager to see the settlement come undone. The problem, Renoir's lawyer told him, was that Yokoi had died before signing the get-out-of-jail letter to French authorities. To Renoir, that letter was an essential part of the deal, Hannigan was told. Hannigan didn't buy it. The way he saw it, Renoir and Kiiko simply saw an opportunity to negotiate a better deal.

But Yokoi's sons, together with Peter Bal, saw little reason to yield much. Trump was now on their side. The deal had already been presented to the judge. Once again, negotia-tions reached an impasse. Renoir told his lawyers to invite Peter Bal for a jailhouse meeting. If he had the chance to rea-son with Bal face-to-face, Renoir said, he could settle the case within hours. His invitation was refused. He grew disgusted with his lawyers.

Kiiko herself waffled. "For a long period of time, no one knew what to do, because Kiiko was undecided," one of her lawyers would later recall.

The death of a real estate magnate can often bring trying times to family members left holding the reins. Estate taxes can be crushing. Sibling rivalries can flare. Kin can stumble, proving themselves incapable successors. After the death of her husband, Leona Helmsley for the most part stayed out of the public eye, shuttling between her Greenwich mansion and Manhattan penthouse with her dog, a lap-size Maltese named Trouble. There was no second generation in the Helmsley family to usher the business into the modern age, to ensure that the Helmsley name would remain a fixture on New York buildings for years to come.

By 1998, the era of New York real estate defined by men like Harry Helmsley was looking increasingly like a bygone one. It wasn't just that the titans of New York's postwar real estate booms were growing old and dying. There was a movement taking hold, heralded by Wall Street promoters as a sea change in the nation's real estate culture. Industry leaders talked of making real estate more like America's other large industries. The change was born, in part, of necessity. Still smarting from the real estate bust of the early 1990s, bankers remained wary of lending to risk-taking developers. Many large property owners were desperate for new financing. Some needed it to pay off debts accumulated during the last boom. Others wanted to put their estates in order for future heirs. Urged on by investment bankers, they began to do the unthinkable: to sell shares to the public, opening themselves to the scrutiny of eagle-eyed professional investors. Shopping mall tycoons Edward DeBartolo and Melvin Simon went public. Chicago real estate magnate Sam Zell did, too. The move was on to transform private real estate fiefdoms into modern businesses. Professionalism was in. Ego, greed, and vanity, in theory, were out.

In this climate of modernization, the feuds swirling around the Empire State Building came to seem almost farcical. In the new order, there was supposed to be no place for strong-willed and eccentric tycoons snapping and snarling at one another with little regard for the consequences. To a more polished generation of real estate entrepreneurs, the Empire State Building, the city's greatest symbol of mid-twentieth-century optimism, had become a burlesque stage, a venue for a dying way of doing business.

In the eyes of some real estate professionals, many Helmsley properties were suffering from too many years of deferred maintenance. Peter Ricker, a onetime Helmsley executive, likened stepping into a Helmsley property to "going back to your childhood." The lobbies, the doors, the detailing, he said, were "stopped in time," steeped in "early Seventies functional."

Yet with the New York economy crackling, Leona had chosen a propitious time to convert her vast inheritance to cash. Even second-tier Manhattan buildings were once again filling with tenants, and property investors, flush with cash raised in the public markets, were on the hunt for turnaround opportunities. Within months of settling her quarrel with Peter Malkin, Leona began inking deals to sell properties Harry had either owned or controlled. Before 1998 was out, Leona agreed to sell 1 Penn Plaza, a 2.4-million-square-foot tower Harry had developed with Larry Wien, for $410 million; 140 Broadway, an office tower Harry built in the financial district, for $191 million; the Starrett-Lehigh Building, a block-size colossus of banded glass and brick, for $152 million; and the Helmsley Building, the gilded 1929 office tower that sits on the Park Avenue office corridor, for $255 million. Within three years, Leona's estate sale would bring in upward of $2 billion, a portion of which went to Harry's partners in the properties.

Yet Leona had no intention of giving up the properties most closely identified with Harry. When one family friend suggested to Leona that Donald Trump would be a logical buyer for the Park Lane hotel, she snapped, "I wouldn't sell anything to that son of a bitch!" She told associates she planned to keep the hotels, as well as her controlling interest in Harry's signature asset: his lease on the Empire State Building.

The reign of Japan's property kingpins among the world's richest men had been brief and had ended with a thud. Consternation over Japanese consumption of American cultural treasures faded rapidly. Japan was now foundering in its own real estate fiasco. Its market showed no signs of bouncing back. Reluctantly, embattled Japanese bankers began to abandon hope.

Savvy American "vulture" investors had notched enormous profits buying defaulted real estate loans from failed American thrifts in the late 1980s and early 1990s, then foreclosing on the properties. As far back as 1993, Americans like Jack Rodman, managing director of E&Y Kenneth Leventhal Real Estate Group, Ernst & Young LLP's real estate consulting unit, had been declaring Japan a gold mine of even greater proportions. Rodman alternately pleaded with and badgered Japanese bankers and government officials to begin selling real estate to the highest bidders. When they eventually began doing so, the men with the money were carrying American dollars.

Investors who had fed off the wreckage of the American real estate industry five years earlier—firms like Goldman Sachs, Merrill Lynch, Morgan Stanley, and Security Capital Group—hurried to Japan. What they found was an industry in even deeper trouble than what they had seen in America. One would-be buyer, Andrew Davidoff of New York–based Emmes & Co., which set up an office in Tokyo, was stunned when he examined a portfolio of 700 real estate loans offered for sale by one bank. It would be impossible to ever collect a single yen on 550 of the loans, the bank told him. Davidoff set out to look at the property backing the other 150. His quest eventually took him to a region of small farms about five hours outside Tokyo. Davidoff found himself walking along a path through a patchwork of farmers' plots. High-tension electrical wires stretched overhead. Davidoff arrived at a half-acre vegetable plot hemmed in on all four sides by other plots and inaccessible by road. The patch of land carried a $2.5 million loan. The bank valued it at $400,000. "It was the most insane thing I ever saw," Davidoff would later recall. "In the U.S., they would call it bank fraud." Davidoff's firm bid for the loans, but another investor offered more. They sold for just 6 percent of face value.

By mid-1998, American investors had snapped up about $20 billion worth of Japanese real estate, according to an E&Y Kenneth Leventhal study. Americans eagerly bought back American resorts and golf courses for a fraction of what Japanese buyers had paid just a few years earlier. They also bought decidedly less glamorous Japanese properties like game arcades, "love hotels," and unfinished golf courses.

Headlines began appearing in Japanese newspapers and magazines decrying an invasion by the Yankee carpetbaggers. "Foreign Companies Hit the Beaches, Occupy the Country," screamed one. "American Capital Runs Roughshod Over Japan," said another. "Japan Defeated Again," said another. One weekly laid the blame on the prime minister: "Hashimoto's Government Puts Country on the Block, Turns Japan into American Colony." Ultranationalists took to the streets with rising-sun flags, their sound trucks blaring martial music, screaming for Americans to "stop meddling in Japan."

"What goes around comes around," crowed one American investor.

As Renoir's detention stretched on for month after month, the pressure on him notched steadily higher. After a hearing in Manhattan federal court in late 1998, federal marshals bused Renoir to Hudson County Jail in New Jersey, where he was locked in a bullpen. Renoir watched three prisoners demand a jail cell occupied by a frightened-looking man busted for marijuana. When the man resisted, the three attacked him with a broom handle, opening a grotesque wound in the man's arm. This wasn't like Westchester, Renoir realized. He was now in a jungle. He determined to keep his cool. His jailers told him to find his own bunk. Four beds were stacked into each cell. To Renoir's relief, a man recognized him from Westchester jail and invited him to share a cell in the bullpen.

Within days, Renoir was moved out of the bullpen into a cell with two of the toughest guys in the jail. One was facing drug and weapons charges. The other, a Latin King gang member, faced a conspiracy charge. Renoir later described his relationship with them as one of "mutual respect." His cellmates, he said, turned to him for advice about the world at large. And Renoir, in turn, sought advice about the hellish world of the jail, a cauldron of racial tension and simmering violence between the Bloods, the Crips, and the Latin Kings. Inmates carried shanks and taped razors to toothbrushes. The stress was intense. Fights would break out daily over television stations, brooms, and other trivial matters. Renoir watched his fellow inmates use their blades on one another with relish.

Renoir's cellmates looked out for him. When a member of one Spanish gang gave Renoir trouble, his cellmates ordered the thug to lay off. When Renoir's protectors shipped out, they instructed other prisoners to look out for him. "Every time some jerk tried to pick on me, I had six other guys trying to protect me," Renoir recalled.

One day, as Renoir talked on the phone to a Manhattan friend, a black inmate began arguing with a Hispanic one about a broom. The Hispanic man hit the black man. Other inmates pulled shanks. "Look, there's a riot starting," Renoir told his Manhattan friend. He hung up the phone. An Irish inmate warned Renoir to return to his cell, and a sympathetic guard locked him into it for protection. When order was restored, jailers ordered a 100-hour lockdown. For one 10-hour stretch, there was no water. The toilets stank. Renoir filed a complaint. Less than two days later, he was moved back to Valhalla, New York, to Westchester county jail. "Valhalla felt like a Holiday Inn compared to that," he later recalled. "I learned that I can survive anything."

Increasingly, Renoir regarded his lawyers at Patterson, Belknap with distrust. Lead lawyer John Winter told Renoir it would be difficult to scrap the proposed settlement merely because Yokoi had died. Renoir vehemently disagreed. Renoir complained about the legal bills and fell behind on payments. During one jailhouse visit, Winter would later complain, Renoir "verbally abused me and physically threatened me." Renoir later maintained that all he had ever done was accuse Winter of trying to screw him and warn Winter that he would not let it happen. With his confidence in Winter eroding, Renoir turned to an expert on extradition, Matthew Herrington, of Washington's prestigious Williams & Connolly.

On January 28, 1999, Herrington met Winter in his New York office to discuss Renoir's arguments for junking the settlement. Winter told Herrington it would be difficult to claim that Yokoi's death made it impossible for the Yokoi family to fulfill its part of the deal. Granted, Yokoi couldn't provide the promised letter. But his heirs could produce a letter revoking any interest in pursuing the French case, Winter said. More important, Winter explained, French authorities had already sent Renoir a chilling signal. Weeks earlier, the French government had filed what Winter described as "a very strong letter" indicating that regardless of how Renoir and the Yokoi family settled their dispute in France, French authorities intended to continue their criminal investigation.

Herrington responded that Renoir could claim that he personally believed the letter was material to the settlement.

What Renoir believed wouldn't matter to the court, Winter maintained. The court would analyze the matter objectively, not subjectively, he said. The court, he predicted, would reject such an argument.

Less than two weeks later, Winter motioned the New York state court presiding over the case for permission to withdraw. Winter complained that Renoir had threatened him, had failed to pay his bills, and had taken "positions not warranted by law." (Herrington, who took over as Renoir's lead lawyer, denied that Renoir had threatened Winter or that Renoir had insisted on pursuing meritless legal theories. Moreover, said Herrington, the Renoirs had already paid Winter's firm millions of dollars in legal fees.) The judge allowed Winter to quit.

Renoir's bid to overturn the extradition ruling stood on two legs: First, Renoir argued, he had not been charged with a crime in France, as required by the extradition treaty, but was wanted only in connection with an investigation. Second, while the French offered a mountain of circumstantial evidence that Renoir had acted with fraudulent intent, Renoir said, they offered insufficient evidence that a crime had been committed.

U.S. district court judge Loretta Preska knocked both legs out from under Renoir. For the purposes of extradition to France, Preska ruled, it is sufficient for someone to be accused of a crime, and not formally charged in the sense of an American indictment. She also ruled that the evidence from France supported a finding of probable cause. Preska dismissed Renoir's petition for a writ of habeas corpus. Renoir's lawyers immediately asked for a stay to appeal to the U.S. Second Circuit Court of Appeals. In the end, Renoir would later maintain, it wasn't the months in jail that broke him, nor was it the string of legal defeats. It was the relentless financial pressure to pay legal bills. He was running out of money. Renoir raged that his lawyers were charging him too much. His and his wife's legal bills were climbing toward $7 million, he said. Kiiko had sold her house in Tokyo and her design studio. She had borrowed bail money from her mother. Renoir had sold his Park Avenue apartment. Twenty-two years' worth of savings was gone. He owed $395,000 to Gary Melius.

In March 1999, lawyers for both sides gathered in Paris to hammer out a settlement. The division of property, they agreed, would remain unchanged: Yokoi's heirs, excepting Kiiko, would get the Empire State Building and the French châteaux; Kiiko and Renoir would get the British castles, the Long Island mansion, the Manhattan apartment, some $7.5 million in cash, and a share of the upside in the Empire State Building if Trump succeeded in breaking the lease. The two sides bickered over the letter. Renoir wanted a statement from Nippon Sangyo to French authorities that after reviewing the evidence, Nippon Sangyo now realized that Renoir and his wife had been acting in accordance with the wishes of her father.

Renoir's French lawyer, Dany Cohen, said later that he simply could not understand why the Yokoi family's lawyers refused to provide such a statement. It seemed, said Cohen, as though "they hoped the letter wouldn't stop the prosecution, that they wanted the prosecution to go on." Cohen said he began to suspect that the family or its lawyers "had something to lose if the prosecution didn't go on. What, I don't know."

Once again, Renoir had to compromise. On October 13, 1999, Hannigan and Herrington penned a joint letter to Renoir's criminal lawyer confirming that Nippon Sangyo and the Renoirs had reached a global settlement. "The documentation implementing the French aspects of this settlement have been completed and delivered in escrow to the head of the Paris bar association. . . . As part of the French settlement, NSKK [Nippon Sangyo] has agreed to withdraw its participation in the criminal complaint in France and furnish the attached letter, which is addressed to the French investigating magistrate."

> We have the honor to inform you that we have concluded with Kiiko Nakahara and Jean-Paul Renoir a settlement to amicably resolve our disputes with them in France and overseas.
>
> Our decision to make this settlement was determined by the explanations furnished by Kiiko Nakahara and Hideki Yokoi on the day of the mediation meeting of March 11, 1998, and also by the overall explanation subsequently furnished by the parties to each other.
>
> Taking into account the explanations we have been furnished, we now realize that we misunderstood the objectives of Kiiko Nakahara and Jean-Paul Renoir and that they considered themselves to have been acting in the interest of NSKK and the members of the Yokoi family.
>
> The death of Hideki Yokoi unfortunately eliminated the person best able to testify about the circumstances in which the alleged false powers of attorney, including the power of attorney of October 20, 1992, were prepared and then delivered to Kiiko Nakahara.
>
> The complexity and international dimensions of the financial situation in this case and the information recently furnished by Kiiko Nakahara allow us to understand why Kiiko Nakahara and Jean-Paul Renoir have not gained any personal financial advantage from the transactions in question.
>
> In consequence, we respectfully hereby irrevocably withdraw our constitution de partie civile.

On its face, the letter, which was signed by Hirohiko Yokoi, seemed to fall short of the unequivocal exoneration that Renoir had long been seeking from his accusers. Nippon

Sangyo asserted only that it "misunderstood" the objectives of the couple and that Kiiko and Renoir "considered themselves" to have been acting in the company's interest. Just what Nippon Sangyo believed Kiiko and Renoir's objectives to be was left conspicuously unstated.

Renoir's lawyer, Herrington, held forth the settlement as evidence that the epic battle was no criminal matter. "An extravagant dramaturgy notwithstanding, this case has always been at bottom a civil dispute among family members," said Herrington. "The Renoirs are pleased that the dispute has been resolved."

Donald Trump, who now had a new partner in the Empire State Building, declared, "Now, instead of having a warring family where I'm partners with one side, now I'm partners with the real owners." Trump said that he and his new partner could focus now on his lawsuit to break the lease, which, Trump insisted with characteristic bluster, was going "real well."

Renoir wasted no time trying to make the best of what he got. The following day, his criminal lawyer motioned the U.S. Court of Appeals for the Second Circuit to add the settlement letter to the record. The new letter, Renoir's lawyer Peter Dolatta asserted, "completely undercuts the probable cause finding in this case." Dolatta termed the letter an "effective recantation of the allegations of wrongdoing by the so-called victims in his case." At a minimum, Renoir lawyers told the court, the letter called out for a rehearing to reconsider the probable cause finding.

Timothy Coleman, the assistant U.S. attorney representing the Department of State, took issue with Dolatta's generous interpretation of the letter. Coleman directed the court to scrutinize the text of the letter carefully. A careful reading, Coleman maintained, would reveal that it fell short of absolving Renoir of anything. "The letter merely states that NSKK has settled its civil disputes with Renoir and his wife, and speculates about the 'objectives' of those two individuals based on unspecified 'explanations' of Nakahara, her late father, Hideki Yokoi, and unidentified other 'parties,' " Coleman wrote. "The letter also implies obliquely that Yokoi, were he alive, might give testimony favorable to Renoir. The letter does not state that the testimony of any witness relied on by the French Government was false. At best, the draft letter suggests that a corporate entity, as part of the compromise of various civil disputes, is now willing to agree that different inferences may be drawn from the facts. That is hardly a recantation." Coleman also noted that in spite of Nippon Sangyo's withdrawal as a party to the French criminal complaint, the French government had certified that its arrest warrant for Renoir would remain in force.

The painstakingly negotiated letter from Japan was proving less than the magic bullet Renoir had wanted. Renoir was still in a serious bind. As he waited for the U.S. Court of Appeals to decide whether to overturn the extradition order, Renoir began his third year behind bars. Although Renoir had always considered himself a strong man, there was little question that the years in confinement were sapping him, both physically and emotionally.

When I visited him in Westchester county jail in March of 2000, he looked drawn. His face had taken on the pallor of a man who had barely seen the sun in years. Renoir seemed to have shrunken into himself, his once-taut physique diminished by prison food and lack of exercise. One of his teeth was broken, but because the jail offered only to pull it out, Renoir let it be. His bitterness over his fate ran deep.

"The insanity I had to face in that family was something else," Renoir complained. "In fighting each other, for something they perceive to have value, but doesn't, they have pissed away millions and millions and millions. If they had just liquidated, and put the money in the stock market, they'd have tripled their money." As he reflected on the battle for the Empire State Building, Renoir harbored no such ill feelings toward his onetime partner, Donald Trump. "I can't expect loyalty from him if I haven't delivered anything in three years."

The visiting room of the Norwood E. Jackson Correctional Center is filled with small, square tables and straight-backed chairs. Nearly all of the tables were occupied by young men. Most of them gazed sadly into the eyes of young women who were visiting them. As I spoke with Renoir in one of the closet-size private interview rooms that ring the main visiting area, a disturbance broke out. Through the window of the interview room, I noticed visitors fleeing in fright from a tumult I could not see. There was shouting and screaming. Within moments, truncheon-wielding guards in riot gear swept through the room.

Renoir barely glanced over his shoulder. He seemed irritated by the distraction. "It happens all the time," he said indifferently. Renoir began to speak of the men he was living among. His long detention, it became clear, had colored his view of humanity. Renoir, his friends said, had always been a blunt-spoken man. But now he seemed to have lost all willingness to abide by the conventions of measured social discourse.

"Ninety percent of people in prison should never have been born," Renoir told me. "These kids should have been aborted." They are unemployable, he said. "They don't even have the attention span to watch a movie."

Drugs, guns, and extortion, Renoir continued, drove the economy of the ghetto. The scarred young men he saw in the jail shower looked as though they had done three tours in Vietnam, he said. "The only power they have is to sell drugs and make babies."

"I've been here 28 months. I was with the worst scumbags you can imagine," Renoir shouted. He pounded the table. "You go to the worst places in the Bronx. I lived with these guys."

17

Donald's Endgame

Early in 2000, hundreds of businessmen flocked to Man-hattan's University Club to be entertained over lunch by Donald Trump's patented brand of self-promotion. Unable to resist an opportunity to case out his adversary, Peter Malkin wangled an invitation from a friend and took a seat in front of the large dining room. When Trump spotted him, he walked over. "What are you doing here?" he asked Malkin. Trump chose a seat at the next table.

After a glowing introduction that identified Trump as part owner of the Empire State Building, Trump strode to the dais.

"What a great crowd," he proclaimed, singling out a hand-ful of Manhattan big shots by name. "Even Peter Malkin is here. He's suing my ass off," Trump deadpanned. "Of course, I'm suing his ass off, too." Laughter rippled through the crowd.

After regaling the crowd with tales about himself, the bronze-haired developer opened the floor to questions. Malkin raised his hand.

"If there is one thing that you could do that you'd like to be remembered for, what would that be?" Malkin inquired.

Trump considered the question, then remarked, "I'd like to own the Empire State Building."

One by one, the men and women who had stirred up so much trouble at the Empire State Building had either walked off the stage or been banished from it. To quiet Yokoi, it had taken death. His sons, in turn, found themselves without the stomachs to fight on. Months of detention had steered Renoir and Kiiko toward compromise. Leona and Malkin had seen the wisdom of a truce. In the end, the one man who could not bring himself to quit was the man who had put the least on the line: Donald Trump.

Trump was no longer caught in the middle of an ugly family row, but he was no closer to his elusive goal of ousting Helmsley and Malkin from the skyscraper. Over the prior year, his fiercely determined adversaries had dealt him a string of legal setbacks. First, New York state judge Edward Lehner rejected Trump's hairsplitting argument that Malkin and Helmsley had improperly acted as "owner" of the Empire State Building when dealing with New York City building authorities. Next, Lehner knocked down, one after another, Trump's most ballyhooed claims of lease violations by Malkin and Leona. The two tycoons were not obligated to install sprinklers in the building, Judge Lehner ruled. There was "insufficient evidence" of rodent infestation. The fire stairs on the eighty-sixth floor were fine and didn't violate the lease, he ruled, nor did the plastic-laminate elevator interiors that Trump had scorned. Insurance coverage on the landmark building was adequate. As for the hundreds of small businesses that occupied the building, they were no less a class of tenant than had ever occupied the building. When Judge Lehner had finished, all that was left standing from Trump's three default notices were a few issues raised in Trump's early 71-page screed about conditions. Judge Lehner directed Malkin to allow another inspection.

Once again, Trump's engineers scrutinized the building. Trump fired off a fresh 15-page notice of default, rehashing complaints about allegedly inferior windows, fire and safety problems, elevator shaft violations, and Malkin's failure to seek approval for "structural alterations." Malkin motioned the court to discard the rest of Trump's case without ever holding a trial.

In October 1999, Trump phoned Malkin. During the five years since Trump had stunned Malkin with the claim that he was buying the building, the two men had spoken no more than a few times.

"You must be as sick as I am about paying these lawyers," Trump told Malkin.

"There's an easy way to stop it, Donald," Malkin responded. "Just stop bringing these lawsuits."

Trump invited Malkin to talk face-to-face about the stand-off. But Malkin had no desire to compromise now. He had been waiting eagerly for a court ruling that would end Trump's threat for good. Trump just wanted to hedge against another setback in court, Malkin figured. Malkin told Trump he was on his way to Europe to visit his son. When he got back, Malkin said, he'd get in touch. He never did.

On December 16, 1999, the New York State Supreme Court granted a summary judgment in favor of Malkin and Helmsley. Replacing all 6,400 windows, Judge Lehner ruled, did not constitute a "structural alteration" requiring Trump's permission. Whether there were better windows on the market, the judge said, was irrelevant. The Landmarks Preservation Commission had approved of the windows, as had the building's prior owner, Prudential. Lehner summarily dismissed all the other default claims. Trump had not presented a single valid ground for breaking the lease, he said, nor had he raised a single issue that would require a trial to adjudicate.

On January 12, 2000, the court entered its final judgment. Trump's lawyer vowed an appeal. Trump, by now in the midst of an even more quixotic campaign for the U.S. presidency, remained uncharacteristically silent about the defeat. His effort to wrest the keys to New York's best-known building from Helmsley and Malkin, it appeared, had ended in a legal rout. The ruling left him with little more a paper stake in the building, a bragging claim. Thus far, it looked to be worthless.

"He picked on the wrong people," crowed lawyer Gerald Fields, who represented Helmsley and Malkin. "To think that he was going to bludgeon Leona Helmsley and Peter Malkin into being scared about a lawsuit. He couldn't have picked two tougher people, with more resources."

Malkin soon discovered that Donald Trump can be a very persistent man.

On January 24, Shamika Petersen, a 20-year-old data entry clerk, left her desk at CarePlus Health Plan on the forty-eighth floor of the Empire State Building and boarded an elevator to descend to the lobby. The elevator stopped on the forty-fourth floor, where 36-year-old Giuseppe Mesoraca, a self-employed travel agent with an office on that floor, got on. After the doors closed, the elevator plummeted in what seemed like a shuddering free fall. It shot past the lobby, then reversed direction, coming to rest on the fourth floor. "I thought I was going to die," Petersen said, likening the experience to "a bungee jump."

That, at least, was what Petersen told reporters the following day when she appeared with her father at a news conference leaning on a wooden cane. Her story, no doubt, was music to Trump's ears. Trump's lawyers argued that the incident, coupled with several elevator violations that had been on file with the city, justified reopening the case.

Malkin and his lawyers offered a far different take on the elevator mishap, which they claimed had been "grossly distorted and sensationalized in the press" and used by Trump "in a transparent attempt to rehash this entire litigation and to continue their bad-faith campaign of harassment." Malkin, in court filings, downplayed the incident as a "minor mechanical malfunction." Some time after Petersen boarded the elevator, Malkin's lawyers claimed, one of six cables attached to the bottom of the elevator to counterbalance its weight became tangled. The car, indeed, had begun falling, but not until it had already descended to the sixth floor, the lawyers said. And a safety switch stopped the plunge by the fourth floor, they said. "This is obviously a far cry from the '400 foot plunge' or 'bungee ride' reported in the press and recycled by Trump," Malkin's lawyers informed the court on March 29.

An inspector from the city buildings department found that the elevator's emergency braking system had stopped the elevator, Malkin's lawyers claimed. After conducting experiments on the elevator, an engineering firm hired by the building estimated that it had dropped only 15 to 20 feet and did not slam into anything, the lawyers said. The other violations cited by Trump related to nonhazardous conditions and had all been corrected, they said.

As for Shamika Petersen, Malkin waved off her complaints of injury. "We have a tape of her leaving the elevator and walking around the building outside, having a smoke, and coming back in again, and one of our people helped her back in the office, and no sign of anything," Malkin said. "Then, a couple of hours later, an ambulance comes, and she comes out claiming terrible injuries, after having spoken to a lawyer, probably."

Malkin's account of the incident differed sharply from those contained in separate lawsuits filed by Peterson and Mesoraca, the elevator's other passenger, who claimed to have sustained a back injury severe enough to require surgery.

Whatever the truth, Judge Lehner found Trump's renewed attack unconvincing. He rejected Trump's motion to reopen the case, claiming that it came too late and was immaterial. Trump, undeterred, pressed ahead with his appeal.

On May 17, 2000, five appellate judges took seats behind an ornately carved bench in New York's stately appellate courthouse on Madison Avenue. A domed stained-glass skylight bathed the marble-walled courtroom in golden light. In the front row of the spectator's gallery, in an oak and leather chair, sat Donald Trump, clad in a dark blue suit and maroon tie. His trademark sweep of hair seemed to glow a strawberry blond.

Trump's lawyer, Jay Goldberg, rose and walked to a lectern. Goldberg offered the five judges a thumbnail history of the Empire State Building, a history that starred, in Goldberg's telling, a heinous villain. Since 1961, he said, the building had been "in the hands of a nasty tenant under a long-term lease." Goldberg reeled off the multitude of alleged defects Trump had uncovered at the skyscraper since 1994. "This is a catastrophe waiting to happen," Goldberg said, his voice rising in calculated outrage. Goldberg spoke glowingly of Trump's record of restoring old buildings, starting with the deal that put Trump on the map, his conversion of the decrepit Commodore Hotel on Forty-second Street. Trump watched intently, his brow furrowed. Goldberg asked the court to reverse Judge Lehner and send the case back for trial. "We are the owner," said Goldberg, as his allotted time for argument ran out. "They are not the owner."

The judges asked not a single question, a worrisome sign for Trump. When Gerald Fields rose to respond on behalf of Helmsley and Malkin, he spoke with the relaxed confidence of a lawyer who had concluded that events were unfolding in his favor. He reviewed Trump's allegations—most of which "border on frivolous," he said—and reminded the judges why Lehner had declared them lacking. Trump scowled.

The hearing drew to a rapid close. Barely a word had been heard from the bench. Trump walked quickly out of the courtroom, traversed the marble foyer, and hurried down the courthouse steps. He climbed into the backseat of a black stretch Lincoln Town Car and sped off up Madison Avenue.

Three weeks later, in a terse two-page ruling, the Appellate Division of the New York State Supreme Court ended Trump's quest to take over the Empire State Building lock, stock, and barrel for himself and the Yokoi family.

Malkin had long since stopped guessing what his foe would do next. "Now it's up to Donald to decide whether he wants to continue being a nuisance," Malkin commented. Trump proposed a meeting. Malkin accepted, curious about whether Trump intended to offer any kind of constructive proposal.

Weeks earlier, Renoir, the man who had dreamed of remaking the Empire State Building into a luxury skyscraper, had decided the time had come to face his accusers in France. His lawyer, Matthew Herrington, had warned him that even though the appellate argument challenging the extradition had gone well, beating extradition remained a long shot. Moreover, the hundreds of days he had piled up in American jails would count for nothing in France. On February 1, 2000, Renoir wrote Timothy Coleman, the assistant U.S. attorney handling the case. "By this letter," Renoir wrote, "I withdraw the appeal presently pending in the Second Circuit Court of Appeals, waive any further right to appeal or review in the courts of the United States, waive review of my extradition by the United States Department of State, and consent to my extradition to France."

On Friday, March 24, federal marshals shackled and handcuffed Renoir and drove him to Manhattan's Metropolitan Corrections Center. One of the marshals treated him, he would later complain, "as if I was a serial killer." That weekend, French agents drove Renoir to John F. Kennedy airport, where they removed Renoir's handcuffs and escorted him onto an Air France plane for a scheduled flight. They carried shopping bags. Renoir decided that they had spent the weekend shopping in Manhattan.

In France, Renoir faced an uncertain fate. French authorities brought him to a jail in the rolling countryside outside Paris, where he was locked into a 10-foot cell with one other man. The trip had exhausted Renoir. He discovered, to his dismay, that prisoners in France were confined to their cells for most of their waking hours. But in other ways, detention in France seemed more humane. The medical care, Renoir found, was better. So was the food. Renoir began eating like a starving man. Within three months, he had put on 25 pounds, which he attributed to tasty baguettes.

"The French jail is less oppressive and more civilized than the American jails," Renoir wrote in a letter from jail. "The inmates are in general less violent and more controlled. The downside is that you are locked in all day and no telephone at all. That is hard to get used to, as I used to spend several hours on the phone every day."

Donald Trump is not the kind of man to readily admit that his deals sometimes don't work out as planned. By the summer of 2000, the only dividends Trump had realized from going into business with Renoir and Kiiko, it appeared, were the gallons of newspaper ink spilled over his "ownership" of the Empire State Building and any pleasure he may have derived from tormenting Leona Helmsley. The latter, of course, was no small compensation for Trump, who, given the chance, consistently leaps to portray his adversary as a malevolent force. "I consider myself to be a nice person," he later told me. "I don't say I'm the best person. But she's a horrible, horrible human being. She's the meanest person. She's not even mean. She's beyond mean. She's sick. I've seen what she's done to certain people, including her own husband. She's a terrible human being."

Trump's Empire State Building venture appeared to be shaping up as little more than an exercise in ego gratification, a misadventure with little promise as a profit-making enterprise. Not surprisingly, Trump portrayed it in a sunnier light. It was, he said, a brilliant deal. "They walked in and said, 'Would you take half of the upside, if you give me nothing?' I agreed. Most people would have done that." It was a no-brainer, he said. "It's a free option. Whether it's great or not, when you get something for nothing, often times you can make something out of it."

The death of Hideki Yokoi, coupled with the settlement of the family row, had thrust Trump into a working partnership with Peter Bal, the man who had once sculpted him as Donald Duck. Within months, Trump and Bal reached a decision that promised to put to the test Trump's bold pronouncements about the value of his interest in the skyscraper.

Trump telephoned Malkin and told him he wanted to discuss the possibility of selling the Empire State Building. Malkin agreed to meet Trump in the office of Benjamin Lambert, a broker who was overseeing the sale of Leona Helmsley's empire. Trump told Malkin that his Japanese partner had authorized him to offer the title to the skyscraper to Malkin and Helmsley. Malkin sensed what was coming. "We think there's going to be a big gap between what you think it's worth and what we do," Malkin said. He asked Trump to get back to him with his formal asking price. Some time later, Malkin received a letter. The price, wrote Trump, was $65 million. Trump wanted a whopping $25 million more than what Oliver Grace had paid on Yokoi's behalf nine years earlier—a price viewed at the time as excessive.

To understand where Trump came up with that number, it is necessary to turn back to the deal he struck with Renoir and Kiiko in 1994. Under the partnership agreement, Trump was entitled to half of any value he could add to the Empire State Building above $45 million. If he sold the building for $65 million, he'd pocket some $10 million. Anything under $45 million would net Trump zero.

Having offered just $35 million for the Empire State Building in 1991, it seemed unlikely that Malkin would be willing to pay anything like $65 million to rid the Helmsley partnership of its landlord problems. Unless, that is, Trump convinced someone else to make such an offer. Trump was in an awkward position. He had spent five years disparaging New York's favorite skyscraper as decrepit, dangerous, and a disgrace to the city. Now, he had to convince an investor to bid for it with the same kind of abandon that Yokoi and his daughter had displayed in the 1991 auction. Trump had to find someone else willing to take a flier.

New York real estate veterans questioned whether any rational outside buyer would offer such a sum. To a buyer paying $65 million, lease payments from Helmsley and Malkin would constitute a minuscule annual return of 2.9 percent. Worse still, when scheduled lease payments dropped to $1.6 million in 2013, the return would diminish further. Nevertheless, by October 2000, Trump was insisting that he had "a very substantial deal" in the works. Several different parties, he claimed, had expressed interest. Who, other than Malkin and Helmsley? Trump wouldn't say.

As Trump saw it, Malkin and Helmsley had every reason to strike a deal with him, and not just to end Trump's relentless troublemaking. The long-term leasehold on the Empire State Building—which runs through 2076—would be worth far more if Helmsley and Malkin also owned the building outright, Trump noted. They could do whatever they wanted with the building, without concerning themselves with the vicissitudes of a hostile owner. More important, Trump reasoned, owning the building would make it far easier for them to cash out. "The value of the building is a lot different if you say, 'I'm selling the building,' rather than, 'I'm selling 75 years of a leasehold,' " Trump said. "The Asians won't buy a leasehold." Helmsley and Malkin "don't own the building," Trump noted with relish. "I own the building."

Trump had begun an endgame with Malkin and Helmsley,

a game of bluff and bluster in which Trump stood to pocket 50 cents of every dollar they bid over $45 million. "I don't lose often," Trump boasted to me in February 2001. "They would buy it tomorrow for over 45 [million]. I want 65 now, but it's going up rapidly. It's going up rapidly." Trump paused theatrically. "I don't even think I'd take 65 now."

But why, I asked Trump, would Malkin pay a nickel over $45 million, much less $65 million, if no one else bids that much, a prospect dimmed by the fact that a third party would stand to earn a paltry 4.2 percent annual return on a $45 million purchase. "Look. The ones that should pay 65 are the ones who own the lease," Trump replied.

Absent a surprise bid from another quarter, why should Helmsley and Malkin do anything at all, given the failure of Trump's attack on the lease? "They know that two things can happen," Trump answered. "As long as we own the land, the building cannot be condominium-ized, which is a huge negative, because that's what's happening today. I don't only mean for apartments, I mean for apartments, hotel, and commercial." Selling condominiums in the Empire State Building, said Trump, is something only the building's owner can do. Trump also insisted that Helmsley and Malkin would be unable to borrow against their leasehold on the building unless they owned it as well.

Never mind that the two tycoons had rarely borrowed against the Empire State Building in the past, having just financed a $71 million facelift out of cash flow alone. Or that Leona was already sitting on a trove of cash, thanks to her sale of many other buildings. Malkin disputed whether Trump had any leverage at all, maintaining there was no reason he and Leona could not obtain a mortgage on their leasehold on the building or sell nonresidential condominiums in the building.

"There are lots of different turns that can happen here," Trump insisted. "Maybe we buy out the lease. That can also happen. It could be that I end up buying out everything."

"No chance!" That was Malkin's blunt assessment of Trump's chances of buying out his archenemy. Malkin explained that Leona would never, ever sell her interests in the Empire State Building to Trump. Indeed, Leona was showing no inclination at all to allow control of the Empire State Building to slip from her grasp. Although she was now 80 years old, she still insisted on approving each and every color change in the building's lights.

The passage of time, Trump stated confidently, would change things. "Some day, they're going to need it," he said. "When Leona kicks the bucket, they're going to need it. Because they're going to have to finance the estate."

Trump's trademark optimism notwithstanding, odds remained long that New Yorkers would be soon be gazing up at a Trump Empire State Building. The leasehold controlled by Leona and Malkin was worth hundreds of millions of dollars. Yokoi's financially struggling heirs were no longer in a position to squander money on overseas trophies, and Trump himself was unlikely to personally commit such a substantial sum to buy out his enemy.

Trump never even bothered to commission architectural drawings for a Trump Empire State Building. "I do drawings in my head," he assured me. "The Empire State Building is not a class A building," he declared. "It's run as a class B or C building, at best. And that's a shame. It's a shame." In his mind's eye, Trump saw a soaring tower filled with blue-chip corporate tenants, Trumpian tenants. At present, he noted with disdain, "when you go up to those floors, instead of having one tenant like American Express, with ten floors, or one quality law firm, you'll have 50 doors in a hallway, with a little individual practitioner in each office. All of these tiny little cubicles. It would have been so good. It should have been so good." Trump, catching himself sounding regretful, brightened. "Doing apartments at the top of that building would be a great idea," he continued. "How about those selling! The floor sizes are great. You'd have people that live on Fifth

Avenue buying apartments there just because it would be so cool."

On the morning of June 16, 2000, a guard came to Renoir's jail cell in France. "Mr. Renoir, you are leaving us," he announced. Renoir packed his possessions slowly, strangely nervous about the sudden prospect of being released. He telephoned his lawyer, but no one picked up. The authorities walked Renoir to the front gate, turned him loose, and slammed the gate behind him.

After 31 months behind bars, Renoir found himself standing in the sunlight on the side of the road, free to do as he pleased. The investigation, he knew, was not over. He could not leave France. But Renoir couldn't help feeling that events were finally breaking in his favor. Renoir began walking down the road toward the train station, lugging an armload of files. At the station, he bought a ticket to Paris and boarded the train. When he arrived in Paris, he was uncertain whether authorities had lifted the prohibition on speaking to his wife. So he grabbed a taxi to the apartment of a friend.

French authorities, in fact, had lifted their restrictions on contact between Renoir and his wife, who had not seen one another in more than two years. Renoir rejoined Kiiko in her modest rental home on the Seine River, intent on rebuilding a relationship that had been torn asunder. Two and a half years without vigorous activity had left the onetime fitness buff feeling weakened. His long ordeal had left him with intractable contempt for Kiiko's father and deep-seated bitterness for Japan.

"I never want to set foot in that country again," he told me in a phone conversation from home. Renoir sounded weary. "Never again. There is no room for individual personality. You're walking on eggshells all the time. They are slave-soldiers. It's a horrible way of life. It's a horror. I tell you, Japan is a horror."

In October, four months after his release, Renoir and his wife picked me up in their white BMW at the train station in Poissy, France. Kiiko, in a white cable-knit sweater and gaudy designer sunglasses, was behind the wheel. She popped a Maria Callas CD into the stereo and sped off into the countryside. It had been years since Renoir had laid eyes on the châteaux. The criminal investigation remained a sensitive subject. His lawyer had forbidden him to talk about the French case. He and his wife were awaiting word on what the investigating magistrate would do next. Would he let the investigation simply die on the vine without bringing formal charges? Or would he press ahead in spite of the Yokoi family settlement?

When Kiiko reached the village of Rosny Sur Seine, she drove slowly down a narrow lane covered with fallen leaves and stopped in front of the spiked, twisting ironwork that formed the front gate to château de Sully. Renoir, dressed in a blue blazer and necktie, gazed out the car window at the first château his wife had bought 15 years earlier. "I haven't been here in eight years," he said. The gatehouses, he saw, were in disrepair, their windows broken out. Hundreds of yards away stood the seemingly abandoned château. Renoir picked up a pair of binoculars and trained them on the forlorn mansion. The roof, destroyed in the suspicious fire several years earlier, had been repaired. Some of the windows had been bricked closed. Kiiko, nervous as a cat, stepped on the gas, and the car lurched forward. Renoir barked at her to slow down, but Kiiko appeared eager to get away from the property that had brought her so much trouble. Kiiko, once strong and defiant like her father, had been transformed by her ordeal, it seemed, into a cautious, even gun-shy, woman. "I lost my life. I lost my reputation. I lost my pride," she had told me after emerging from prison.

Renoir, on the other hand, appeared determined not to be cowed by the weight of the pending investigation. Renoir directed his wife to drive on to the village of Louvenciennes, near Versailles, where Kiiko had spent 30 million francs for the historic château de Barry. Kiiko and Renoir drove in circles through the winding, nearly deserted streets of the town, unable to even locate the property. Eventually, Renoir asked for directions.

"Someone is looking," said Kiiko, her discomfort growing by the minute.

"So, someone is looking," replied Renoir testily. "They're going to remember eight years later?"

Finally, Renoir and his wife located the château's driveway, and Kiiko timidly drove in. There was work being done on the muddy road leading to the stately seventeenth-century home, which was itself being renovated. A dump truck backed down the road. Kiiko threw the BMW into reverse, and backed rapidly toward the road. Renoir commanded her to stop.

"What, are you afraid to go to jail?" he asked her, his voice edged with anger.

"He's sick in the head," Kiiko replied, more to Renoir than to me.

Renoir and I climbed out of the car and began walking back toward the château. "You can see she's got a temper," he told me, with fondness and exasperation. Renoir walked back up the driveway to look at the château, apparently unafraid.

Back on the road, as we drove toward Yokoi's grandest French property, a sign for Bois D'Arcy caught Renoir's eye. "Why do I know that name?" he wondered aloud. Abruptly, Renoir laughed, then offered the answer: "That's where I was in jail." French jail, he reflected, would have been "a horror if you've never been to jail. But compared to Hudson County, it's like Club Med." Renoir ignored his wife's attempt to change the subject. "You don't know what it is never to have had a piece of cheese in your mouth for two and a half years, never to have had a piece of fish," he said.

Abruptly, Renoir turned defensive. It was important, he said, that I understood. "I didn't go to prison," he declared. "I didn't go to jail." True, he had spent nearly three years behind bars. But it was, he continued, "preventive custody." The French never charged him, in the American sense of the word, with a crime. "I don't have a criminal record," Renoir said.

It seemed like an artful dodge, a matter of semantics. But to Renoir, it was a deadly serious distinction. His involvement with the Empire State Building and the European castles had, by many measures, ruined his life. His refusal to bow to his father-in-law's demands had cost him his savings and, for many months, his liberty. He now faced the Olympian challenge of restoring his reputation.

Renoir directed his wife to drive to the château Millemont. Kiiko turned onto a narrow country road that knifed through the forest. Abruptly, we arrived in a tiny village where rustic buildings crowded the road. Not a soul was about. Kiiko slowed. Renoir pointed out a stately château surrounded by acres of meadows. Most of the building was shuttered. The meadows were unmowed. Deadwood lay fallen beneath tall trees. It was easy to understand why a scrappy Japanese billionaire who had risen from poverty would find such a place beguiling.

Renoir's misadventure with the Empire State Building—and the gauntlet of horrors that it brought upon Kiiko and him—had taxed his marriage in ways that few couples are ever called upon to endure. Renoir and his wife had been barred from speaking to one another for more than three years. Yet Renoir told me that, appearances to the contrary, the ordeal had brought them closer together.

As for the Empire State Building, Renoir now spoke of it with a curious mixture of contempt—for the stupidity of the purchase—and regret over a lost opportunity. For Renoir, like many of the men associated over the years with the New York landmark, had allowed himself to dream of the Empire State Building as the foundation of a personal empire. Renoir

wanted to do more than just remake the Empire State Building for the new millennium. He aspired to make it the centerpiece of a new public company. "My secret ambition," he
told me one day, "was to make it the core of a real estate
investment trust. I would have co-managed it with Trump."
What did Trump think of the idea? "It depends on when you
were talking to him. Trump is a rational opportunist. If you
create something that's rational and makes sense, he'll support it."

The mayhem that broke out within his wife's family, however, dashed Renoir's hopes. "If I hadn't been shut down, it
would have gone somewhere," Renoir assured me. The lease
held by Helmsley and Malkin, he said, was a surmountable
problem. "I always, always find a solution. I had another card
up my sleeve with Malkin. I won't tell you, not now." But what
about Leona's avowed intention to hold onto the Empire
State Building, I asked him, and her nearly rabid refusal to
consider selling anything to Trump? "I think she would have
sold it," he said confidently. "Maybe it was a mistake of mine
to let Trump lead. But after they sued us, what could I do? I
stepped on a booby-trap."

There are those who say that with old-style tycoons like
Harry Helmsley and Hideki Yokoi dying off, the years in
which family fiefdoms dominate the real estate industry are
drawing to a close. Yet in many ways, despite efforts to modernize the industry, the real estate sector remains a world
unto itself, as far from the cutting edge as Harry Helmsley was
from Silicon Valley. In what other business could an aging
relic from the 1930s—the Empire State Building—loom so
tall and inspire such covetousness at the turn of the twenty-
first century?

By almost any rational business measure, Hideki Yokoi
paid more for the Empire State Building than it was worth.

And when a new owner comes forth—and odds are one will within the decade—it is safe to assume that that owner will pay too much for the building as well. That few in the industry find that surprising is testament to how a certain kind of real estate mogul measures success.

As a native New Yorker, Trump seems to grasp that the Empire State Building exerts a pull over people like no other building. "The building is magic. It's got a unique place in people's hearts," Trump said. What Trump ultimately makes of his wildcat grip on the building remains to be seen. For now, at least, Trump holds something that is difficult to value. It is the right to boast. "Hey, I own the Empire State Building. They don't own it. I own it, with my partners," Trump told me after he had put the building back on the market. "Peter Malkin made a tremendous mistake when he didn't buy it."

The known facts about the fray within the Yokoi family over the Empire State Building leave the most baffling mystery without an answer. Who betrayed whom? Did Yokoi secretly promise his daughter the Empire State Building as a gift, as Kiiko later claimed, then betray her? Or did Kiiko more or less steal the building, as Yokoi later insisted? "Only father and me know the facts," Kiiko told me when I visited her in France in 1998, seven months before the death of her father. "The others don't know anything. His instructions were never written down." The death of Yokoi left only one person, Kiiko, knowing for certain whose version of the tale is correct. The settlement of the lawsuit ensured that neither a judge nor a jury will ever be called upon to pass judgment on who was telling the truth.

Relationships between fathers and their sons and daughters perhaps color the real estate industry more than any other sector of the business world. Real estate lore is rife with tales of children not living up to the expectations of their fathers, of tragic family breeches, of fortunes lost. The truth about the outlandish fight within the Yokoi family over the

Empire State Building is in the end buried somewhere in the complex relationship between Kiiko and her father.

In October 2000, over afternoon tea at a Paris hotel, Kiiko tried to impress upon me the depth of the ties between herself and her father. "My father always said, 'We have the same lifelines,' " Kiiko explained with utter seriousness. From her bag, she retrieved a small hardcover book. The book mapped the lines on the hands of well-known people. "My father gave it to me a long time ago," she said. She opened the book to a map of her father's hand and laid it on the table. She opened her own hand next to the book, palm up. "Look," she said. I asked Kiiko how she had felt in 1991 when her father had finally recognized her on his official family registry. She paused. "It's very complicated," she said at last, and lapsed into an awkward silence. It was something Kiiko was not willing—or perhaps not able—to discuss.

Through the years, real estate markets have shown a remarkable ability to shrug off crises brought on by the ego and greed of property tycoons, to survive their rapid ascents and crashing falls. The buildings themselves, after all, remain standing. While the Empire State Building lacks the surface sheen of more pampered buildings—thanks both to its age and the cast of characters charged with its care—it remains largely undiminished in the public eye. Unlike nearly every other building erected during the storied early waves of twentieth-century Manhattan development, it has not slipped into irrelevance, to be cherished only by architectural historians. Unique among office buildings, it lives on as a monument, a sturdy lighthouse on the New York skyline for generations of travelers dropping down out of the clouds after a long-distance flight or cresting New Jersey's palisades on the way home.

The days have passed when the U.S. State Department called regularly to arrange visits for foreign heads of state. But the Empire State Building remains etched into the popular imagination as the essence of New York. On a typical day, between 4,000 and 6,000 people descend an escalator to the basement, where they move through charmless, fluorescent-lit corridors to a ticket office that looks to belong in an old ballpark. There they fork over $9 per adult for a ticket to the apex of the midtown skyline. Day in and day out, they are drawn to the observatory to marvel at the world, furtively penning on its rails messages like "Hector-n-Sonia 2000" and "Jessica, I Love you forever." At dusk, from the street, it is possible to make out the nearly ceaseless twinkling of tourists' flashbulbs that form a glittering necklace around the observation deck.

Blue-chip companies—the kind of tenants held in esteem by Donald Trump—may not consider the Empire State Building an acceptable place to do business. But that has never been part of the building's appeal. The tenant directory posted in its lobby reflects its status as a building for the masses—Round the Clock Socks and Hoisery, Travel Goods Association, Empire Chiropractic, Grandma Sylvia's Funeral, and so on. Occupancy has climbed back up to 99.5 percent. Some 25,000 people report to the building for work each day. For Malkin and Helmsley, who have poured $72 million of partnership money into the nearly completed renovation, the building is a cash cow. After two lean years in the mid-1990s, it is once again pumping out profits to investors in the partnerships that control the lease. If the Empire State Building weren't saddled with that lease—and Leona has told acquaintances that she has no intention of giving up her stake in it—it might fetch as much as $1 billion on the open market.

The Empire State Building has weathered the tempest of envy and greed that swirled around it for a decade with its allure intact. As another wave of building washes over Manhattan, it seems unthinkable that the Empire State Building will lose its power as a symbol of New York's grandeur. In the

69 years that have passed since he first rented space in the sky-scraper, diamond and precious metals dealer Jack Brod has watched from the windows of his small, drab offices as New York changed, as new generations of tall buildings rose around him. But he has never once considered leaving. The building has been his calling card.

"I've spent most of my life here," says Brod, now 91. He shuffles into his disheveled, sixty-seventh-floor corner office, which is stuffed with merchandise and mementos. It is getting late, after hours, so Brod has tucked an old .38-caliber police special into his waistband. Gold chains hang from tabletop jewelry racks. Tarnished silver platters and tea sets, piles of silver spoons, and boxes of old watches clutter the tables. Silver ingots are stacked on the floor, and a 1,000-ounce block of Mexican silver holds open the door. A layer of dust blankets the room. Brod, shrunk into his suits by age, his long white hair slightly askew, eases into an old chair. Over the years, Brod says, he traveled the world, and he never met a literate person who didn't know of the Empire State Building. Brod figures he has taken thousands of visitors to the observation deck, and people remain as thrilled at present as they were when the building was the loftiest on the planet.

To Brod, the events of the last decade were an affront to the building he loves. Brod felt he had done his part to defend his beloved skyscraper against the attacks of the big wheels. The campaign to malign the building was "complete hogwash," he says, and Donald Trump was "full of crap."

Brod fixes his rheumy unblinking eyes on lower Manhattan at twilight and gestures to the twin towers of the World Trade Center, rising like a pair of twinkling ingots. "They're like two shoeboxes on end," he says contemptuously of the towers that once nosed the Empire State Building out of the record books. His home skyscraper "may not be quite as up-to-date as some of the brand-new buildings," he admits. "But I don't think they'll ever build a building this beautiful again."

S eventy years after its completion, the Empire State Building still retains its inestimable hold on the imagination, along with a mysterious power, it seems, to bring out the worst in those who seek to make it their own. The courses charted by many of the men and women who fought to control the landmark during the last decade of the twentieth century sent them winding toward self-destruction. In the end, nearly all of them came away with some lasting tarnish. Some were left with scars they will carry for a lifetime. In their stories, one can almost divine the wages of ego, greed, and vengeance.

Although much of the legal warfare had run its course by mid-2001, controversy continued to swirl around the New Yorkers who had been embroiled in disputes over the building. On March 30, 2001, Peter Malkin, who seemed to have navigated the decade of skirmishes with his reputation intact, suffered a blow to his standing. In a 134-page ruling, an American Arbitration Association panel derailed Malkin's cam-

replace Helmsley-Spear, now controlled by Harry
y's longtime partner Irving Schneider, as manager of
ire State Building and 10 other buildings. After hearing from 50 witnesses and sifting through a record of nearly 2,000 exhibits, the arbitrators ruled that Malkin had failed to prove his accusation that Helmsley-Spear had grossly mismanaged the great skyscraper or any of the other buildings in question.

Malkin's case, of course, had not been helped by his vigorous defense of the Empire State Building from Trump's accusations of mismanagement. But the arbitrators, it appeared, were also distressed by the skullduggery that had colored the long fight. A private investigator hired by Wien & Malkin, they discovered, had secretly taped a luncheon meeting with a Helmsley-Spear employee, then sent a transcript that was "riddled with omissions and inaccuracies" to the district attorney. Malkin later said he had been unaware of the taping, but that it was justified due to his lawyers' concern that Helmsley-Spear was trying to entrap Wien & Malkin, an accusation he did not elaborate upon. ("That's a laugh," said Schneider's lawyer, Howard Graff.) Worse still for Malkin, the ruling added a stinging rebuke to his law firm for blurring the line between its legal and business activities in dealing with partnership investors. Malkin later complained that the arbitrators hadn't backed their negative conclusions with evidence, and he argued that several courts had discounted similar accusations. Malkin motioned in New York state court to vacate the ruling.

It is impossible to know what Harry Helmsley or Larry Wien would have made of Malkin's crusade to strip management of the Empire State Building from Helmsley-Spear. Forty years earlier, Wien and Helmsley had structured their partnership so that neither of them could make such a move without the approval of the other. That long-ago commitment still yokes Malkin and Leona to one another. Malkin needs support from Leona Helmsley to get rid of Schneider. He's unlikely to get it. When Leona settled her own legal battle with Schneider in 1997, she struck a secret alliance with Schneider against Malkin. She vowed to take all necessary actions to ensure that Helmsley-Spear would continue to manage the Empire State Building for as long as Schneider was alive and actively controlled the company.

Malkin, nonetheless, has vowed to carry on his fight. His stalemate with Schneider, Malkin said in May 2001, would not last forever. Schneider was 81 years old, he noted, and Leona would turn the same age within months.

But Leona, for her part, has shown no signs she is ready to cede much of anything to Malkin or to anyone else. The increasingly private life that she sought after the death of her husband was shattered in early 2001 by embarrassing reports about a dispute with a 45-year-old optometrist from Florida whom she had named a top executive at Helmsley Enterprises. Leona had begun socializing with the man, Patrick Ward, and had sold him 60 Manhattan apartments at a steep discount. Gossip columnists took note. Shortly after she learned the man was gay, she abruptly cut him out of her life, and ultimately opted to pay him $1 million to return the apartments. "I'm starting to mistrust my judgment," she confessed to *Wall Street Journal* reporter Peter Grant. A trace of self-pity seemed to color her remarks. "I don't have a life," she stated.

Although Leona's nemesis, Suzy Smith, has long since left the building, she has not been able to easily escape the turmoil she stirred up years earlier. In April 2001, Smith was subpoenaed for questioning by a lawyer defending the Empire State Building against a lawsuit brought by a victim of the terrorist shooting. According to Smith, she was peppered with questions about her involvement with Trump. The session became so confrontational, she said, that she later dashed off a letter to the judge handling the case. "At one point this attorney was yelling so loudly for me to answer only yes or no that I 'refused to answer.' (How can anyone think straight when they are being verbally harassed.)," she wrote. "It was a horrible experience which has left me very shaken."

As of May 2001, Renoir was still awaiting indication from French investigators about whether they intend to proceed toward prosecution. He has grown to loathe his native land. "I want to go back to the U.S.," he said. "I've got nothing to do here. If I touch anything here, who knows what they might arrest me for? I'm trying to keep my sanity." Renoir is eager, of course, to restore his reputation. Shortly before his release from jail, several of his friends wrote open letters attesting to his character. "It is inconceivable to me that he has had to endure this type of torture while lawyers, judges, politicians, and journalists look on and do nothing," wrote Lee Miller, the Greenwich, Connecticut, investor who has counted Renoir as a friend since the late 1970s. "Mr. Renoir is not, and never has been, a threat to society. Maybe I am naive but I thought that that is what prisons were for."

Kiiko Nakahara has also been trying to restore normality to her life. She has exhibited some of the paintings she produced while her husband sat in jail, portraits of a woman with wild raven hair and furious eyes, and landscapes filled with heavy, dark clouds, stark trees, and volcanoes. Unlike her husband, Kiiko has grown reticent to discuss her travails.

In the wake of Hideki Yokoi's death, his once impressive empire has unraveled at breakneck speed. By July 2000, Nippon Sangyo, the holding company through which Yokoi had assembled his foreign portfolio, was nearly bankrupt, with liabilities of more than half a billion dollars, according to Teikoku Databank Limited, a credit research agency. Banks stopped doing business with it, and courts seized company real estate, according to Teikoku. In October 2000, Yokoi's primary lender during the bubble years, Chiyoda Mutual Life Insurance Company, filed for bankruptcy protection, listing nearly $27 billion in liabilities, making it Japan's largest postwar bankruptcy. Japanese newspapers cited loans to Yokoi as the best-known example of its reckless lending.

Because Nippon Sangyo has not sought to reorganize under court protection, it is difficult to ascertain which overseas buildings it still owns. It is believed, however, that the settlement of the New York litigation left the family's interest in the Empire State Building invulnerable to Japanese creditors. In France, at least six of the châteaux have been sold, with a considerable chunk of the proceeds going to creditors, according to Dany Cohen, Renoir's French lawyer.

The Yokoi family real estate portfolio in Japan is also in decline. By late 2000, the Toyo Yusen bowling center, once the largest in the world and the pride of Hideki Yokoi's Tokyo holdings, looked to be going to seed. Cracks spidered across the exterior of the eight-story building. Its sign, a neon bowling pin, was broken. Several of its upper floors appeared all but abandoned, a dust-covered repository of cardboard boxes, old office furniture, even an old motorcycle. The cosmetics and diet guru who purchased Yokoi's valuable residential compound in Denenchofu had bulldozed his homes to the ground, leaving not a trace of the buildings that had housed his peculiar family for more than half a century.

In America's treacherous real estate markets, Yokoi had discovered that trophy buildings are not tickets to Tiffany-class profits. From an investment standpoint, Yokoi's $80 million global shopping spree had proven a farce, serving to illustrate that old adage, "Let the buyer beware."

Yet Hideki Yokoi never lost his passion for the kind of buildings that fill people with awe—a passion that fueled his obsessive quest for the world's most famous skyscraper and shattered his family, seemingly beyond repair. Yokoi took his taste for grandeur with him to the grave.

On April 29, 2000, about a dozen workmen gathered in Tokyo's Tama Cemetery at the underground tomb of Hideki Yokoi, according to *Shukan Bunshun,* a Tokyo magazine. Thirty years earlier, Yokoi had seen to it that his final resting place would be like no other. He had built a trophy tomb. Inside the carpeted chamber, which was decorated with chandeliers, lay the cremated remains of Yokoi, his mother, and eight other members of his family. After a prayer by a monk, the workmen began lifting the stone lids off the coffins holding the remains. "It is suspected that my father hid the money somewhere, and we have been searching for it everywhere at the request of the creditors," Kunihiko Yokoi told the publication. "But we have not been able to locate the money. The grave, built by my father, was the last place we could think of." But Yokoi, in death, had added a final footnote to his book of secrets. There was no money there, either.

M any of the characters in this story were interviewed at length, both for my coverage of the events for *The Wall Street Journal* and for the preparation of this book. The following list of those interviewed does not include people who requested anonymity or those to whom I spoke only briefly. People appearing in the book who chose not to speak to me were made aware of information I had gathered about them and given an opportunity to comment on it. Some chose to do so, others didn't. Some of the following people granted numerous lengthy interviews.

Peter Bal, Jack Brod, Edward Brodsky, Jacques Catafago, Duke Chapman, Dany Cohen, Timothy Coleman, Lester Crown, Andrew Davidoff, Gerald Fields, Edward Gordon, Oliver Grace Jr., Howard Graff, Donald Grossmann, Charles Guigno, Raymond Hannigan, Philip Hawkes, Patricia Hawkes, Stephen Heyman, Matthew Herrington, Mitsuo Hishida, Hisakazu Honjo, Jesper Koll, Charles Lindsay, Peter Malkin, Carol Mann, Bernard Mendik, Heath McLendon, Gary

Melius, Lee Miller, Atsushi Mizoguchi, Richard Morano, Kiiko Nakahara, Pascal Narboni, Naomi Okada, Hiroshi Okuyama, Stephen Rathkopf, Kurt Reich, Jean-Paul Renoir, Peter Ricker, Steven Rosen, Charles Ross, Lydia Ruth, Tsuneji Sato, Alvin Silverman, Alex Smirnoff, Suzy Smith, Julien Studley, Thomas Sullivan, Robert Tinker, John Trainor Jr., Donald Trump, Charles Urstadt, Fred Uruma, Abraham Wallach, Gregory White, John Winter.

Several collections of historical material proved invaluable for reconstructing events of long ago. The Avery Architectural and Fine Arts Library, Columbia University in the City of New York, contains an extensive archive on the Empire State Building, including early newspaper clippings, publicity materials, and photographs. The Hagley Museum and Library in Wilmington, Delaware, has a comprehensive collection of the papers of John Raskob and Pierre S. du Pont. The New York State Library in Albany houses the papers of Al Smith. Columbia University's Rare Books and Manuscripts Library contains the papers of Lawrence Wien. The Foreign Correspondents' Club of Japan has an impressive newspaper file, from which I unearthed considerable information about Yokoi's business career, his shooting, and the fire at the Hotel New Japan.

The disputes that form the spine of this narrative were fought out in a number of separate lawsuits:

- *Nihon Sangyo Kabushiki Kasisha v. Kiiko Nakahara, Jean Paul Renoir, et al.,* 130874-94, Supreme Court of the State of New York, County of New York.
- *Empire State Building Associates, et al. v. Trump Empire State Partners, et al.,* 103694/95, Supreme Court of the State of New York, County of New York.
- *Empire State Building Associates et al. v. Donald Trump, Hideki Yokoi, Kiiko Nakahara, Jean Paul Renoir, et al.,* 113519/95, Supreme Court of the State of New York, County of New York.

- *In the Matter of the Extradition of Jean-Claude Perez, a/k/a "Jean-Paul Renoir," to France,* U.S. District Court, Southern District of New York.
- *Jean-Paul Renoir v. Madeline Albright, Sec. of State, et al.,* 98 Civ. 1898, U.S. District Court, Southern District of New York; 99-2026, U.S. Court of Appeals for the Second Circuit.
- *Wien & Malkin LLP et al. v. Helmsley-Spear, Inc.,* 603145/97, Supreme Court of the State of New York, County of New York. *Wien & Malkin LLP et al. v. Helmsley-Spear, Inc.,* American Arbitration Association Commercial Arbitration Tribunal, case numbers 13-180-00976-97, 13-180-00964-97, New York City Regional Office.
- *Leona Helmsley v. Peter Malkin,* 104708/97, Supreme Court of the State of New York, County of New York.
- *Irving Schneider v. Peter Malkin, et al.,* 600163/98, Supreme Court of the State of New York, County of New York.
- *Irving Schneider and Alvin Schwartz v. Helmsley-Spear Inc., et al.,* 95/118033, Supreme Court of the State of New York, Appellate Division, First Department.

The papers filed in connection with these lawsuits, along with the depositions and affidavits given by participants and witnesses, amount to many thousands of pages and were a vital source of information. Among the people who made extensive statements under oath were Hideki Yokoi, Jean-Paul Renoir, Kiiko Nakahara, Hirohiko Yokoi, Kunihiko Yokoi, Peter Bal, Peter Malkin, Mitsuo Hishida, and Henry Bubel.

Nearly all of the dialogue in this book was taken from interviews and court records. Much of it came verbatim from transcripts of depositions and court hearings. In other cases, I have reconstructed conversations through interviews with those involved. Their words are reported exactly as told to me by those people, to the best of their abilities to recall. I always attempted to check comments they attributed to others with those people. Thoughts are attributed to characters only when those people recalled, in interviews with me, having such thoughts. The limited amount of dialogue attributed to historical characters is taken from direct quotations contained in newspaper articles or books.

In the following notes, I have chosen not to list the many newspaper articles that I read, only the ones from which I used quotations or data.

Prologue

Yokoi's visits to the Empire State Building were described in interviews with four people who accompanied him: Hannigan, Bal, and his two bodyguards, Henry Olsen and Jerry Galgano. Yokoi's unsavory reputation in postwar Tokyo was detailed in numerous newspaper and magazine articles written over the years by Japanese reporters.

Chapter 1: The Deal and the Deception

Reich and White recounted in interviews the marketing of the building, the meetings and discussions with Renoir and Kiiko, and the events that followed. Renoir said he recalled very little about his meeting with Reich. Malkin described in interviews his discussions with Salomon bankers and his telephone conversation with Trump. Reich and Grace recalled their meeting in separate interviews.

Chapter 2: Reaching for the Sky

Much of the material for this chapter was drawn from the archives of the Avery Architectural and Fine Arts Library at Columbia University, the Hagley Museum and Library in Wilmington, Delaware, and New York State Library in Albany. A more comprehensive account of the early history of the building is contained in John Tauranac's *The Empire State Building* (New York: Scribner, 1995; St. Martin's Griffin, 1997).

Smith's announcement of the project was described in the *New York Times* (hereafter *NYT*), 8/30/29. Smith's financial motives were discussed in *Al Smith: Hero of the Cities,* by Matthew and Hannah Johnson (Boston: Houghton Mifflin Co., 1969). The quotation about Smith's sales skills came from "Al Smith: Four Times Governor," the *New York Times Magazine,* 1/2/30. Biographical material at the Hagley Museum detailed Raskob's career. Historian Oscar Handlin's *Al Smith and His America* (Boston: Northeastern University Press, 1987) discussed Smith's relationship with Raskob. Details of du Pont's family and career were drawn from newspaper articles, including "Du Pont Clan Advances to New Conquests Under Pierre, a Strong Yet Gentle Leader," *The World,* 8/7/27.

The pencil story appeared in Jonathan Goldman's *The Empire State Building Book* (New York: St. Martin's Press, 1980). "Skyscrapers: The Paper Spires," *Fortune,* September 1930, described planning by Raskob and Smith. The height contest with the Chrysler Building was detailed in "The Chrysler Building, As I See It," by Kenneth Murcheson, *The American Architect,* 1930, and in *NYT,* 5/2/31.

Smith's comments announcing the zeppelin mast appeared in the *NYT,* 12/12/29; his remarks at the start of demolition, *NYT,* 10/2/29; and his statements at the cornerstone ceremony, *NYT,* 9/10/30. Smith's comments on his visit with ironworkers appeared in the *New York Sun,* 5/6/31. Smith's daughter, Emily Smith Warner, wrote of his concern about the economics of the project in her biography, *The Happy Warrior* (Garden City, N.Y.: Doubleday & Co., 1956). Smith's expression of confidence that the building would be fully rented appeared in the *Telegram,* 1/7/30, and Eckener's reservations about the mooring mast in the *Evening Post,* 2/6/31.

Smith's remarks to Roosevelt concerning the opening date appeared in *NYT,* 5/2/31. His opening day radio speech is contained in his papers at the New York State Library in Albany. Aloysius's account of visitors to the observatory appeared in the Associated Press, 7/26/36. The story about peeping toms appeared in the *Pittsburgh Post-Gazette*, 7/7/31. Aldrich's comments were contained in the *New York American*, 2/10/37. Accounts of early suicides and attempted suicides were taken from the *NYT*, 11/4/32, 9/20/33, 2/14/35, 5/11/47, and 7/15/47.

Documents and correspondence related to the building's early financial woes, including the letter to tax authorities and Smith's letter urging the federal government to buy it, are contained in the papers of Raskob and du Pont at the Hagley Museum. Quotations related to the plane crash appeared in the *NYT*, 7/29/45.

Chapter 3: Trophy Hunting

Interviews with Renoir and his colleagues and acquaintances, and Renoir's deposition, provided information about his life and career. Patricia and Philip Hawkes described the châteaux market and their dealings with Nakahara in interviews. Renoir recalled his early contacts with Yokoi in an interview and in written reflections.

The development of Japan's bubble economy is discussed in historian Walter LeFeber's *The Clash—U.S.-Japanese Relations Throughout History* (New York: W. W. Norton & Co., 1997), and by Marcus Brauchli in articles in *The Wall Street Journal*.

Nakahara discussed her father's net worth in a deposition. Information about Nakahara's European property search was drawn from interviews with her, Renoir, and Hawkes, and from Nakahara's deposition and affidavit. A letter from Yokoi's lawyer to a French investigating magistrate discussed the purchases, as did the French extradition complaint against Renoir.

Data on Japanese investment in U.S. real estate came from annual reports by E&Y Kenneth Leventhal Real Estate Group.

The high-profile purchases, were described in *The Wall Street Journal* and in Christopher Wood's *The Bubble Economy* (New York: The Atlantic Monthly Press, 1992). Okada described his meetings with Nakahara, Yokoi, and Trump in an interview. Robert King's self-published 1985 monograph, *Raising a Fallen Treasure,* recounts the history of Oheka castle. Melius described his involvement in an interview. Nakahara told of her other attempted purchases, and of her father's comments on losing the Saks deal, in a deposition.

Yokoi's first discussions with Nakahara about the Empire State Building, his alleged offer to give it to her, and his reaction to the collapse of the deal were described by Kiiko in a deposition. Renoir, White, and Lindsay described their involvement in interviews. Grace's involvement, and the structure of the deal, was detailed in the depositions of Renoir and Bubel and in interviews with Grace and Renoir. Malkin described his lunch with Grace in an interview.

Chapter 4: Yokoi's Secret

Details about the postwar climate in Tokyo were drawn from John Dower's *Embracing Defeat* (New York: W. W. Norton & Co./The New Press, 1999) and from LaFeber's *The Clash.* The rise of the *yakuza* was explained in David Kaplan and Alec Dubro's *Yakuza* (New York: Collier Books/MacMillan Publishing Co., 1986) and in Robert Whiting's *Tokyo Underworld* (New York: Pantheon Books, 1999).

Information about Yokoi's early life came from interviews with his longtime associates, Hishada, Sato, and Honjo, from Nakahara and Renoir, and from the depositions of Hishida and Nakahara. Numerous Japanese newspaper and magazine articles have chronicled Yokoi's rise, his controversial business practices, and his personal life. One article that proved especially useful was "Yokoi's Disgraceful Resume," by Atsushi Mizoguchi, in *"Gendai,"* June 1982. Yokoi's early takeover activities were described in articles in *Japan Times,* the *Daily Yomiuri, Mainichi Daily News,* and *Asahi Evening News* in 1958 and 1982.

Yokoi's family tree was discussed in an affidavit by Nakahara and by Hishida in a deposition. Yokoi's official family registry supplied details about his recognized children. There are many Japanese press accounts of his womanizing, with Mizoguchi's being among the most rigorously researched. Interviews with Renoir, Hiroshi Okuyama (Yokoi's former son-in-law), and an illegitimate daughter who now lives in New York yielded information about Yokoi's relations with his various households. Nakahara told of her early life and career in interviews and in a deposition.

Hishida, Sato, and Okuyama recalled in interviews the shooting of Yokoi. Additional details were drawn from newspaper coverage of the shooting, manhunt, and trial in *Mainichi Daily News, Japan Times, Daily Yomiuri,* and *Asahi Evening News,* and from *Tokyo Underworld.*

Sato and Honjo discussed their meeting with Yokoi prior to the hotel fire in separate interviews. Details about the fire and its aftermath were drawn from the newspapers cited above, from *Shukan Shincho* magazine, and from an interview with Hiroko Hanaoka, who was widowed by the fire. Hishida discussed Yokoi's feelings about the response of his sons to the fire in an interview. Nakahara and Renoir discussed Nakahara's growing involvement in interviews and in depositions. Sato, Honjo, and Renoir provided details about Yokoi's daily life. *Shukan Shincho* reported on the adoption of Yokoi's mistress by his brother.

Chapter 5: Yokoi Meets His Match

Honjo recalled Yokoi's problems with bankers in an interview. The beginning of Japan's economic slide was discussed in a series of *Wall Street Journal* articles in 1990 and 1991 by

Marcus Brauchli and Clay Chandler. Renoir described Yokoi's debt problems in a deposition and in interviews. The Hotel New Japan debt was detailed in correspondence between Yokoi and Trump. The exposure of Hirohiko Yokoi, Kunihiko Yokoi, and Kiiko Nakahara to Yokoi's debts was discussed in the depositions of Hirohiko, Kunihiko, Nakahara, Hishida, Bubel, and Yokoi's bookkeeper. Yokoi's financial problems in France, and Renoir's increasing involvement, were enumerated in the depositions of Renoir and Nakahara and in interviews with them.

The complex ownership structure for the Empire State Building was delineated in documents filed in the lawsuit. Ohashi recalled her concerns about the deal in a deposition. Charles Lindsay described his trip to Tokyo and his subsequent meetings about the Hotel New Japan in an interview. Trump's letters about the project and the subsequent draft agreement surfaced in the lawsuit. Trump's trip to Japan was described in deposition testimony by Nakahara, Renoir, and Bubel, and in interviews with Renoir, Nakahara, and Trump.

Chapter 6: Old Guard, New World

Details about Wien's life and career were taken from "Reminiscences of Lawrence Wien (9/16/1988)," from the Columbia University Oral History Research Office Collection. The lives and careers of Harry and Leona Helmsley were described in Michael Moss's *Palace Coup* (New York: Doubleday, 1989), Richard Hammer's *The Helmsleys* (New York: NAL Books, 1990), and Tom Shachtman's *Skyscraper Dreams* (Boston: Little, Brown and Co., 1991). Leona Helmsley declined to speak about any of the events described in this book. All of the material about her was shared with her publicist, Howard Rubenstein, who declined to comment for the record on any of it.

Information about the partnership between Wien and Malkin was taken from interviews with Malkin, Silverman,

Tinker, Heyman, Ricker, and Mendik. Malkin's 1958 Harvard Law School thesis on real estate syndication provided additional details.

The sale of the building to the Stevens group was detailed in the original press releases, newspaper coverage, and by Malkin in conversations. The Crown sale was recounted by Malkin, Silverman, and Lester Crown in interviews. The circumstances surrounding the 1961 sale to the Wien/Helmsley group were described in interviews by Malkin, Silverman, and Tinker. Terms of the deal were described in the original prospectus.

Opposition to the World Trade Center was recounted in Leonard Ruchelman's *The World Trade Center* (Syracuse, N.Y.: Syracuse University Press, 1977.) Toobin's criticism of Wien was drawn from *NYT,* 4/27/66, and Jones's comments about his plan to increase the height of the Empire State Building, *NYT,* 10/11/72. Further details came from "Memoirs of Harold C. Bernhard, Architect" (unpublished), and interviews with Malkin and Donald Grossmann.

Leona Helmsley's rise in the Helmsley organization and harsh treatment of employees were described by Guigno, Tinker, Mann, Heyman, and Ricker in interviews. Harry Helmsley's declining health was recounted by Malkin and Trainor in interviews and in doctors' reports referred to in Malkin's lawsuit against Helmsley-Spear. Details of Trump's early career were taken from his own *Trump: The Art of the Deal,* written with Tony Schwartz (New York: Random House, 1987) and Wayne Barrett's *Trump: The Deals and the Downfall* (New York: HarperCollins Publishers, 1992), from which Trump's comment about surpassing the Helmsleys was taken.

The King Kong stunt was recounted in interviews by Tinker and Ann Wawer, co-owner of the balloon company. Leona Helmsley's trial was described in a series of *NYT* articles, from which the quotes from Koch and Leona were drawn. Trump's comment about the verdict was reported in Hammer's book. Trump recounts his early confrontations with Leona in his book, written with Charles Leerhsen, *Trump: Surviving at the Top* (New York: Random House, 1990).

Chapter 7: East Meets West

Trump referred to Yokoi as "Nokoi" in a 2000 interview and in Bryan Burrough's "Emperors of the Air," *Vanity Fair,* May 1995. Renoir described Trump's way of introducing Nakahara in an interview. Trump's pitch to the Renoirs and the reactions to it were detailed in interviews with Renoir, Lindsay, and Trump. A copy of the subsequent agreement with Trump is contained in the court record. The deposition testimony of Renoir, Nakahara, and Bubel, and interviews with Nakahara and Renoir, detailed how the deal came about, what each party contributed, and what each stood to gain.

Yokoi's judicial setbacks in Japan, and his subsequent prison sentence, were recounted in Japanese newspaper and magazine articles, including reports in *Mainichi Daily News* and *Asahi Evening News,* and in interviews with Honjo and Sato. Setsuichi Akiba's comment about the Yokoi family was contained in a December 1993 article in *Shukan Asahi,* a weekly. The description of Hachioji Medical Prison came from Burrough's 1995 *Vanity Fair* article and from an interview with Hishida.

Renoir explained his vision for the Empire State Building, and Trump's suggestions for improving it, in interviews. The reactions of Yokoi and some of his family members to the deal were described in an affidavit by Hirohiko Yokoi, in the deposition of Hishida, and by Rosen in an interview. Hishida recounted his meeting with Nakahara in a deposition. The Yokoi family's search for a lawyer was described by someone involved in the search, who requested anonymity. Rosen detailed his involvement in interviews.

Wallach recalled his trip to Tokyo in an interview, and Bubel described his meeting with Hishida in a deposition.

Chapter 8: Who Owns the Empire State Building?

Kunihiko and Hirohiko Yokoi, who declined to be interviewed, described in depositions their actions after their father's imprisonment. Hirohiko's statement that Nippon Sangyo had neither agreed to give the Empire State Building to Nakahara nor authorized her to form a partnership with Trump was contained in his affidavit.

Smith described in interviews her confrontations with Helmsley-Spear representatives and her conversations with Trump, and she shared all of her correspondence related to the dispute. Trump confirmed details in an interview.

Rosen described the filing of the lawsuit and his trip to Japan in an interview. The activities in France of Bal, Takenosuke Sakakura, and Chizuko Sakakura were recounted in Bal's deposition and in an interview with him. A French police report and a letter from Yokoi's French lawyer to an investigating magistrate provided further details.

Chapter 9: Trump's Broadside

Smith discussed her escalating campaign against the building, and her encounters with Helmsley-Spear representatives, in interviews. Trainer described his meeting with Smith, and the presence of a man with a concealed tape recorder, in an interview. Emanual and Sullivan recounted their meeting in separate interviews. Guigno and Trainer described the hearing resulting from Smith's complaints about them.

Documents related to Trump's effort to break the lease are contained in court records. Smith's encounter with Brod was described by both of them in interviews. Trump's meeting with Liman was described by Charles Bagli in the *New York Observer*, 2/27/95. Studley recounted his meeting with Trump in an interview. Smith described Trump's admonitions to her, and the mystery phone call, in an interview.

Chapter 10: The French Front

Copies of the letters quoted in this chapter were entered as exhibits in the lawsuit. Details about the property transfers in France were drawn from documents filed in the subsequent extradition case against Renoir. Bal described his escalating involvement in a deposition and interview. The testimony of Sothy, Tant, Bordenave, and Bal to French investigators is contained in the record of extradition case.

Kiiko recalled her questioning and detention in an interview. A French report on the session contained further details. Renoir described his response to being summoned for questioning in a deposition and interviews. Bubel recalled Hernot's warning in his deposition.

Hishida recalled in an interview his discovery that Yokoi could not speak, and Bal described Yokoi's jailhouse comments to him in a deposition. The French extradition record contained information about the magistrate's trip to Japan and Yokoi's medical examination.

Chapter 11: Fall of the House of Harry

Schneider's comments about Harry Helmsley's health were contained in an affidavit by Malkin. Guigno recalled his encounter with Leona in an interview. The dispute between Malkin and Leona Helmsley was detailed in court documents and in interviews with Malkin and the lawyers for each side conducted in 1997 for *The Wall Street Journal*. The court record of the ensuing lawsuit contains additional statements and correspondence by the lawyers. The circumstances of Harry's death were reported in the *New York Times*. Copies of his 1974 and 1994 wills detailed the planned division of his assets.

Details about the 1997 shooting on the observation deck were drawn from the original police reports on the incident, obtained through a Freedom of Information Act request, and from the *NYT,* 2/24/97–2/27/97.

Chapter 12: Sibling Rivalry

Renoir and Nakahara provided explanations for the property transfers and for the legal attack on them by other family members in depositions and interviews and in an affidavit by Nakahara. Bubel added concurring details in his deposition.

Details about the libel suits in France were drawn from translations of the suits and judgment contained in the record of the New York lawsuit brought by Renoir and Nakahara against Bal.

Sato described his conversation with Yokoi after Yokoi's release from prison in an interview. Information about Yokoi's trip to New York was drawn from interviews with Hannigan, Renoir, Yokoi's two bodyguards, and his daughter who lives in New York. The description of his deposition was drawn from a videotape, from the transcript of the proceeding, and from interviews with some of the lawyers involved. Nakahara's deposition testimony was contained in a transcript.

Chapter 13: Behind Bars

Information about Renoir's arrest and detention was drawn from interviews with Renoir and a prison official.

Trump's continuing effort to break the lease was described in court records. Renoir recounted in an interview his phone conversation from jail with Trump.

Malkin recalled his first meeting with Bal, and the deal that was proposed, in an interview. Hannigan and Rathkopf described their negotiation with Trump in interviews.

Chapter 14: A Meeting with Daddy

Details about the financial problems of Japanese investors and the fate of their American investments were drawn from articles in *The Wall Street Journal* by Clay Chandler, John Bussey, Jathon Sapsford, and me.

The courtroom comments of Eaton and Ross were contained in a transcript of the hearing.

The account of Yokoi's activities in Paris was pieced together from interviews with Nakahara, Hannigan, Wallach, Bal, and Narboni.

Chapter 15: Yokoi's Last Stand

The settlement of the Yokoi family lawsuit bars participants from discussing it. The account of the settlement discussions was compiled from information supplied by several people familiar with the proceedings. Hannigan described in an interview Yokoi's rejection of the first settlement proposal.

Yokoi's economic slide was detailed in Japanese newspaper and magazine articles. Kunihiko Yokoi recalled his conversation with his father in a deposition.

Trump's effort to block the family settlement was detailed in court records and transcripts and described by Hannigan in an interview.

Details about Yokoi's death were taken from an obituary in *Nihon Keizai Shimbun*. Hishida described his gift to Chizuko in an interview.

Chapter 16: Heirs

Leona Helmsley's property sales were detailed by David Dunlap in *NYT,* 11/26/00. The activities of American real estate investors and advisers in Japan, and the backlash against them, were described by Jathon Sapsford in *The Wall Street Journal.* Davidoff described his experience in Japan in an interview.

Settlement negotiations following Yokoi's death were described by several people familiar with the details. Renoir recalled his days in Hudson County Jail in interviews. Court documents and affidavits by Winter and Herrington detail Winter's departure from the case. Renoir described the financial costs of the case in an interview.

Dolatta's and Coleman's interpretations of the settlement letter are contained in the appellate court record of Renoir's extradition.

Chapter 17: Donald's Endgame

Malkin offered his recollection of Trump's speech, and his subsequent phone conversations and meetings with Trump, in interviews. Details about the elevator incident were drawn from lawsuits filed by the passengers, the record of the Trump litigation, *NYT*, 1/26/00, and a conversation with Malkin.

Renoir described his extradition, his French jail stay, and his eventual release in an interview and letters written from jail.

Trump offered his views on the value of his position, and his ability to negotiate a sale, in interviews.

ACKNOWLEDGMENTS

This book could not have been written without the assistance of many of the people who appear in it. As I attempted to reconstruct key portions of the story, I often faced starkly different perspectives on the same events. I am grateful to those who were willing to share their stories in exchange for no more than a vow from me to be accurate and fair to everyone involved. In particular, my thanks are due to Jean-Paul Renoir, who spent many hours with me at Westchester County jail and, later, in France. His wife, Kiiko Nakahara, was likewise generous with her time, in spite of the pummeling she had suffered in the French press. Raymond Hannigan, Hideki Yokoi's New York lawyer, tolerated many phone calls from me and helped open the door to the Yokoi family, if only a crack. Peter Malkin gave generously of his time and was always prompt and courteous in answering my many questions, no matter how irritating or ill-informed they were. I hope I have succeeded in depicting all of their stories in a truthful way.

This book arose from articles I wrote for *The Wall Street Journal* between 1994 and 1999. That newspaper has been my professional home for more than a decade, and I have benefited immeasurably from the talented reporters and editors I have worked with there. I would like to thank, in particular, Paul Steiger, the *Journal's* managing editor, who generously granted me a leave to write this book. My colleagues at the paper's Tokyo bureau provided valuable help with my reporting in Japan. Bill Spindle, in particular, introduced me to important sources of information about Yokoi. *Journal* reporter Jathon Sapsford, who spent many years covering Japan, and his wife, Yuka Hayashi, also a journalist, offered me much-needed guidance in understanding contemporary Japan. Makiko Tazaki, an energetic and talented freelance interpreter, translator, and reporter, provided invaluable assistance during my stay in Tokyo and beyond. In the end, my research into Yokoi's life was made infinitely richer by her efforts.

I could not have pieced together the stories of the creation of the building and the rise of Yokoi without help from several libraries. Janet Parks, curator of the department of drawings and archives at the Avery Architectural and Fine Arts Library at Columbia University, guided me through a fragile collection of material on the early days of the Empire State Building. Marjorie McNinch, reference archivist at the Hagley Museum and Library in Wilmington, Delaware, made available the papers of John Raskob and Pierre S. du Pont. The Foreign Correspondents' Club of Japan generously allowed me to go through its old newspaper clippings about Yokoi. Ace *Wall Street Journal* librarian Bruce Levy helped me to track several elusive people. I also owe thanks to Lydia Ruth, director of public relations at the Empire State Building, for sharing historical photos of the building, some of which have been used in this book.

I would not have begun this book without the encouragement and support of my agent, Esmond Harmsworth, and his partner Todd Shuster, who provided invaluable advice every step of the way. The unwavering enthusiasm of Airié Deki-djiev, my tireless editor at John Wiley & Sons, sustained me as my deadline loomed, and her deft editing enriched this book. James B. Meigs, an old friend and a talented magazine editor, lent his incisive editing hand to an early draft of the story, helping me to sharpen the text and puzzle out the pac-ing of the tale. Thanks also to all those at Wiley for their extra efforts, including Michelle Patterson, Jessica Noyes, Helene Godin, Lori Sayde-Mehrtens, and Linda Witzling.

My largest debt, without doubt, is to my wife, Laura Schnell, who persevered through my absences in Japan and France and the long hours of writing. My two sons warrant special recognition for putting up with my seemingly irra-tional prohibition on pounding around the house while their father was trying to write.

INDEX